ATTACK OUT OF THE SUN

LESSONS FROM THE RED BARON FOR OUR BUSINESS AND PERSONAL LIVES

Durwood J. Heinrich, Ph.D.

iUniverse, Inc.

New York   Bloomington

ATTACK OUT OF THE SUN
LESSONS FROM THE RED BARON FOR OUR BUSINESS AND PERSONAL LIVES

iUniverse books may be ordered through booksellers or by contacting:

iUniverse
1663 Liberty Drive
Bloomington, IN 47403
www.iuniverse.com
1-800-Authors (1-800-288-4677)

Because of the dynamic nature of the Internet, any Web addresses or links contained in this book may have changed since publication and may no longer be valid. The views expressed in this work are solely those of the author and do not necessarily reflect the views of the publisher, and the publisher hereby disclaims any responsibility for them.

ISBN: 978-1-4502-5740-4 (pbk)
ISBN: 978-1-4502-5742-8 (ebk)
ISBN: 978-1-4502-5741-1 (hbk)

Library of Congress Control Number: 2010914501

Printed in the United States of America

iUniverse rev. date: 10/04/2010

DEDICATION

To all military aviators and soldiers who have made the Ultimate Sacrifice and also to those who risk their lives daily in the service of their Country.

CONTENTS

PREFACE

The year was 1966. The author had not yet been airborne, but he was fascinated with flying. Therefore, there was never a question that he would go see the then recently-released film The Blue Max starring George Peppard cast in the leading role as fictional German pilot, Bruno Stachel. Not only was the author captivated by the action-packed flying sequences, but he also developed a deep interest in the Pour le Merite ("The Blue Max") medal, which Stachel sought throughout the movie. The Orden Pour le *Merite* (Order of Merit) was established three hundred years earlier by King Frederick I, and the medal was subsequently presented by Frederick William III as Prussia's highest military honor to officers for repeated and continual gallantry in action during World War I. It was equivalent to the United States Medal of Honor and the British Victoria Cross.

Although he was never a pilot, the author's father worked in a defense plant in Dallas and had helped build many of the military aircraft that his family watched takeoff, maneuver, or land—separately or in spectacular air shows—at nearby Hensley Field or Carswell Air Force Base on Sunday afternoons. Occasional performances by the Air Force Thunderbirds and the Navy Blue Angels were especially impressive because of the precision displayed by the airmen, whether they were marching sharply to their aircraft or flying in close formation with their wingtips literally just inches apart. The author was intrigued with the freedom, the control, and the power these masters of the sky seemed to possess. In spite of his mother's concerns, he set his mind early on to venture into an aviation career. As a child, he assembled plastic models and later built and flew airplane models using his own designs. But it would be 1967 before the author would himself take the controls for the first time in a slow single-engine Cessna and two more years before he would graduate from the USAF Undergraduate Pilot Training Program, culminating with the requisite mastery of the dual-engine supersonic T-38A "White Rocket."

Years later, a James Dietz limited edition print—"Last Word"—hung on the wall opposite the author's desk in the airport hangar where he served as Director of Aviation and Chief Pilot for a multi-national corporation. The print depicts *Rittmeister* (Cavalry Captain) Manfred von Richthofen briefing his men of *Jagdstaffel 11* (Fighter Squadron 11) beside his all-red Fokker DRI triplane just before takeoff from Cappy airfield on April 21, 1918. Richthofen's dog, Moritz, is waiting patiently at the feet of his master for an anticipated playful goodbye. As a special touch, the individual who framed the print had included a replica of the Blue Max medal beneath the picture. The handsome medal consists of a striking Maltese cross of deep blue enamel with eagles between the arms trimmed in gold; and even this replica brightly radiated the streaks of sunlight in the office. That very picture was presented to the author when he retired from that company.

Because of its size, the picture of von Richthofen is now hanging in the hallway just outside of the author's home office. But even there it catches the light from the array of windows in the high-ceiling formal dining room. As always, it remains a colorful and fascinating piece that continues to draw admirers and questions—and that's how it has affected this author. In fact, the author reflected one day, why not learn more about the intriguing hero that it portrays? Why not investigate the imposing Wing Commander who is standing in the picture with his walking stick—fashioned from an opponent's propeller and the symbol of the office of *Jagdgeschwader I* (Fighter Wing I)—obviously the focus of the admiring eyes of his pilots? Why not examine further why the Red Baron seems as alive today as he was ninety-two years ago and is featured not only in numerous films, documentaries, and books but also in everything from comic strips and pizza sales to electronic games and racing? Instead of simply writing another history of the Baron, why not explore the real person behind the mystique and the enduring principles that Richthofen apparently championed for application to business and everyday living for those of all ages? Why not use quotes from the Baron himself, his family members, his superiors, and his comrades to establish his personality and philosophies and then expand and explore them further? Why not utilize this author's strengths: a long career in aviation and pilot instructing; degree in aeronautical engineering, advanced degree in business, and doctorate in organizational psychology; proven management and leadership skills; years of teaching and lecturing experience; numerous published articles and presentations; and lifelong determination to learn and improve as an individual? Why not use some time, now primarily devoted to speaking and consulting, to record these concepts that can potentially be a benefit to many (including the author) for their personal and business lives? Why not write about the Red Baron? Accordingly, the author has accumulated a sizable Richthofen library—hundreds of books, articles, and videos—and has been researching and giving presentations on the Red Baron for several years. You now hold the envisioned product in your hands.

As an example of the book's content, Chapter 9 is entitled *Attack Out of the Sun (Secure the Upper Hand)*. The German fighter squadrons were greatly outnumbered throughout the war, and Richthofen—as did his mentor Oswald Boelcke before him—taught his pilots the importance of securing the advantage before charging head-on into battle. One of those tactics, utilized by both sides, was to dive out of the sun's blinding glare to produce a surprise attack that could not be easily detected or defended. Another method was to approach the opponent from behind or below, again making defense more difficult. However, a critical strategy to achieve victory, recognized early on by both Boelcke and Richthofen, was the necessity of recruiting the best pilots, providing them with proper and extensive training, and supplying them with superior aircraft and equipment. Richthofen constantly demanded these elements when he was in command of his squadron and later his wing. Richthofen also knew that his planes were typically in the minority, his pilots fatigued, and that the opponents' aircraft and crews were becoming increasingly more capable as the war progressed. He instructed his men when attacked to remain clear-headed, focus, be innovative, and seize the offensive as quickly as possible following the assault.

These concepts, then, as applied to employees and businesses— given a particular goal or mission—imply that success is more probable if we utilize the right machines and provide the proper tools to carefully-chosen, well-trained workers. As did Richthofen, however, we must also understand our strengths and weaknesses, the dynamic environment, and our competition. Lessons for us as individuals include: selecting and learning from an appropriate mentor; recognizing the importance of enhancing our skills and continuing our education; disciplining ourselves to be calm; avoiding procrastination; focusing; and permitting ourselves to secure healthy nourishment and adequate rest. Less obvious lessons are developing core strengths, establishing trust, supporting our teams, and tapping external resources as required. Developing visioning and goal-setting skills; management and leadership qualities; team-building capabilities; operational and competitive strategies; personal strengths; and much more are all topics covered in the other chapters.

~

So who really was *Rittmeister* Manfred Albrecht von Richthofen, affectionately known as the "Red Baron?" How could a man who only lived to be twenty-five years old have had such a brilliant career and have been so highly decorated? How was it that he was such an admired and beloved commander and also a feared and yet respected foe? He was clearly idolized by his comrades and a famous hero to the German people who anxiously followed his prowess in their newspapers. The British Royal Flying Corps referred to him as the "dear old baron" or the "jolly old baron," even drinking toasts to his health in their messes. What can we learn from his personality, skill sets, management style, leadership ability, strategy formation, focused determination, and family-focus? How can we apply his legacy to our own personal lives and businesses? That is what this book is about.

This volume is not meant to be another typical motivational or self-help book. Rather, as mentioned, it was conceived with the idea of presenting an informative history of the legendary Manfred von Richthofen while attempting to paint his footprints as potential templates for lessons in our personal lives and businesses. It is often easier to learn through examples, particularly those taken from real-life stories, and especially if those stories are about famous heroes. Further, although you will most likely recognize many of the timeless principles and concepts presented, the author hopes that looking at them from an "airborne" perspective will help bring them into greater focus for easier application. In this context, it must be remembered that Richthofen only lived two and a half decades. Obviously, in that short span of time—more than ninety years ago—we are only able to glimpse a minute segment of who he really was and how he lived. Accordingly, there are many aspects of daily living and characteristics of the business world that are not part of this treatise. Even so, Richthofen's life was lived to its fullest and there is much to be learned.

The author has made a considerable effort to present the material in this book as accurately as possible using quotes from many sources and historical facts to support the fundamental concepts in each chapter. However, it should be remembered that the memoires written by Richthofen and others of the time were subject to wartime censorship. Similarly, material written after the war, even by those who were actually there, most likely resulted in some recollection or reconstruction errors. Nonetheless, readers are encouraged to interpret the character of Richthofen and other heroes of the time in the context of other materials and testimonies as well as their own.

Additionally, in some cases because of the time element involved and because information that may have been initially incomplete, the author came across some inconsistencies in facts, especially those related to documentation of combat victories. Although there is little dispute as to whether or not Richthofen actually achieved eighty or even more victories, there are at times discrepancies as to exactly which specific aircraft were credited or on what dates those air battles actually occurred. In the "dogfights," sometimes consisting of hundreds of aircraft, it was difficult at best for aerial and ground observers to always make accurate identifications. Further, there were inconsistencies regarding any romantic relationships Richthofen may have had. Regardless, while the author utilized all available sources to provide the most accurate information, some details are not critical to the overall thrust of the book. In cases of contradictions in historical information, the author either used material that has been later proven to be accurate or commonly accepted over time. "History" that was considered to be based on rumors or questionable in its own right, he either excluded or referenced in endnotes for the reader to judge.

By nature, the author tends to be a positive person, but he is well aware that the Baron, like any of us, was not perfect. In his significant research in writing this book, however, the author was pleasantly surprised to find that Richthofen apparently possessed numerous attributes and characteristics of personality to which many of us aspire. The author concentrated primarily on those. If you happen to be an individual who hoped for an argument of Richthofen's positive traits contrasted with some envisioned "dark side," you will be disappointed. That said, there was no intention to glorify in any way the horrors of war. Again, this book is about the numerous positive attributes of a wartime hero of the skies who fought his battles in defense of his beloved country. When one is driving down the highway, concentration on not running over the yellow lines and the shoulder markers will inevitably result in just that! Why not just simply follow the course that the construction crew has laid out and enjoy the journey?

The "course" is straightforward. It consists of the introduction, which provides a complete biography of Manfred von Richthofen, meant to serve as a broad glimpse of the Baron and foundation for the chapters. The next sixteen chapters that follow are essentially divided into three sections: preparation and planning for success (Chapters 1–5), execution for results (Chapters 6–13), and evaluation and renewal (Chapters 14–16). The section that follows, *Debriefing (Conclusions)*, is a general summary.

The author wishes to thank the countless individuals who have gone before him in writing about Richthofen, beginning, of course, with Manfred von Richthofen himself in his 1917 autobiography, *Der Rote Kampfflieger* (The Red Fighter Pilot); and his mother, Kunigunde Freifrau von Richthofen, in her 1937 *Mein Kriegstagebuch* (My War

Diary). An important earlier work in English was that of Floyd Gibbons *The Red Knight of Germany* in 1927. William Burrows published *Richthofen: A True History of the Red Barron* in 1969. Numerous other outstanding authors have also studied Richthofen extensively and published excellent works. These include Suzanne Fischer, Norman Franks, Hal Giblin, Peter Kilduff, Nigel McCrery, Greg VanWyngarden, Nicolas Wright, and many others, most of whom are included in the bibliography.

I want to thank my lovely wife, Charlene, who patiently endured the many hours I spent barricaded in my office, bent over my laptop, beneath stacks of books, reference materials, and notes in putting together this book. I also wish to thank my good friends, James W. Robertson and Paul H. Smith, whose encouragement and support enabled this book to be written.

Durwood J. Heinrich, Ph.D.
Austin, Texas USA
April 2010

INTRODUCTION

It is early in the morning of March 27, 1918. A red German Fokker DR.1 triple-winged "triplane" has taken off with five additional triplanes of *Jasta 11* (Fighter Squadron 11) from their new base at Lechelle in northern France.[1] Each aircraft's engine cowling, wheel covers, and wing struts are painted bright red, but only the leader's machine also has a red upper wing, upper fuselage, aft fuselage, horizontal tail, and vertical tail. The wingmen have chosen various individual colors and markings of their own to facilitate quick identification by their comrades in aerial combat and also by observers on the ground. Pilots of the Red Baron's colorful "Flying Circus" glance back through the scattered low clouds at the rapidly-receding aerodrome. The airfield had been chosen by the Wing leader because it is closer to the Front. It had only recently been abandoned by the British 3 Squadron in the wake of what would arguably become the largest and most important offensive of World War I. *Jagdgeschwader I Kommandeur* (*JGI* Fighter Wing Commander) Manfred von Richthofen is focused and determined as he leads his *Kette* (flight section) to seek out the English aircraft that are taking advantage of the good weather to conduct low bombing and strafing sorties against the advancing Germans near Albert. This is particularly disturbing to *Rittmeister* (Cavalry Captain) von Richthofen because he holds a special mutual connection not only with his men of *JGI*, but also with the field-grey uniformed soldiers who are forced to fight in the trenches and on the battlefields below.

At 0900 hours, Richthofen singles out a Sopwith Camel biplane fighter of 73 Squadron Royal Flying Corps (RFC) being flown at low altitude by six-victory ace, Captain Thomas Sharpe. Even though the Camel is slightly faster than the triplane, the battle is typical of most of Richthofen's victories—brief, at close range, and with prudent and effective use of precious ammunition. Additionally, the *Rittmeister* attacks using the bright morning sun and scattered low clouds as a cover. He expends only 150 bullets, equating to several quick bursts from his twin Spandau 7.92 mm machine guns. White gasoline vapor streams from the crippled Camel, confirming that the fuel tanks have been hit. Wounded and forced to shut down his engine to avoid a fire, Sharpe goes down into a flooded part of the Ancre River area northeast of Albert, now controlled by Germany, where he is promptly taken prisoner.

It is late afternoon the same day, and Richthofen is now flying another, but newer, triplane. This aircraft sports red on its cowling, wheel covers, struts, all three upper wings, upper horizontal tail, and vertical tail. The weather has turned somewhat misty and hazy. This time the Red Baron is leading six triplanes of *Jasta 11*. At 1630 hours, he attacks an Armstrong Whitworth AWFK8 two-seater bomber/ reconnaissance aircraft of 2 Squadron RFC being piloted by Lieutenant Edward Smart and observer/gunner Lieutenant Kenneth Barford, who are once again making life even more miserable for the advancing German army personnel. Approaching unnoticed from below and behind, Richthofen is able to quickly dispatch the AWFK8 following some one hundred shots from less than fifty meters. The aircraft falls near Foucaucourt, along the main road from Amiens to St-Quentin.

Just five minutes later, at 1635 hours, northeast of Chuignolles, Richthofen notes that one of his pilots is being attacked by a formidable Sopwith Dolphin fighter of 79 Squadron RFC flown by Second Lieutenant George Harding. Incessantly vigilant and fiercely protective of his men, Richthofen swiftly positions his highly maneuverable triplane behind the Dolphin and registers his 73rd victory, his third of the day!

Richthofen's Fighter Wing, *JGI*, consisting of *Jastas 4, 6, 10*, and *11*, would conduct 118 combat flights by the end of the day and down thirteen enemy aircraft without a single corresponding loss. Richthofen would post another victory the following day against a new AWFK8 from 82 Squadron RFC crewed by Second Lieutenants Joseph Taylor and Eric Betley. The Red Baron would go on to achieve eighty combat victories by April 20, 1918, to punctuate his place as the greatest pilot and ace of World War I.

~

Manfred Albrecht von Richthofen was born on May 2, 1892, in Kleinburg, a suburb of Breslau, Selesia, Germany (now Wroclaw, Poland). He was the eldest son of a Prussian aristocratic family whose father, Albrecht von Richthofen, born in 1859, was a professional military officer. However, Richthofen's father was forced to retire early following the rescue of one of his men who had fallen off his horse while crossing the icy Oder River. He had leapt from the bridge in full uniform to save the young dragoon. The severe cold that he subsequently sustained left him deaf in one ear. His mother was Baroness Kunigunde von Richthofen, born in 1868. Manfred's siblings included Elisabeth Therese Luise Marie (called Ilse), born on August 8, 1890; Lothar Siegfried, born on September 27, 1894; and Karl Bolko, born on April 16, 1903.

Manfred was a very healthy and athletically-gifted child and could easily turn standing somersaults and climb the pine trees in the forests of Silesia. He especially enjoyed swimming, horses, dogs, and shooting. He was a natural marksman and took pride in his ability to deliver clean shots that precluded suffering of his prey. When his father retired with the military rank of Major to Schweidnitz, a small industrial city southwest of Breslau in the Weistritz Valley, Manfred's love for hunting continued to grow. He made frequent hunting trips with his father into the forested mountain ranges that bordered the valley where game was abundant. Manfred was also fascinated with the hunting stories told by his mother's brother, Uncle Alexander, who had claimed trophies in Europe, Asia, and Africa, and who frequently visited the Richthofens.

Manfred's father—probably frustrated that his own military career had been interrupted and also recognizing Manfred's considerable leadership, horsemanship, marksmanship, and athletic abilities—sent him to the Germany Military School at Wahlstatt in 1903 at age eleven. Manfred was not sure that he desired a military career, but thoughts of military adventure leading his men into battle on horseback with sabers drawn certainly had its appeal. Regardless, his personal wishes were not considered and it never occurred to Manfred to oppose his father. Although he was intelligent, Manfred studied only enough to get by, but excelled in athletics, vaulting horse, parallel bars, and ropes. He won several awards for his skills. One day, deciding to test his abilities to the limit, he scaled the famous church steeple at Wahlstatt using the lightning conductor as a rope and tied his handkerchief to the top. He noticed that the handkerchief was still in place ten years later when he visited his brother Bolko at the school. While the strict, Spartan regimen at Wahlstatt certainly wasn't to his liking, he later felt new freedom at the senior school at the Royal Military Academy at Lichterfelde in 1909, where cadets were treated more like adults. He became wholly enthusiastic about the military when he was finally able to wear his epaulettes and be addressed as "*Herr Lieutenant.*"

Upon completion of cadet training at Lichterfelde on April 27, 1911, Manfred von Richthofen was commissioned as a Second Lieutenant. Following final training at the War Academy in Berlin, he was assigned to the elite *Uhlan* (cavalry) Regiment Number 1 (Emperor Alexander III's) at Ostrovo, some six miles from the Russian frontier. Because Ostrovo was in his beloved Selesia, Manfred took advantage of the frequent opportunities to hunt. Further, his regiment included a number of friends and relatives, so the officer's mess was in many ways like a family reunion. Generous leave provisions provided him with ample opportunities for sporting activities at the estates of other Richthofens. Also, to his pleasure, he was able to get all the riding he wished, and officers in the German army were encouraged to ride their own horses in races and steeplechases. Manfred regularly competed, often with success. His last win was the Imperial cross-country race for army officers in the Kaiser Prize Race in 1913, in spite of suffering a broken collar bone in the middle of the race when his mount (*Blume*) encountered a rabbit hole.

On June 27, 1914, Archduke Franz Ferdinand, heir to the ruler of Austria-Hungary, and his wife, were assassinated while visiting Serbia. Austria-Hungary subsequently declared war on Serbia on July

28th. When Russia—an ally of Serbia—mobilized its armed forces, Germany—an ally of Austria-Hungary—declared war on Russia on August 1st and then on France August 3rd. Britain declared war on Germany and Austria-Hungary August 4th. Italy—previously an ally of Germany and Austria-Hungary—declared its neutrality but then joined Britain, France, and Russia on May 24, 1915. World War I had begun. The Central Powers included Germany, Austria-Hungary, Ottoman Empire, and Bulgaria. The United States would not join the Allied Powers (Russia, UK, France, Canada, Australia, Italy, Japan, Portugal, and the United States) until April 6, 1917.

Manfred von Richthofen experienced some cavalry action on the Eastern Front in August of 1914 and was subsequently awarded the prestigious Prussian Iron Cross on September 12, 1914. However, following his unit's transfer to the Western Front, Richthofen's vision of leading horse-mounted charges against the enemy soon faded with the reality of the trench and barbed wire stalemates of the war. His subsequent service as a communications officer in the Signal Corps, *Ordonnanzoffizier* (assistant adjutant), and finally supply officer proved unacceptable to the young *Uhlan*. Visualizing possibilities flying with the "cavalry of the air," he applied and was accepted to aircraft observer school at Cologne, Aviation Replacement Section No. 7, in May 1915. At the time, the observers were the officers and were responsible for the two-seat aircraft, while the NCO (non-commissioned officer) pilots served as chauffeurs. Besides, Richthofen was anxious to get into the air and was afraid the war might be over by the time he had obtained his pilot's certification, which would take three months versus two weeks for that of observer. Even though the observer program was difficult and few survived the extensive training, the focused Baron studied hard and was the first in his class of thirty to graduate. He was assigned to *Flieger-Abteilung 69* (No. 69 Flying Squadron) June 21,1916, on the Eastern Front, flying in a large Albatros BII three-bay biplane with *Oberleutnant* (First Lieutenant) Georg Zeumer, a reckless individual dying of tuberculosis. Zeumer was known as the "Black Cat" because of his almost total disregard for caution. Richthofen performed his reconnaissance work from the front cockpit and was armed with only a rifle and a pistol.[2] When Zeumer was transferred, Richthofen crewed

5

with *Rittmeister* Erick *Graf* (Count) von Holck flying the Albatros CI, which looked somewhat like the BII but positioned the observer in the rear cockpit. There the observer could easily perform his reconnaissance duties and more effectively protect the aircraft. Richthofen and Holck were well suited to each other because of their similar tastes and a common background as cavalrymen.

In August 1915, Richthofen was transferred to the *Brieftauben-Abteilung Ostende (BAO)* on the 4th Army Front in Flanders, where once again he was teamed with *Oberleutnant* Zeumer. This time Richthofen was flying in the twin-engine AEG G-type *Grosskampfflugzeug* (Big Combat Aircraft) bombers. In the G-II, the observer/bombardier sat in the *Kanzel* (pulpit) that protruded from the front of the fuselage and was equipped with a machine gun. This gave Richthofen's air-cavalry machine a lance, and he set his mind to put the weapon to good use!

Richthofen took a quick course in machine-gunnery at Ostende and was excited when he and Zeumer encountered a French Farman bomber on September 1, 1915. Unfortunately, after a few maneuvers and unsuccessful bursts of fire at the opponent, Richthofen learned that to be more successful at securing victories he would also have to be in control of the aircraft.

It was also in Ostende where Richthofen purchased his "little lap dog" Moritz for five marks. As a puppy, the Great Dane initially slept in the same bed as his master, but later became too big. He even flew once with the Baron, calmly assisting with observer duties.

Richthofen would have another opportunity for an air fight in mid-September when his *BAO* unit was transferred to the 3rd Army Front at Vouziers to support the *VIII.Reserve-Korps* aerial unit over the Champagne Front. This time, Richthofen found himself flying with *Oberleutnant* Paul Henning von Osterroht in the smaller and more maneuverable Aviatik CI. Like Richthofen, Osterroht had attended the schools at Wahlstatt and Lichterfelde. Richthofen's Parabellum 7.9 mm machine gun could be attached to mountings on either side of the cockpit as necessary. When Osterroht positioned the Aviatik CI alongside a Farman S.II, the two aircraft traded machine gun fire. Richthofen's machine gun jammed at first, but then he managed to exhaust his entire supply of one hundred rounds and the enemy aircraft fell. However, because the aircraft crashed behind enemy lines, he would not receive credit for the victory.

On October 1, 1915, Richthofen was posted to the other German bomber unit, *Brieftauben-Abteilung-Metz (BAM),* in Rethel, some 30 kilometers northeast of Vouziers. En route by train to his new assignment, Richthofen by chance met *Leutnant* Oswald Boelcke in the dining car, recognizing him from pictures he had seen in the newspapers. At the time, the Fokker *Eindecker* (single-wing monoplane) had been Oswald's platform for four aerial combat victories, and he was rapidly becoming famous throughout Germany.[3] Anxious to find out how the great Boelcke was able to shoot down his opponents, Richthofen merely asked. Boelcke replied: "Well it is quite simple. I fly close to my man, aim well and then he of course falls down."[4]

Richthofen was confused because he felt that he used the same technique but his opponents seldom fell. Nevertheless, he realized that Boelcke flew a Fokker while he was an observer on a large battle plane. He therefore resolved to also fly a Fokker. During the journey on the train, he spent many hours getting to know Boelcke and asking him countless questions. Because Boelcke was also on his way to Rethel to fly barrier patrols—lone aircraft scouting along the Front to intercept enemy aircraft—Richthofen would have many more opportunities to learn about aviation fighter techniques from his humble new friend and mentor.

Once his unit was installed at Rethel flying in the Albatros CI, Richthofen wasted no time in convincing Zeumer to teach him how to pilot an old two-seater available at the Metz airdrome. Finally, on October 10, 1915, following twenty-five instructional flights, Zeumer sent Richthofen up on his first solo. The aircraft behaved differently with only one crewmember aboard and Richthofen hit the ground hard, bounced back into the air, and then nosed over. Zeumer assisted the embarrassed, but unhurt pilot out of the cockpit. Two days later aboard the repaired aircraft, the determined Baron made a series of successful landings, and on November 15th found himself on the way to Doberitz, near Berlin, to train as a fighter pilot. Desperately wanting to be a pilot, Richthofen once again applied his Prussian resolve in academics and flying, and on Christmas Day 1915, passed his third and final examination for pilot certification.[5]

Following a short cross-county flight to Doberitz, the Fokker factory in Schwerin, and then to Breslau as part of his final examination, Manfred was able to catch a train and arrived in Schweidnitz by evening to spend Christmas with his family. He returned home again on February 1st, this time with a passenger, his brother Lothar, who had been glad to get a break from training new troops in Luben. Local officials had authorized Manfred to land on the parade ground across the road from his family home. Not surprisingly, most of the townspeople showed up to have their first close look at an airplane and to welcome and admire the dashing brothers who climbed out of the fascinating machine. The attention, awe, and glamour of it all convinced Lothar and he soon applied for training as an observer.

It was nearly two months later before Manfred von Richthofen finally received orders to return to the Front. He reported on March 16, 1916, to No. 2 Combat Wing (*Kampfgeschwader 2–Kagohl 2*), Battle Squadron 8 (*Kampfstaffel 8–Kasta 8*) based at Metz, flying the Albatros CIII. Richthofen was disappointed on two levels: one, that he was as yet unable to fly the faster, more maneuverable Fokker; and two, that he was now the pilot of a two-seat aircraft of which only the observer had a machine gun to fire at the enemy. However, this did not deter von Richthofen. In the manner of the French Nieuport aircraft, he attached a machine gun to the upper wing of his reconnaissance aircraft so that it could be fired over the propeller arc. His fellow pilots, who had laughed at the clumsy installation, were silenced on April 26, 1916, when the German official communiqué noted that two hostile aircraft had been downed in aerial combat above Fleury, southwest of Douaumont. One of these was a French Nieuport II scout pursued and shot down by the Baron himself, although once again he would not receive official credit for his victory because the plane came down behind Allied lines.

Richthofen's unit, *Kasta 8*, was commanded by *BAO* veteran *Hauptmann* (Captain) Victor Carganico. Its sister unit, *Kasta 10*, based close by at Mont, near Landres, was commanded by Oswald Boelcke's brother *Hauptmann* Wilhelm Boelcke. This gave Richthofen occasional opportunities to learn more from his mentor Oswald, "the great man" as Richthofen referred to him. Meanwhile, Richthofen was determined to fly the single-seat Fokker *Eindecker*. He continued to press Carganico to secure one for him so that he could be designated the fighter pilot for *Kasta 8* when he wasn't flying reconnaissance flights. As a result of previous urging, Carganico had already allowed Richthofen to attend a three-day single-seat fighter instruction program at the Air Park in Montmedy, and then permitted the Baron to fly his personal single-seater.

Finally one day, two Fokker *Eindeckers* arrived at Landres. One was assigned to *Leutnant* Erwin Bohme, and, perhaps because of a good word from Oswald, the other was to be shared by Richthofen and *Leutnant* Hans Reimann, for morning and afternoon patrols respectively. In an encounter with a Nieuport on the second day, Reiman had to force-land between the lines in "No Man's Land," set fire to his *Eindecker*, and finally crawl back to the German trenches after dark. Manfred lost his engine on takeoff several days later when a replacement aircraft was received. Like many other engines of the period, the *Eindecker* motor had a history of unreliability. Once again the aircraft was destroyed.

In June 1916, Richthofen's No. 2 Combat Wing (*Kagohl 2*) was transferred to the Russian Front to an airfield outside the Ukrainian city of Kovel. Richthofen and two of his friends pitched a tent in the nearby forest rather than live on the hot train that traveled with the unit. During the day, he flew the Albatros CIII on bombing runs, and at night the always-energetic Baron hunted game.

Meanwhile, Richthofen's mentor, Oswald Boelcke had been grounded by Kaiser Wilhelm II. Boelcke was sent on an extended tour because of the loss of *Oberleutnant* Max Immelmann—Oswald's competitor and squadron comrade—on June 18, 1916. Both had steadily added to their combat victories and had been decorated, not only with the Knight's Cross of the House of Hohenzollern with Swords but also with the prestigious *Orden Pour le Merite*, the Prussian highest award for bravery, which came to be known as the "Blue Max."[6]

Upon returning from his trip in mid-August 1916, Boelcke stopped at Kovel to visit his brother, Wilhelm. Before departing on his tour, Boelcke had pressed his idea for new air fighter squadrons (*Jastas*) that would utilize his combat principles—*Dicta Boelcke*—to regain air superiority in the West. Apparently, his arguments to the *Feldflugchef* (Chief of Field Aviation) had been successful. Taking Wilhelm's recommendations into consideration, Oswald chose two pilots of *Kagohl 2*, *Leutnants* Erwin Bohme and Manfred von Richthofen to join his new unit, *Jasta 2*, at Bertincourt (southwest of Cambrai) in northern France. The *Jasta* fighter squadrons were formed to support each Army, and *Jasta 2* was assigned to the 1st Army sector on the Somme Front. The first seven *Jastas* were created in August 1916, an additional eight in September, plus eighteen more in October and November.

Richthofen was overjoyed that he had been selected by Boelcke and arrived at Bertincourt, on the Somme Front, on September 1st. *Jasta 2* only had a pair of Fokker DIIIs and a lone Albatros DI brought over from *Jasta 1* by *Offizier Stellvertreter* (Acting Officer) Leopold Reimann, although they would receive a refurbished Halberstadt on the 11th. While they were waiting for their new Albatros fighters, which didn't arrive until the 16th, Boelcke spent countless hours teaching his pilots about fighter tactics, formation flying, navigation, and gunnery. They also began flying the four aircraft in small group sorties behind German lines to sharpen their skills. Typically before breakfast, Boelcke flew solo patrols in his Fokker DIII rotary-engine biplane. He scored *Jasta 2's* first victory, and his personal 20th combat success, against a DH2 on September 2nd. Boelcke forced the pilot, Captain R.E. Wilson of 32 Squadron RFC, to land, arrested him, and then gave him a cordial coffee-tour of *Jasta 2* at Bertincourt.

On September 14th, Boelcke forced down another DH2 aircraft, this time intact, from 24 Squadron. He had it delivered to *Jasta 2* for additional instruction for his eager fledglings. Boelcke personally achieved seven victories for *Jasta 2* before his pilots were ultimately allowed to leave the nest.

Richthofen's first opportunity to fly a combat sortie occurred on that same day, September 14th, when along with Boelcke and Bohme, they attacked several Sopwith Strutter two-seaters of 70 Squadron. Boelcke sent one down for his first of two victories for the day, but Richthofen and Bohme, although engaging the enemy for several minutes, were left only with valuable experience.

Finally, on September 16th, *Jasta 2* received six new Albatros DI and DII fighters.[7] *Leutnant* Otto Hohne got lucky during a practice flight that evening and downed an 11 Squadron FE2b. Late the next morning, on the clear day of September 17th, Richthofen was in close formation with the inaugural *Jasta 2* flight of five aircraft with Boelcke in the lead. Piloting his new Albatros DII, Richthofen selected one of seven FE2b two-seat fighters of 11 Squadron RFC supporting BE bombers from 12 Squadron who were attacking the Marcoing railway station near Cambrai.[8] The Baron's FE2b attempted evasive maneuvers and the crew thought they had escaped. However, Richthofen suddenly attacked from behind at only ten meters and forced the pilot to land at the German airfield at Flesquieres, giving the Baron his first official confirmed victory.

The fledgling *Jasta 2* pilots amazingly chalked up three other victories by the end of the day in addition to Richthofen's. Even though he was late getting into the skirmish because he was watching over his pilots, Boelcke increased his tally to twenty-seven, dispatching a FE2b as well. Typically, a victorious pilot received the one-liter silver *Ehrenbecher* goblet honoring his first victory, but it was too soon after Richthofen's first success.[9] Therefore, Richthofen marked the occasion by ordering a plain silver cup, two inches tall by one inch wide at the brim, from a jeweler in Berlin inscribed: "1. Vickers 2. 17.9.16."[10] Richthofen would order a cup for each subsequent success, until silver was no longer available—due to both scarcity and price—after his 60th victory in September of the following year.

Jasta 2 had a very successful September with 186 combat flights, twenty-one confirmed victories, and four more unconfirmed. But it would also experience losses—Winand Grafe, September 19th; Hans Reimann, September 23rd; and Ernst Diener, September 30th. Richthofen achieved three victories in September, followed by four in October (plus one more unconfirmed). The Baron's third victory on the last day of September was against a very capable FE2b crew whose gunner, Sergeant Albert Clarkson, had already shot down three German aircraft.

Jasta 2 was forced to relocate to Lagnicourt, some nine kilometers north, September 22–23 because of British artillery fire. On October 28th, the unthinkable happened when *Jasta 2's* leader, Oswald Boelcke, then with forty victories, crashed fatally following an aerial collision with one of his unit's pilots. He and Erwin Bohme were forced to pull up and lost sight of each other when a British aircraft crossed their path. Bohme's wheel struck Boelcke's left wing causing the aircraft to lose its top wing, resulting in total loss of control.

News of Boelcke's death quickly spread, and a brave British pilot, Second Lieutenant T.S. Green, dropped a laurel wreath over *Jasta 2's* airfield inscribed: "To the memory of Captain Boelcke, our brave and chivalrous foe. From the British Royal Flying Corps."[11] A funeral service was held at the Cambrai Cathedral on October 31st, and von Richthofen—deeply saddened over the loss of his leader and mentor— was given the honor of carrying Boelcke's medals on his *Ordenskissen* (cushion with decorations) at the head of the procession. *Oberleutnant* Stefan Kirmaier, the unit's senior officer, technical officer, and leading scorer with seven victories, was given command of *Jasta 2*, subsequently designated *Jasta Boelcke*. In spite of the loss of "the great man," Boelcke had taught his students well. By the time he fell, *Jasta 2* had amassed more than fifty victories, and von Richthofen, Bohme, Kirmaier, and Reimann had all achieved the status of "ace," with five or more victories each.

Richthofen scored five times in November, two victories of which occurred on the 20th. On November 9th, he shot down a British BE2c fighter/bomber that apparently intended to drop its bombs on the headquarters of Duke Carl Eduard of Saxe-Coburg-Gotha. When Richthofen later landed and rushed across the muddy field to survey his all-important eighth victory, he was met by a very grateful Duke who subsequently awarded the Baron the Saxe-Ernestine Ducal House Order, Knight 1st Class with Swords. Richthofen was pleased to receive the award from the Duke, but he hoped that he would soon be receiving the famed *Pour le Merite* now that he had achieved his eighth aerial success. However, although both Boelcke and Immelmann had received their "Blue Max" awards after eight victories, the bar had been raised. Richthofen believed that victories were now more difficult to achieve than nearly a year earlier when his predecessors were faced with fewer opponents with less armament. Nonetheless, he would not receive his Blue Max until two months later following his 16th triumph. Further, another intermediate award became a prerequisite for the Blue Max— the Prussian Royal Hohenzollern House Order. However, Richthofen received that award on November 11, 1916 and thus cleared the way for the coveted Blue Max.

On November 22nd, *Jasta Boelcke* lost its second leader when Kirmaier was shot down behind British lines while pursuing a FE2b. Although the unit's administrative officer, *Oberleutnant* Karl Bodenschatz, took charge until a new commander could be identified, Richthofen was the most decorated and highest-scoring pilot, and served as the de facto leader. The next day, on November 23rd, von Richthofen would avenge the death of Kirmaier and go up against Major Lanoe Hawker, the "British Boelcke."

Major Hawker was the Commander of 24 Squadron RFC, Britain's heroic first ace, and a recipient of both the Victoria Cross (VC) and Distinguished Service Order (DSO). He was well known, not only to the British but also to the Germans who had already lost seven aircraft to his combat skills. In what was one of the longest "dogfights" of the war, with both participants highly-experienced, Richthofen would ultimately be victorious. Because both aircraft, Hawker's DH2 and Richthofen's Albatros DII, were able to fire straight ahead, each pilot attempted to get on the other's tail. This resulted in a series of "curves" or tight turns to arrive at the opponent's "6 o'clock" for optimum positioning (close firing) or alternatively at a less-advantageous angular shooting solution (if further away). At one point, Richthofen noted that his opponent even "merrily waved" at him.[12] The DH2 was light and maneuverable, but the Albatros was faster and possessed a better climb rate. Because the prevailing winds were from the west, the battling pilots were being blown eastward over German lines, in Richthofen's favor.

The conflict began at eight thousand feet, but the high bank angles, g-forces, and resulting loss of lift forced the dueling aircraft lower and lower. Losing altitude and running low on fuel, Hawker ultimately chose to attempt an escape rather than be forced to land behind the German lines. Hawker hoped that his zigzag path, coupled with an anticipated increase of thrust at lower altitude, would be sufficient to fend off the relentless German Baron and his faster Albatros. However, the DH2's unreliable single-valve rotary engine failed to deliver the anticipated needed power, and Richthofen's skillful flying and shooting brought down the British ace south of Bapaume.

On November 29, 1916, *Oberleutnant* Franz Josef Walz was appointed to succeed Kirmaier as commander of *Jasta Boelcke* because of his seniority and perceived similarity to Boelcke. The *Jasta* was relocated to Pronville aerodrome, southeast of Queant, on December 5th. Meanwhile, Richthofen continued to add to his victories, scoring four times in December, another "double" coming on December 20th. His 13th success and first victory that day was against a former squadron member of Major Lanoe Hawker, Captain Arthur Knight who was an eight-victory ace. Like Hawker, Knight flew the DH2 and had been awarded the DSO and Military Cross (MC). Knight was the pilot that Boelcke and Bohme had been pursuing at the time of their deadly collision on October 28th.

When 1916 ended, *Jasta Boelcke* had posted eighty-six enemy aircraft destroyed and led, by far, all other *Jastas*. Von Richthofen had personally delivered fifteen victories and was the premier living German ace.

Manfred celebrated Christmas at the Pronville airfield with Lothar and his father who had taken leave from the small garrison he commanded outside Lille. Lothar made his first solo flight on the 26th as his father and Manfred observed from the ground.

The 1916–1917 winter was one of the most severe on record, but in spite of low clouds and rain in the morning, the afternoon of January 4th was sunny. The Baron's 16th victory against Flight Lieutenant Allan Todd in a Sopwith Pup of 8 Squadron Royal Naval Air Service (RNAS) would be his last with *Jasta Boelcke* and the one needed, as it turned out, to qualify for the Blue Max.[13] However, Richthofen did not immediately receive the coveted *Orden Pour le Merite*. Instead, on January 10, he was appointed commanding officer of *Jasta 11* based at La Brayelle airfield just outside of Douai, northeast of Arras, on the 6th Army Front. Finally, two days later, von Richthofen received a welcome telegram informing him that he had been awarded the *Orden Pour le Merite*.[14]

Jasta 11 eagerly awaited Richthofen's arrival at La Brayelle the first month of 1917 to take command of his new unit. The *Staffel* had been formed on September 28, 1916, but because of marginal leadership and inadequate training, had not scored a single victory. Of the three *Jastas* assigned to the 6th Army, *Jasta 11* had been the least aggressive and the least successful. Even *Flieger-Abteilung 18*, a neighboring two-seater reconnaissance unit, had a better victory record. On January 15, 1917, Manfred von Richthofen—the living ace of aces, with an incredible sixteen aerial combat victories to his credit—skillfully maneuvered his Albatros DIII to a perfect landing and stepped out of the sleek new machine, wearing the impressive *Pour le Merite* at his collar.[15] To further add to the *Jasta's* amazement, Richthofen's DIII was painted bright red.[16] Before the month ended, Richthofen would already become known as "The Red Baron," *Le Petit Rouge* (The Little Red One), and *Le Diable Rouge* (The Red Devil). Richthofen's famous red machine was an inspiration to his comrades and a challenging warning to his adversaries.

Richthofen was not thrilled about leaving *Jasta Boelcke*, but he was always eager to embrace a new challenge. As *Kommandeur* of *Jasta 11*, he could combine his unrelenting drive for personal combat with the challenge of transforming his dozen pilots into a team of disciplined expert aviators with an aggressive hunting spirit. He began immediately to coach his men and lead by example, utilizing the lessons learned from his mentor Oswald Boelcke. As did Boelcke before him, Richthofen drove his pilots hard to learn and refine tactics, master formation flying, and use armament effectively. He emphasized the requirement for vigilance, attacking at close range, shooting accuracy, and the ineffectiveness of acrobatics that surrendered precious speed and altitude. Finally, he cautioned his men that because they were outnumbered in the skies (typically 3-to-1), they had to choose their battles carefully, maintain an escape option, and to break off a fight if battle conditions were not right.

Richthofen wanted his men to fight as he did, and on a clear 23rd of January led six of his men for the first time to an area over the trenches near Lens. There they came upon two FE8 Scouts that had just shot down two German reconnaissance aircraft. Richthofen charged one FE8 head on, but it promptly dove and sped away. He then attacked the other, flown by the experienced, three-victory British pilot, Second Lieutenant John Hay of 40 Squadron RFC. As his pilots looked on, the Baron quickly dispatched his opponent, following 150 shots from fifty meters, to score *Jasta 11's* first victory.

The next day, Richthofen scored again against a FE2b when he went up to evaluate the performance of *Feldwebel* (Sergeant) Hans Howe as a potential pilot for his *Jasta*.[17] In a classic assault out of the sun, Richthofen attacked Lieutenant John MacLennan and Captain Oscar Greig of 25 Squadron RFC while they were photographing Vimy Ridge. Because the British crew's machine gun had jammed, Richthofen elected not to shoot the aircraft out of the air and forced the crew to land west of Vimy. However, the Baron, although not hit by machine gun fire, was also forced to land with wing structural damage to his Albatros DIII. Richthofen was delighted to speak with his adversaries, and, when he asked if either had seen his red aircraft, one replied: "Oh, yes. I know your machine very well. We call it 'Le Petit Rouge.'"[18]

Two *Jasta Boelcke* pilots, Hans Imelmann and Paul Ostrop, also experienced structural failures in their DIIIs and lost their lives on January 23rd. Finally, following complaints from Richthofen and other *Staffel* commanders, the DIIIs were grounded on January 27th.[19] With the exception of victory number twenty-five—when he used *Leutnant* Lubbert's Albatros DIII—Richthofen flew the much slower Halberstadt DII for his next thirteen scores through March 25th. He had "double" victories on February 14th, March 4th, and March 17th. Although most of these victories were against opponents with equal speed capability, three were against aircraft with as much as a twenty-nine mph advantage.[20]

Richthofen continued to fly with individuals and with groups of his men in January and the first part of February. Soon, like his mentor Boelcke, he developed the amazing ability to take note of essentially everything going on around him, even when engaged personally in a deadly one-on-one battle. This allowed him to effectively evaluate his pilots' performance and suggest improvement. He was challenging with his men, but he never asked them to do anything more than he demanded of himself.

On February 4th, with the weather closing in and increasingly more comfortable with his *Staffel's* rising stars such as Kurt Wolff, Karl Allmenroder, and Sebastian Festner, Richthofen went on home leave for ten days.[21] He also stopped in Berlin to discuss the problems with the Albatros DIII. During his visit home, Manfred's mother asked him why he risked his life every day, to which he replied: "For the man in the trenches. I wish to lighten his hard lot, to keep enemy fliers away from him."[22]

Following his brief rest at Schweidnitz, Richthofen landed his Halberstadt DII at *Jasta Boelcke's* aerodrome for conferences. On February 14th, he wasted no time getting back into combat on his return trip to his *Staffel*. During the subsequent short flight from Pronville to La Brayelle, he recorded his 20th victory against a BE2d fighter/bomber flown by Second Lieutenants Cyril Bennett and Herbert Croft of 2 Squadron RFC. Later that afternoon, with five aircraft of his *Staffel*, Richthofen scored again, this time against a BE2c, also of 2 Squadron, flown by Captain George Bailey and Second Lieutenant George Hampton.

Typical rainy and snowy weather in northern France and Belgium in February and March 1917 often kept aviators on both sides of the Front grounded. Richthofen used the time to further develop his men, refine Boelcke's *Dicta*, and write a series of reports to the Chief of Field Operations that would later become the basis of his own *Air Combat Operations Manual*. It was during this time that the members of *Jasta 11* began to paint their aircraft. They had heard rumors that their leader's all-red machine had become the target of a special "anti-Richthofen" squadron, and they implored him to allow them to paint their aircraft with red markings as well. Richthofen consented but reserved the all-red paint scheme as his own.[23] Individual colors allowed the pilots to identify each other during swirling dogfights and made confirmations of victories easier for ground observers.

As Britain prepared for the Battle of Arras, aerial combats increased. *Jasta 11* scored twenty-seven victories in March—ten by Richthofen, including two "doubles" on the 4th and 17th—outscoring all other *Staffels*, even though the Albatros DIIIs were still temporarily grounded for lower wing failures.[24] The British First & Third Armies amassed some 385 operational aircraft on the Arras Front, split between twenty-five squadrons. The Germans had 114 aircraft of the 6th Army—*Jasta 11* plus seven other *Staffeln*—but typically only seven aircraft were functional from each unit on a daily basis.

On the snowy morning of March 6th, von Richthofen would get a taste of his own mortality. He and four members of his *Jasta* attacked a group of Sopwith Strutters of 43 Squadron, but quickly found themselves outnumbered 3-to-1 when 40 Squadron joined in. Richthofen singled out an opponent and closed in. Briefly failing to look aft, the Baron was suddenly hit in both fuel tanks of his Halberstadt by an aircraft that had momentarily moved into firing position behind him. The Baron quickly dived away, switched off the engine to avoid a fire, and landed within the German lines. Just as he did in the days when he was thrown by his horse, von Richthofen took to the air again that same afternoon, this time in *Leutnant* Lubbert's Albatros DIII. Using only one hundred rounds, he secured his 25th victory against a DH2 flown by Lieutenant Arthur Pearson of 29 Squadron RFC, who had been a previous victor and holder of the Military Cross.

On March 10th, Manfred's brother, Lothar, was assigned to *Jasta 11*. On March 23rd, Manfred von Richthofen was given an early promotion to the rank of *Oberleutnant* (First Lieutenant).

April 1917 was the most successful month of Richthofen's career and also that of his *Staffel*. The Baron downed twenty-one enemy aircraft and his unit claimed a total of ninety, once again outperforming all other *Jastas*.[25] Bad weather precluded flying on the first day of April, but Richthofen, using his newly refitted Albatros DIII, opened the April scoring with two victories the next day and ended the month on the 29th with an incredible four successes in less than eight hours. He also had additional double victories on April 5th and 8th and a "triple" on the 13th. Major Albrecht von Richthofen proudly witnessed his sons' six-victory day when visiting the aerodrome on April 29th.[26] Manfred ended the month with fifty-two total aerial combat successes, surpassing his mentor Oswald Boelcke's total of forty by mid-month. *Jasta 11*, the lowly *Staffel* without a victory just three months earlier, achieved its one hundred victory milestone on April 22nd. Unfortunately, *Jasta 11* would not escape tragedy, losing Sebastian Festner on April 23rd and Hans Hintsch on the 24th. On April 26th, the Kaiser ordered the unit to be designated *Jagdstaffel Richthofen*, although after three weeks the humble Baron would not allow the designation to remain in place.

Bringing further satisfaction to his month's work, von Richthofen was promoted to *Rittmeister* (Cavalry Captain) on April 7th. That same day, *Jasta 11* set up seventeen captured English machine guns in the vicinity of the officers' mess in order to counter a second night's bombing raid by 100 Squadron RFC.[27] The next morning, Manfred, Schafer, and their comrades were informed by military intelligence that they had forced down three British FE2b aircraft close to the aerodrome by putting their engines out of action. On April 15th, Richthofen, constantly looking for improved strategic locations for his operations, relocated his unit from La Brayelle to Roucourt, some twelve miles southeast of Douai.

On April 30th, the Baron received a wire that he was to meet with the Kaiser on May 2nd. Richthofen had been ordered to take leave after surpassing Boelcke's record of forty victories in mid-April. However, Richthofen, refusing to miss the action during the Battle of Arras, protested and was ultimately allowed to remain at the Front until the end of the month. By then, he had recorded fifty-two combat victories!

On May 1st, Manfred transferred command of *Jasta 11* to his brother Lothar with an informal handshake. He departed Roucourt with his Technical Officer Konstantin Krefft—also going on leave—in the *Staffel's* all-red two-seat Albatros CIX bound for German Army Headquarters at the resort city of Bad Kreuznach. They landed in Cologne where they received a public reception, complete with crowds, flowers, and speeches by town dignitaries. After lunch and a short rest, the crew flew on to Bad Kreuznach—enjoying an aerial sightseeing tour of the Rhine River en route—where Richthofen met briefly with *General* (General) Ernst von Hoeppner, Commanding General of the German Air Service. The next day, his 25th birthday, Richthofen met with Field Marshall Paul von Hindenburg, *General* Erich von Ludendorff, and then had lunch with Kaiser Wilhelm II, who gave him a birthday gift consisting of a full-size bronze and marble bust of the Emperor in full martial splendor. That evening, Richthofen was the guest of honor at a dinner party hosted by *General* von Hoeppner. Richthofen was seated to the right of von Hindenburg, who he learned had also begun his military career at Wahlstatt, coincidentally in Barracks Room 6. The following day, Richthofen flew with *Oberleutnant* Fritz von Falkenhayn in an Aviatik CII to Bad Homburg, another old spa city, where he had lunch with Empress Auguste Victoria. Later, Richthofen returned to Bad Kreuznach for a formal dinner hosted this time by Field Marshall von Hindenburg. Finally, on May 4th, Richthofen was able to hunt wood grouse in the Black Forest near Freiburg.

Following his stay in the Black Forest, Richthofen was off to Berlin where weather forced his plane down in a meadow outside of Leipzig, southwest of his destination. Completing the journey by train, Richthofen spent several days in Berlin where he posed for a formal portrait photo, met with various dignitaries, and spoke with the major publisher Verlag Ullstein about commencing work on his memoirs.[28] Finally, on May 16th, Richthofen was able to visit the aeronautical test center at the Adlershof section of Johannisthal airfield. There, still concerned about the lower wing problems on the Albatros DIII, he flight-tested the LFG Roland DIII.

At 0700 hours on May 19th, Richthofen arrived in Schweidnitz where he was met by his sister, Ilse, for the short walk home. However, even at such an early hour, news of the hero's arrival spread quickly.

For the next several days, the shy Baron graciously accepted the overwhelming attention he received from the residents of the city, dignitaries, delegations, reporters, and photographers. Richthofen gave special attention to the children and various youth groups, and he patiently satisfied the numerous requests for autographs from both young and old. Finally, when the intensity of the visitors never seemed to let up, Richthofen's long-time friend and fellow hunter, *Herr* Schwanitz, rescued him one afternoon and they sought the peacefulness of the forest.

Richthofen also began work on his book during his leave at Schweidnitz. The publisher sent a stenographer and she stayed in the Hotel Crown in the city center. There, he would dictate stories to her in the mornings. Later, she would type the notes and then bring them to the house where he, his mother, and Ilse would review them in the evenings. Even though the arrangement was strictly professional, the situation generated rumors that there was a romantic relationship between the pretty stenographer and the handsome pilot. Once, just after he had brought the stenographer to the garden gate, two very inquisitive ladies happened to pass by and paused to speak with him. He mischievously introduced the modest, smiling woman as his fiancée.[29]

On May 26th, Richthofen was welcomed as the honored guest at the estate of Hans Heinrich XI, the Prince of Pless, where he had been invited to hunt bison. After a successful hunt, Richthofen returned to Schweidnitz. Then on May 31st, he departed in a Halberstadt single-seat aircraft, on his way to Vienna to begin a programmed "tour" of aviation facilities in Austria and then in Turkey.

On June 5th, Richthofen learned that his protégé, *Leutnant* Karl-Emil Schafer, who had gone on to command *Jasta 28* on April 26th, had been killed in combat. Richthofen cancelled his remaining appointments in Vienna and travelled by train to attend the funeral in Berlin. While there, the Baron also worked to persuade the Inspectorate for Military Aviation to expedite an appropriate successor to the Albatros DIII and DIV. Not only were the machines continuing to have wing failures, but they were no longer a match for the newer British and French aircraft.[30]

Before returning to the Front, Richthofen was ordered back to Bad Kreuznach. There he again had lunch with Kaiser Wilhelm II and met with Czar Ferdinand of Bulgaria, who presented him with the Bulgarian Bravery Order 4th Class, 1st Grade. On June 10th, Richthofen arrived at Harlebeke, *Jasta 11's* new base of operations, northeast of Courtrai, selected because it was closer to the 4th Army Front. On June 17th, Richthofen's friend and former pilot, Georg Zeumer, was killed in air combat as a pilot with *Jasta Boelcke.*

Richthofen was back into aerial combat in an Albatros DIII on June 18, 1917, for his 53rd victory. He scored against a RE8 reconnaissance aircraft of 9 Squadron flown by Lieutenants Ralph Ellis and Harold Barlow. On June 23rd and 24th, flying his new Albatros DV, Richthofen added two more victories against Spad VII and DH4 fighters, flown respectively by Second Lieutenant Robert Farquhar of 23 Squadron and Captain Norman McNaughton and Lieutenant Angus Mearns of 57 Squadron. Farquhar had six victories to his credit, while McNaughton had claimed five and had been awarded the Military Cross.

It was also on June 24th that Richthofen was given command of the first *Jagdgeschwader* (Fighter Wing) comprised of *Jastas 4, 6, 10,* and *11* and chartered to achieve aerial superiority over critical battle zones, reporting directly to the 4th Army High Commander. The new *JGI Kommandeur's* four *Jasta* leaders included *Oberleutnant* Kurt-Bertram von Doring (*Jasta 4*), *Oberleutnant* Eduard Dostler (*Jasta 6*), *Oberleutnant* Ernst *Freiherr* von Althaus (*Jasta 10*), and *Leutnant* Kurt Wolff (*Jasta 11*).[31] *Leutnant der Reserve* Konstantine Krefft, *Jasta 11's* Technical Officer, was given the corresponding assignment in the *Jagdgeschwader,* and Richthofen selected *Oberleutnant* Karl Bodenschatz from *Jasta Boelcke* to serve as his adjutant. True to form, "Richthofen's Traveling Circus" would relocate to Marcke, southwest of Courtrai on July 2nd.[32]

On June 25th, the Baron, flying with *Oberleutnant* Karl Allmenroder just two days before the latter's death, was victorious against his 56th opponent, a RE8 reconnaissance biplane of 53 Squadron RFC flown by Lieutenant Leslie Bowman and Second Lieutenant James Power-

Clutterbuck. Allmenroder also logged his 29th victory against a Sopwith Triplane.

On the cloudy morning of July 2nd, Richthofen took off with *Jasta 11* and joined in on an attack on a pair of RE8s, once again of 53 Squadron. From only fifty meters, the Baron quickly sent the aircraft, flown by Sergeant Hubert Whatley and Second Lieutenant Frank Pascoe, out of control over Deulemont for his 57th victory.

On the morning of July 6th, Richthofen personally led a contingent of *Jasta 11* Albatros DVs against six ground-strafing FE2d pusher biplane bombers from 20 Squadron reportedly heading for Deulemont. After joining with additional German fighters in the area, Richthofen and his formation maneuvered to get behind the enemy aircraft, which then suddenly turned to meet the Albatrosses head-on. Richthofen took note that the observer in the FE2d approaching him began firing from long range (some twelve hundred feet away). In fact, because of the interval, the *Rittmeister* had just begun to arm his guns. While he was reflecting on the poor chance the gunner had of success at that distance—especially protected as he was by the engine in front of him—he suddenly felt a blow to the head.[33] The Baron was completely paralyzed and blinded! He fought mentally and physically to regain muscle control and his vision. As he felt the aircraft spinning and rapidly losing altitude, he was finally able to grip the control wheel and instinctively switch off the engine to minimize the possibility of a fire. Using sheer willpower, he was able to slowly regain his eyesight, restart the engine, and locate a landing area within German lines. Feeling himself weakening again, he hurriedly set his Albatros down near Wervicq, tumbled out of the cockpit, but was unable to gather the strength to move further. Fortunately, two of his comrades, *Leutnants* Otto Brauneck and Alfred Niederhoff, followed his aircraft and protected its pilot as it spiraled down. Another officer, *Leutnant der Reserve* Hans Schroder, had watched the descent using an alert post telescope and, together with a corporal, was able to get to the scene quickly. Richthofen was taken to Field Hospital No. 76 (St. Nicholas) at Courtrai.

That afternoon, when Richthofen was finally allowed to receive visitors, Adjutant Bodenschatz and the leaders of *JGI's Staffels* were immediately at his bedside.[34] Although exhausted and pale, the Baron assured his staff that he would be back soon. Meanwhile, *Oberleutnant* Kurt-Bertram von Doring served as acting *Kommandeur* of the *Jagdgeschwader*. The day after the Baron was forced down, the pilots of *JGI* sought their revenge and scored nine victories with no losses of their own. Kurt Wolff was the first to score that nearly cloudless day. Four days later on July 11th, Wolff would share the hospital room with his mentor after he was severely wounded in the hand in a conflict with twelve Sopwith Triplanes. He would not see action again until September 11th.

Meanwhile, Richthofen continued to do battle even from his hospital bed. Counter to Richthofen's operational orders that had been previously approved by the Commanding General of the German Air Service (*Kogenluft*), *Hauptmann* Otto Bufe—the Air Officer in Charge of Aviation for the 4th Army—directed von Doring to utilize the *Geschwader* in squadrons on "barrier flights" to keep British aircraft from crossing German lines. Further, he expected the single German *Staffels* to fly late in the evening and at night against the large British formations that used the sun behind them to mask their attacks. The inevitable result was that the heavily outnumbered German aircraft could not be as effective and also became easy targets. Richthofen was furious and used his influence in his letter to his friend *Oberleutnant* Fritz von Falkenhayn, the *Kogenluft* staff's Technical Officer. At about this same time, the Commanding General of the 4th Army, *General der Infanterie* Fredrich Sixt von Armin, ordered increased attacks against British tethered observation balloons, thereby essentially freeing up the fighter units.[35] The Baron also continued to push for more improved fighters to counter the Sopwith Triplane, the SPAD VII, and the Sopwith Camel. The Baron was particularly frustrated that the Albatros DIII and DV aircraft continued to have occasional wing problems.

In spite of continuing headaches and periodic procedures to remove residual small bone fragments, Richthofen—as well as his equally impatient hospital roommate, Kurt Wolff—was determined to get back to his *Geschwader*. Finally, on July 20th, the *Rittmeister*, although embarrassed, was allowed to visit his men with his pretty brunette nurse, Katie Otersdorf, insisting that she be in attendance.[36] Thus, Karl Bodenschatz drove Manfred, Nurse Otersdorf, Major von Richthofen, and Wolff to the airfield. Along the 15-minute route, they passed a long column of soldiers on their way back to Courtrai. When one infantryman spotted the *Rittmeister* with his *Uhlan* jacket, *Pour le Merite*, and head bandage, he cried out "Richthofen!!!"[37] The roar of the name spread faster than Bodenschatz's car and the excited and grateful soldiers waved and shouted hurrahs to the great fighter ace as he passed by.

When the *Rittmeister* arrived at Marckebeke, he shook hands with *Oberleutnant* von Doring, but said little as he toured the facilities and the flight line with its shot-up and frequently patched machines.[38] Finally, he addressed his assembled pilots with some welcome news: "You are getting new Fokker triplanes. They climb like monkeys and they're as maneuverable as the devil!"[39] The *Geschwader* also had good news for its *Kommandeur*. The weather had been bad for several days, but that morning the *JGI* pilots had claimed five victories, two pilots achieving their first scores.[40] He didn't say it, but the members of *Jagdgeschwader I* could tell by his movements and the look in his clear, focused eyes that the *Rittmeister* would be back, very soon.

Indeed, Richthofen returned just five days later, on July 25th, and resumed command of his *Geschwader*, even though he would not be allowed to fly for three more weeks. At last, on the morning of August 16th, the Baron took to the sky again in his all-red Albatros DV with four other aircraft of *Jasta 11*. The *Geschwader* had lost Otto Brauneck on July 26th and Alfred Niederhoff two days later. The *Rittmeister* was anxious to again see action and, in spite of fighting fatigue, a headache, and nausea, quickly dispatched a Nieuport 23 of 29 Squadron RFC flown by Second Lieutenant William Williams for his 58th victory. When the exhausted Baron returned to the field, he had to be assisted out of the aircraft and carried to his quarters.

As he slowly recovered, fortunately not all of the *Rittmeister's* activities were as strenuous as flying. Following *Oberleutnant* Eduard

Dostler's 21st aerial victory, it was announced on August 6th that he was to receive the *Pour le Merite*. In his visit to the *Jasta 6* mess to congratulate the *Staffel* leader, Richthofen demonstrated his fierce loyalty and support of his men and their successes when he placed his own Blue Max around Dostler's neck because the latter's award had not yet arrived.

There was also a special *Geschwader* celebration the evening of August 17th. In addition to three other victories that day, a new *Jasta 11* pilot, *Leutnant* Hans-Georg von der Osten, had achieved his first victory. But that first victory also marked the 200th victory for *Jasta 11* in only seven months of operation. The day before, *Leutnant* Werner Voss—who had been designated commander of *Jasta 10* on July 30th—achieved his 37th victory.

On August 21st, the leader of *Jasta 6*, *Oberleutnant* Dostler, was killed in action. Then early on the morning of August 26th, the three *JGI* airfields—Marcke, Heule, and Bisseghem—were attacked by British SPAD VII fighters of 19 Squadron. Interpreting the situation severe enough to offset the directive that he not fly unless "absolutely necessary," the *Rittmeister* went after his attackers. Within an hour of the last strafing run, Richthofen, with four members of *Jasta 11*, came out of the sun on a lone SPAD VII of 19 Squadron RFC flown by Second Lieutenant Coningsby Williams and sent it down for his 59th. The *Rittmeister* had to make an emergency landing following the attack because some faulty incendiary ammunition rounds caused damage to his pressure line, intake manifold, and exhaust manifold. He was forced to switch off his engine and glide his aircraft back to Marcke. Once again, he had to be helped from his aircraft.

On August 28th, two pre-production Fokker FI Triplanes finally arrived at Marckebeke. The designer Anthony Fokker, as well as 4th Army General Sixt von Armin, and Chief-of-Staff Major General von Lossberg were on hand to mark the occasion. Richthofen gave the honor of demonstrating one of the new Fokkers to *Leutnant* Werner Voss. The Baron was still suffering from the effects of his head injury and admitted that he was "not quite right" in a letter home that evening. In fact, the doctors had removed another fragment of bone from his head just the day before.

On the night of August 31ˢᵗ, British bombers again made a direct assault on Richthofen's airfields west of Courtrai. Thus, on a cloudy, rainy September 1ˢᵗ, Richthofen flew the Fokker Triplane for the first time and used only 20 rounds from a distance of fifty meters to defeat a RE8 of 6 Squadron RFC flown by Lieutenant John Madge and Second Lieutenant Walter Kember. Afterwards, the Baron ordered his 60ᵗʰ, and last, silver victory cup from the jeweler in Berlin. Two days later, the *Rittmeister* scored his 61ˢᵗ aerial victory, this time charging his triplane against a Sopwith Pup of 46 Squadron, damaging its engine and forcing the uninjured pilot, Lieutenant Algernon Bird, to land near Bousbecque.[41] Anthony Fokker arrived at Marcke not long after Bird was forced down, and the famous aircraft designer filmed the two smiling adversaries as they visited following the battle. The *Geschwader* claimed ten other aerial victories that day. Although *JGI* suffered no loses, *Leutnant* Bockelmann of *Jasta 11* sustained a leg wound.

Richthofen was this time firmly dispatched on recuperative leave beginning September 6ᵗʰ. He had been invited by Carl Eduard—the Duke of Saxe-Coburg-Gotha—to *Schloss* (Castle) Reinhardsbrunn, the Duke's hunting lodge southwest of Gotha in the Saxon Duchy of Thuringia.

On September 15ᵗʰ, recently-promoted *Oberleutnant* Kurt Wolff, flying Richthofen's Triplane FI 102/17, was shot down by a Sopwith Camel. He had been victorious in the air thirty-three times. Then on September 24ᵗʰ, *Leutnant* Werner Voss—Richthofen's chief rival for aerial victories with forty-eight to his credit—was shot down in his triplane in an epic battle against no less than seven SE5s of 56 Squadron.[42] Richthofen, struck hard when he heard the news of the loss of two of his dearest friends, dealt with his grief in the solitude that the East Prussian retreat afforded. Lothar von Richthofen, who had been wounded in the hip by anti-aircraft fire on May 13ᵗʰ following a victory over a BE2e, resumed command of *Jasta 11* on September 26ᵗʰ, thereby boosting the unit's morale brought low by the recent losses.[43]

At the end of September, Richthofen journeyed to Berlin where he met with *General* von Hoeppner and *Oberst* (Colonel) Thomsen. He also visited Adlershof to evaluate several new scout fighter designs. While in Berlin, Richthofen learned that on September 22nd, he had been awarded the Lubeck Hanseatic Cross, and on September 24th the Brunswick *Kriegsverdienstkreuz* (War Merit Cross). On September 23rd, the Baron was given a bronze bust by Kaiser Wilhelm II inscribed: "To The Glorious Fighter Pilot *Rittmeister Freiherr* von Richthofen. His Grateful King. 10 Sept 1917."[44] In October, the Baron received two additional awards—the Cross for Faithful Service 1914 of Schaumberg-Lippe (dated 10 Oct 1917) and the Princely Lippe War Honor Cross for Heroic Deeds (dated 13 Oct 1917).

On October 9th, Richthofen was able to use the Wing's all-red, two-seat reconnaissance aircraft to fly home to Schweidnitz, flying over the city to waving swarms of people and then landing on the barricaded parade ground across from his home. His mother, surprised that his head wound was still far from being healed and that he looked ill, implored him to stop flying. Manfred replied: "Who should fight the war then, if we all thought that way? The soldier alone in the trenches?! If those who are competent refuse to lead, it will soon be like in Russia."[45]

During his visit home, the Baron spent some time making a few final adjustments to the text of his book. He also accepted invitations from the War College in Danzig and to the Neu-Sternberg game reserve in Labiau, East Prussia. On October 18th, Richthofen traveled back to the Reinhardsbrunn Castle in Thuringia where he attended the wedding of his friend *Hauptmann* Fritz Prestien. Subsequently, a confused journalist for the *Gothaisches Tageblatt* reported that it was Manfred von Richthofen who had married the former *Fraulein* von Minckwitz. This obviously created quite a stir throughout Germany. When the Baron returned to the Hotel Continental in Berlin, he was inundated with congratulatory greetings and telegrams.

The *Rittmeister* was delighted to finally get back to the Front on October 23rd where his new Fokker DRI triplane awaited him. Unfortunately, the new Fokkers began having problems shortly after entering service. On October 30th, *Staffelfuhrer* Heinrich Gontermann of *Jasta 15*, flying DRI 115/17, was injured and died later that day following aircraft wing and aileron problems.[46] That same day, Manfred and Lothar, flying their triplanes, led a flight of *Jasta 11* aircraft on an early morning patrol. First Lothar and then Manfred experienced engine problems and were forced to land. After covering his brother's glide down from enemy fire, Manfred lost his engine and crash-landed, catching one wheel in a hole. He was able to climb out unharmed, but to his amazement, the triplane was totally destroyed, literally collapsing around him. The next day, *Leutnant* Gunther Pastor of *Jasta 11* was killed in his triplane DRI 114/17 when he experienced wing problems similar to *Leutnant* Gontermann's. On November 2nd, all Fokker triplanes were grounded for modifications.[47] The Fokker wings were strengthened and the ailerons redesigned, but the triplanes would not be cleared to return to service until November 28th. Meanwhile, Richthofen went back to flying the Albatros DV. However, an old problem resurfaced when *Leutnant* Erich Loewenhardt, a seven-victory ace with *Jasta 10*, sustained a wing failure in his DV on the morning of November 6th. Fortunately, Loewenhardt was not injured, but confidence in the Albatros fleet suffered again. The *Kommandeur* was forced to put in a request from his friend Fritz von Falkenhayn in Berlin for better hangar facilities to protect his moisture-sensitive aircraft. *JGI* pilots, meanwhile, continued to fly the Albatros DIII, Albatros DV, and the new Pfalz DIII biplane.[48]

On November 4th, the *Rittmeister* was presented with the Turkish War Medal (Iron Crescent), but for several weeks in November, Richthofen was once again barred from flying. With the triplanes grounded and the Albatros DVs under investigation, his superiors sought to protect their greatest asset.

On November 20th the Battle of Cambrai began with the British First and Third Armies launching a surprise attack—using 381 tanks, infantry, and support aircraft—against the 2nd Army sector from Gonnelieu to Havrincourt. In mid-November, the *Geschwader* had already been in the process of relocating to the 2nd Army Front in anticipation of a major Allied offensive, but the airfields couldn't be readied in time. Therefore the *Staffeln* flew, for staging, to the training field (*Jastaschule*) at Valenciennes on November 21st and then to the La Briquette airdrome on the 22nd. During mostly bad weather the next three days, the *Circus* finally moved to their new airfields at and around Avesnes-le-Sec, 20 kilometers northeast of Cambrai.[49]

Richthofen was back in action in his Albatros DV on November 23rd when he led combined flights from *JGI* and *Jastas 5* and *15* to challenge British fighters over Bourlon Wood supporting infantry attacks on that city. He attacked two Airco DH5s from 64 Squadron, forcing the first, flown by Captain Henry Russell, to land west of Bourlon Wood. At low altitude, he fired on the second, flown by Lieutenant James Boddy, causing it to crash southeast of Bourlon Wood. The Baron only submitted a claim for the second aircraft and subsequently received credit for his 62nd victory.

On November 29th, Richthofen learned that his good friend *Oberleutnant* Erwin Bohme, leader of *Jasta Boelcke*, had been shot down by a British Armstrong Whitworth FK8 two-seat reconnaissance aircraft.[50] The loss was particularly difficult for Richthofen because Bohme had been the last surviving member of the very close group of comrades that made up the original roster of eleven men at Boelcke's *Jasta 2*.

The next day, on a cloudy afternoon, the *Rittmeister* led a *JGI* flight that included Lothar and *Leutnant* Siegfried Gussmann against a formation of ten superior SE5a fighters of 41 Squadron. At an altitude of three hundred feet and close range using only one hundred rounds, the Baron sent SE5a pilot Lieutenant Donald MacGregor down in the vicinity of Steinbruch Forest near Moevres. MacGregor had claimed a German Albatros over Douai on the previous day. Later that day, in addition to celebrating his 63rd victory, Richthofen learned that *Leutnant der Reserve* Hans Klein (*Staffel* Leader of *Jasta 10*) was to become the Baron's seventh protégé to receive the *Pour le Merite*. *Leutnant der Reserve* Kurt Wusthoff (*Staffel* leader of *Jasta 4*) had received notice of his *Pour le Merite* award on November 27th.

As winter set in and activity slowed, the *Rittmeister*, still concerned about the dependability of the Fokker and Albatros machines, visited the Pfalz *Flugzeugwerke* (Aircraft Works) in Speyer on December 12th to evaluate the Pfalz DRI Triplane. He returned ten days later, disappointed that the Pfalz did not handle as well as the Fokker, and the allegedly more powerful Siemens-Halske SH III rotary engine failed to meet the manufacturer's claims.

The *Rittmeister* spent Christmas 1917 with his men at Avesnes-le-Sec. His father was able to join his two aviator sons for the Holiday, to the delight of everyone in *JGI*. The members of the Wing treated Major Albrecht *Freiherr* von Richthofen as a father and affectionately referred to him as *Fliegervater* (Father of the Flyers).

On December 28th, Manfred and Lothar, at the invitation of *Prinz* Leopold of Bavaria—Commander in Chief of German Forces in the East—were sent to Brest-Litovsk to attend the peace conference where the Central Powers were dictating terms with representatives of Bolshevist Russia.[51] However, it was ultimately determined that having the Richthofens in attendance resulted in little propaganda value on the Russians, and following an invitation and acceptance to visit the late Czar Nikolai II's hunting lodge in the Bialowicz Forest to hunt rare game, the brothers were sent back to Germany on January 5th.

In Berlin, Richthofen was called on to address workers at various munitions factories who were protesting working conditions and shortages of food and other commodities. He was able to communicate to them the importance of their work, and they generally called off their strikes.

On January 19, 1918, Richthofen was on hand at the Adlershof airfield outside of Berlin for *Idflieg's* new aircraft type competitions.[52] He had been instrumental in formalizing these *Typenprufungen* (aircraft type tests) in order to give the frontline pilots the opportunity to evaluate the most appropriate designs to be placed into production. Of the twenty-eight aircraft from various companies, one of the most promising was the Fokker V.11 biplane, which when modified according to the Baron's suggestions, ultimately proved to be the most formidable aircraft of the war, the Fokker DVII.[53]

At the end of January, Richthofen flew from Berlin to visit Schweidnitz, but first "buzzed" the parade grounds at Wahlstatt where his younger brother, Bolko, was gathered with his cadet classmates. In an uncharacteristic display of his acrobatic skills performed specifically for his proud youngest brother, the Baron followed the low pass with a loop. Nevertheless, Bolko was disappointed that his brother had never landed at the parade field and later complained to his mother. Later, on his flight back to the Front, Manfred conducted another low pass and then a "bombing run" on Wahlstatt, dropping chocolates for the delighted cadets.

On February 2nd, Richthofen returned to *JGI* to prepare for the spring offensive that would officially begin on March 21, 1918. That same day because of the success of *JGI*, two more *Jagdgeschwader* fighter wings were formed.[54] Understanding the importance of the fighter wings and skilled pilots in combating the superior air forces of the Allies, Richthofen refined and published the Air Combat Operations Manual he had begun formulating a year earlier to aid both *Jagdgeschwader Kommandeurs* and individual pilots.

On March 12th, Richthofen, flying with Lothar and *Leutnant* Werner Steinhauser of *Jasta 11*, attacked a squadron of ten Bristol F2B Fighters of 62 Squadron at 5500 meters between Caudry and Le Cateau.[55] The pilot of the British aircraft selected by Richthofen, Second Lieutenant Leonard Clutterbuck, and observer/gunner Second Lieutenant Henry Sparks, immediately dove to one thousand meters in an attempt to escape.[55] However, the Baron kept the F2B in his sights and, hitting both fuel tanks, forced his 64th combat victory to land inside German lines north of Nauroy, where the crew was immediately captured. Two days later, Second Lieutenant Sparks, who was hospitalized with injuries to the left shoulder and arm, happily accepted half-a-dozen cigars, compliments of *Rittmeister* Manfred von Richthofen.

The following day, Richthofen and three of his *Staffels* encountered eleven Bristol F2B Fighters escorting several Airco DH4 bombers. These aircraft were joined by a flight of Sopwith Camels of 73 Squadron. Richthofen engaged a Bristol F2B, damaged its engine, and then left it to two Albatrosses from another *Staffel* to finish off, climbing back up to 3200 meters to battle several Camels. When he noticed a Camel attacking a member of his *Geschwader*, he quickly attacked, punctured its fuel tanks, and caused its pilot, Lieutenant Elmer Heath, to crash-land between Gonnelieu and Banteux for his 65th victory. During this same battle with the Bristol Fighters, Lothar von Richthofen lost the center section of the upper wing of his triplane and was forced down near Awoingt. Lothar's injuries to his jaw and right eye would keep him grounded for four months.

On March 15th, the *Rittmeister* handed his adjutant Bodenschatz a sealed envelope and instructed him, "If I do not return, open."[57] That same day, Richthofen visited *Jasta 37's Staffelfuhrer Leutnant der Reserve* Ernst Udet at the Le Cateau airfield. Udet had achieved twenty combat victories and was very successful in his own unit, but he immediately accepted Richthofen's request that he join *JGI*. Udet later remarked: "There are many good squadrons in the Army, and *Jasta 37* is far from the worst. But there is only one Richthofen group."[58] When Udet reported to *JGI's* new airfield at Awoingt, east of Cambrai, on March 25th, Richthofen took him on a mission to observe his flying. When they returned, the *Rittmeister* gave Udet command of *Jasta 11*.[59]

Late morning on March 18th, Richthofen led thirty aircraft of his *Geschwader* and scored his 66th victory, forcing a Sopwith Camel of 54 Squadron flown by Second Lieutenant William Ivamy to land with a ruptured fuel tank. *JGI* scored nine victories in the twenty-five minutes between 1100 and 1125 hours.

On March 24th and 25th, Richthofen was the only pilot of *JGI* to score, with victories respectively over a SE5A of 41 Squadron and a Sopwith Camel of 3 Squadron. The SE5A had been flown by Lieutenant John McCone, who claimed two combat victories. On March 26th, the *Geschwader* moved its operations to Lechelle, southeast of Baupaume. That same afternoon, Richthofen scored twice in fifteen minutes, once against a SE5A of 1 Squadron for his 69th, and then against a RE8 two-seater of 15 Squadron for his 70th.

On March 27th, the *Rittmeister* registered three successes (described earlier in the opening paragraphs of this Introduction). The Baron closed out a very successful March by logging his 74th victory the next day against an Armstrong Whitworth FK8 bomber/reconnaissance aircraft of 82 Squadron crewed by Second Lieutenants Joseph Taylor and Eric Betley.

Approaching his target at only ten meters, Richthofen scored his 75th victory on April 2nd against a RE8 of 52 Squadron crewed by Lieutenant Ernest Jones and Second Lieutenant Robert Newton. On April 6th, flying with *Jasta 11*, the *Rittmeister* dispatched a Sopwith Camel flown by five-victory ace and Flight Commander Captain Sydney Smith of 46 Squadron, intent on attacking German ground targets northeast of Villers-Bretonneux. That same day, Manfred von Richthofen received a congratulatory telegram that he had been awarded the unusually high decoration, the Prussian Red Eagle Order, Third Class with Crown and Swords in recognition of his 70th aerial victory.

On April 7th, in a thirty-five minute span just before noon, the Baron claimed his 77th and 78th victories against pilots of 73 Squadron flying Sopwith Camels. The first pilot, Second Lieutenant Albert Gallie, was able to walk away from his totally-destroyed aircraft near Hangard. The second, Lieutenant Ronald Adams, was forced to land north of Villers-Bretonneux and taken prisoner.

On April 12th, *JGI* was relocated to an airfield just south of Cappy. Then on April 20th, the *Rittmeister*, flying his red Fokker Triplane, claimed his last two victories in the span of three minutes.[60] On that cloudy and overcast Saturday evening, Richthofen lead five other aircraft of *Jasta 11* seeking targets near the old Roman Road. Forty minutes into the flight, the Baron dove on a Sopwith Camel that was attacking one of his pilots (*Leutnant* Hans Weiss). Maneuvering from below, the *Rittmeister* quickly sent down the Camel flown by 3 Squadron Commander Major Richard Raymond-Barker, who was a six-victory ace and had been awarded the Military Cross. Moments later, Richthofen attacked another Camel flown by Second Lieutenant David Lewis, forcing it down northeast of Villers-Bretonneux, only fifty yards from the first aircraft. Although the entire aft fuselage burned away in the air, Lewis was able to escape with only minor burns and bruises. Richthofen made a pass, waved to Lewis, and then continued over the infantrymen in the trenches and column of men on the road. The German soldiers waved to the Red Baron and flung their caps into the air. *JGI* would claim thirty-eight successes (including Manfred von Richthofen's six victories) in April 1918, with only three corresponding losses.

The next morning, Sunday, April 21, 1918, *JGI's* airfield at Cappy was fogged in. As usual, the pilots of the *Geschwader* were dressed and ready for action, waiting for the weather to clear. Meanwhile, their spirits were still high from the previous evening when they had celebrated their *Kommandeur's* 79th and 80th victories, along with the recent successes of the *Geschwader* itself. Even though the ever-modest Richthofen mentioned little about his 79th and 80th triumphs, he too was in a good mood. He and *Leutnant* Hans Joachim Wolff of *Jasta 11* had been invited to go hunting in the Black Forest by the fallen *Leutnant* Werner Voss's father and they had already purchased their train tickets in the event that the weather wouldn't allow them to fly. Playfully, the *Rittmeister* turned over a cot occupied by the resting and unsuspecting *Leutnant* Richard Wenzl. Moments later, another pilot met the same fate, tumbling over onto the damp grass. In retaliation, two officers tied a wheel chock to the tail of Richthofen's beloved Great Dane, Moritz, who, dragging the anchor behind him in circles, subsequently sought some measure of comfort from his master.

By 1030 hours, that day's uncharacteristic strong east wind succeeded in blowing the low stratus clouds away, and the pilots rushed to their aircraft. About the same time, they received word that there were two flights of Sopwith Camels approaching the Front. In less than five minutes, the first wave of Fokker triplanes was airborne, which included the *Kommandeur*, his cousin *Leutnant* Wolfram von Richthofen, *Vizefeldwebel* (Vice Sergeant Major) Edgar Scholz, *Leutnant* Hans Joachim Wolff, and *Oberleutnant* Walter Karjus.

On this particular morning, new pilots from both sides had been told to remain clear of any action and to simply observe—specifically the *Rittmeister's* cousin Wolfram and the Royal Air Force 209 Squadron's Lieutenant Wilfred May.[61] However, in the excitement of the ensuing battle between the *Rittmeister's* flight and Captain Arthur "Roy" Brown's flight, May fired on the triplane flown by Wolfram. May was soon drawn further into the fray, but he was quickly outclassed and then effectively unarmed when his guns jammed due to constant triggering. Richthofen, noticing the attack on Wolfram and the subsequent break-away by May to return to British lines, quickly dived on potential victory eighty-one. Soon May was flying extremely low over the Somme River being chased by the Baron. May's Camel was faster than the triplane, but his erratic maneuvering and Richthofen's superior flying soon narrowed the interval. Typically, May would have been an easy mark, but one of Richthofen's guns was hopelessly jammed and the other had a broken firing pin and was jamming intermittently. Richthofen was forced to release his shoulder harness and constantly lean forward to operate the cocking handle to be able to get off any rounds at all. Meanwhile, Brown saw that his fledgling pilot was in trouble and initiated a steep dive from one thousand meters to intercept the red Fokker. Finally, with about a 40 mph speed advantage, Brown swung southwards to position the sun behind him and then briefly attacked Richthofen above and from the left, west of Vaux-Sur-Somme. Brown then broke south with a climbing turn over the ridge near Vaire-Sous-Corbie.

Richthofen continued the pursuit of May for a few moments, but with his guns now both totally inoperable, he abandoned the chase and turned east. Situated on the top and south-facing slope of the Morlancourt Ridge west of Vaire-Sous-Corbie was an Australian anti-aircraft Lewis machine gunner, Sergeant Cedric Popkin. He fired on Richthofen twice, once as the Baron approached his position head-on; and then again, at long range from the right.[62] It was a single bullet from his machine gun that passed through the heart of the Red Baron.[63] In spite of the fact that he was mortally wounded, Richthofen was still at low altitude and apparently managed to make a controlled, side-slip landing in a field near the Bray-Corbie road, just north of the village of Vaux-sur-Somme, in a sector controlled by the Australian Imperial Force (AIF). *Rittmeister* Manfred von Richthofen died moments later, probably some 15–20 seconds after he was shot—remaining undefeated by his many adversaries in the air.[64]

Rittmeister Manfred Frhr. von Richthofen

1 SEEK THE BLUE MAX
(Formulate Your Vision)

Quite early somebody knocked at my door and before me stood the great man [Oswald Boelcke] with the *Ordre Pour le Merite*. I knew him ... but still I had never imagined that he came to look me up in order to ask me to become his pupil. I almost fell upon his neck when he inquired whether I cared to go with him to the Somme. Three days later I sat in the railway train and traveled through the whole of Germany straight away to the new field of my activity. At last my greatest wish was fulfilled. From now onwards began the finest time of my life. At that time I did not dare to hope that I should be as successful as I have been. When I left my quarters in the East a good friend of mine called out after me: "See that you do not come back without the *Ordre Pour le Merite*." [Richthofen, 1918, pp. 95–6]

The *Orden Pour le Merite* (Order of Merit) was Prussia's highest military award during World War I. The Order's badge consisted of a striking Maltese cross of deep blue enamel with eagles between the arms trimmed in gold and worn at the neck, a requirement when in uniform. It was awarded to officers for repeated and continued gallantry in action. The *Pour le Merite* was to become informally known as "The

Blue Max" because of its predominantly blue color and its first pilot recipient, *Oberleutnant* Max Immelmann.[1]

~

In 1966, Twentieth Century Fox Film Corporation released the movie *The Blue Max*, starring George Peppard as the fictional pilot, Bruno Stachel, who was obsessed with winning Germany's most coveted medal. In contrast to Stachel's misguided determination to win the Blue Max honorably or dishonorably, von Richthofen's vision was to serve his country by transferring to the "cavalry of the air" when his traditional *Uhlan* (cavalry) role was altered by the war's trenches and barbed wire. Richthofen's friend on the Eastern Front had helped plant the *Pour le Merite* seed in the Baron's mind. The Baron was intrigued by the possibility of one day actually being awarded the Blue Max, but he was also concerned with making a difference in the air war by shooting down enemy aircraft. Richthofen looked to the sky, visualizing the new battleground as an opportunity to contribute. As in his game hunting conquests, his aerial victories would be his trophies and the *Pour le Merite* a measure of his success.

Look to the Sky

What are we doing? We're reaching for the stars. **Christa McAuliffe, Astronaut, 1986.**

I joined the Flying Service at the end of May, 1915. My greatest wish was fulfilled. [Richthofen, 2005, p. 60]

Richthofen, stymied by the inability to conduct traditional cavalry operations at the Verdun Front in the spring of 1915, was bored and acknowledged his "restless spirit."[2] During a visit home to Schweidnitz in late May, Manfred announced to his mother that he was going to "join the fliers."[3] His mother noted the unmistakable elation in Manfred's voice when he spoke of becoming an airborne observer in the Flying

Service. She also knew that once he had verbalized his intention, there was no turning back—it was already a fact to him. He had made up his mind, and, even though she knew little about aviation, she knew him well enough to know that it he would soon make his dream a reality.

Richthofen literally looked to the sky and formed his initial vision! He understood that his envisioned "cavalry of the air" would provide the same sense of freedom and demand the enterprise and skill that he could no longer exercise in the ground war. He felt that his training as a cavalryman would allow him to do well as an aerial observer, and he was not yet interested in becoming a pilot. Richthofen was anxious to get into the air and was afraid the war might be over by the time he received his pilot certification.

In the air, Richthofen found the autonomy and challenge he was seeking. He could serve his country, and yet he could also enjoy his work:

The glorious thing in the flying service is that one feels that one is a perfectly free man and one's own master as soon as one is up in the air. [Richthofen, 1918, p. 56]

I was full of enthusiasm and would have liked to be sitting in an aeroplane all day long. I counted the hours to the next start. [Richthofen, 2005, p. 62]

Even though Richthofen enjoyed reconnaissance work in the Albatros BII and CI with his pilots Zeumer and von Holck, respectively, he was excited when he was transferred to the Western Front to fly in a "large battle-plane." Sitting in the nose of the two-engined AEG GII aircraft, he was now armed with a machine gun, could more-effectively protect the aircraft, and most importantly, could begin to collect aerial victories. Richthofen even took a short course in machine-gunnery. Unfortunately when he and Zeumer unsuccessfully battled a French Farman aircraft on September 1st, 1915, the Baron decided that to secure a victory he would also have to pilot the aircraft so that he could better control his aim.

Richthofen had another opportunity for an air fight in mid-September flying with von Osterroht in the smaller and more maneuverable Aviatik CI. When Osterroht positioned the aircraft alongside a Farman S.II, Richthofen exhausted his entire supply of one hundred rounds and the enemy aircraft fell. However, because the aircraft crashed behind enemy lines, he would not receive credit for the victory.

When another two weeks passed, Richthofen was transferred to the German bomber unit, *Brieftauben-Abteilung-Metz (BAM)*, in Rethel. On the train to his new assignment was where he met *Leutnant* Oswald Boelcke. When queried, Boelcke modestly explained how he was able to shoot down four hostile aircraft. Richthofen was frustrated because he felt that he used the same technique but his opponents seldom fell. Yet he realized that Boelcke flew a Fokker while he was an observer on a large battle plane. He therefore resolved to also fly the more maneuverable Fokker. Richthofen had *redefined* his vision!

At last I formed a resolution that I also would learn to fly a Fokker. Perhaps then my chances [to shoot down a hostile aircraft] would improve. [Richthofen, 1918, p. 64]

Luck is what happens when preparation meets opportunity. **Oliver Wendell Holmes**

A *vision* is a clear and concise image of a desired future state, either in your personal life or in your business. What is *your* vision? Are you "looking to the sky" to a dream you never really felt was within your grasp? Is your vision innovative, conceivable, challenging yet achievable, but even previously unimaginable? Is it truly a passion and a source of pride for you, your family, your team, or your company? Will it provide freedom, challenge, growth, and, yes, fun? If pursuing your vision is not fun—given that there will always be highs and lows pursuing anything that is worthwhile—then perhaps it's not the right dream for you. Remember that motivation, "luck," and success grow out of a clear sense of direction and a challenge for which you or your team are prepared. As Oliver Wendell Holmes and others have pointed out, *luck* occurs when *preparation* and *opportunity* come together. This author likes to suggest that luck can be found at the intersection of preparation and opportunity. Don't be afraid to modify your vision as it gradually comes more into focus. Richthofen visualized flying as the means of becoming a cavalryman of the air, but he soon realized that he could be more effective by personally flying a single-pilot aircraft with its machine gun as his personal lance. "Luck" and ultimate success came for Richthofen after he had taken to the air, diligently worked on his aerial gunnery skills, and then, during a chance train ride, noticed the "Blue Max" around the neck of German hero *Leutnant* Oswald Boelcke.

Climb the Steeple (Be Ambitious)

Shoot for the moon. Even if you miss, you'll land among the stars. **Les Brown**

From the beginning of my career as a pilot I had only a single ambition, the ambition to fly in a single-seater fighting machine. [Richthofen, 2005, p. 84]

Manfred von Richthofen's ambition was to fly a single-seat fighter and become the "first of the chasers."[4] To be given an opportunity to fly in a single-seat aircraft was aggressive enough in its own right. But to aspire to become the best of the best was beyond nearly every pilot's ambitions and expectations. This was true not only because of the skills required, but also because of the tremendous odds against even surviving combat long enough. If a pilot was well-trained, skillful—or even just plain lucky—it was possible to achieve the status of *Kanone* ("ace") with five aerial victories. In fact, 1863 WWI pilots (all nationalities) were credited with five or more victories. However, only twenty-eight pilots (1.5%) had forty or more victories. At forty victories—the total achieved by Oswald Boelcke at the time of his fatal collision with one of his men—the potential victory curve flattened, apparently due to pilot aging, burnout, and administratively-enforced leaves to protect valuable, experienced aviators.[5] Yet, Richthofen refused to allow the *system*, the doubts of others and even those of his own to force him to abandon his dream to fly a Fokker and become Germany's highest-scoring ace. This took tremendous ambition, courage, and conviction. One of Richthofen's biggest supporters, his mother, knew that Manfred possessed both the courage and the stamina to realize his dreams. She observed that he was capable of making "lightning-fast" decisions.[6] He knew instantly what he wanted to do, never vacillated in his resolutions, and never looked back.

~

It is commonplace to allow ourselves to be influenced by others, especially by those who are close to us. If we are fortunate, we have had family, friends, mentors, managers, or co-workers who have encouraged our most lofty dreams. Richthofen was fortunate to have a father, mother, and a grandmother who were all supportive. One place this was apparent was at the home of Manfred's grandmother, Marie, in the country. Following the strict regimen in the corps, holidays were particularly pleasing to the young cadet. His arrival at the *Gute Romberg* was typically greeted with the welcome greeting from his grandmother, "Now you are free … here everything is permitted."[7] The Richthofen boys especially enjoyed the county where they could swim, ride, and hunt as much as they wanted. Similarly, Manfred's mother was not an anxious parent. She too had enjoyed a childhood that permitted freedom and enterprise. She felt that nervous mothers could hinder the development of their children.

More than likely, however, we have been surrounded by others who may have been disappointed in achieving their own dreams and have settled for something less. They may have experienced their share of disappointments and thereby may even be trying to "protect" us from potential failure ourselves. As humans, it is far too easy to accept obstacles as the reality of life that stymie our ambition and block the achievement of our most-cherished aspirations. Too often we lower our sights or simply give up. Richthofen was undoubtedly ambitious, energetic, and enthusiastic, but he also possessed the bravery and courage to choose, pursue, and ultimately realize his dreams and destiny.

As noted earlier, the author had always wanted to be a pilot. Unfortunately, his mother was concerned about the hazards of flight and clearly expressed her wishes that he not put himself in danger. However, by September, 1968, the pull was so strong that he decided to pursue his dream with or without the approval of his parents. Once he made up his mind, accomplishing his objective was relatively easy. In only six weeks, while taking a full course load in college, he earned his private pilot's license. One sunny afternoon, less than three months later, his apprehensive parents climbed aboard a four-place Cessna Cardinal at Redbird Airport with their young son at the controls to experience their first-ever departure from the ground and personal airborne tour of the Dallas Metroplex.

One fine day, with my friend Frankenberg, I climbed the famous steeple of Wahlstatt by means of the lightning conductor and tied my handkerchief to the top. I remember exactly how difficult it was to negotiate the gutters. [Richthofen, 1918, p. 23]

What is your dream, your *steeple*? Are you ambitious enough to "climb the steeple" and to take command of your "aircraft?" Don't settle for less than the "highest point" or allow others to pilot your "plane" to its destination. Expect and insist on the freedom to achieve your vision. Isolate yourself from negativity. Likewise, don't allow walls (or glass ceilings!) to be built up around your family members, employees, or co-workers. Give them the support and freedom to be creative and realize their own dreams at the same time. Further, there does not have to be a dichotomy between your company's vision and that of your employees or colleagues. Help them "see" the vision and take pride in its achievement. Allow them to be creative and remain motivated. For those who don't think employees are motivated, hide out in the company parking lot on a Friday afternoon at 5:00 PM!

Insist on Flying a Fokker (Be Determined)

After the third flight with him [Manfred's brother, Lothar] I suddenly noticed he parted company with me. He rushed at an Englishman and killed him. My heart leapt with joy when I saw it. The event proved once more that there is no art in shooting down an aeroplane. The thing is done by the personality or by the fighting determination of the airman. [Richthofen, 1918, p. 150]

Although von Richthofen's strong resolve helped him prepare for and then pass his pilot's examination on Christmas day, 1915, it was nearly three months later before he finally received orders to return to the Front to fly the Albatros CIII. He was disappointed that he was as yet unable to fly the faster, more maneuverable single-pilot Fokker. Worst of all, he was again in a two seater aircraft, but this time in the pilot seat, the one without the machine gun! However, undeterred and ignoring the ribbing from the other pilots, he attached a machine gun to the upper wing of his aircraft so that it could be fired over the propeller arc. Subsequently, on April 26, 1916, the German official communiqué noted that two hostile aircraft had been shot down in aerial combat. One of these was a French Nieuport II scout pursued and shot down by the Baron himself!

Meanwhile, Richthofen continued to implore *Kasta 8's Kommandeur, Hauptmann* Carganico, to obtain a single-seat Fokker *Eindecker* so that he could be designated the unit's fighter pilot when not flying reconnaissance missions. Finally one day, two Fokkers were delivered to Landres. One was assigned to Erwin Bohme, and, perhaps because of a good word from Oswald Boelcke, the other was handed over to Richthofen and *Leutnant* Hans Reimann, for morning and afternoon patrols respectively.

It is one thing to have a vision and ambition. It is quite another to possess the *determination* or resolve to achieve your dream. To assert that Richthofen was an excellent pilot, as well as having dedication and determination would be an understatement. For any pilot to achieve forty victories in World War I—*the right stuff*, if you will—tremendous skill and determination were required. Richthofen would ultimately post eighty official victories!

But the Baron was also logical and calculating in what he did. Generally, the German pilots were outnumbered in the air by a ratio of 3-to-1. It was critical under such circumstances that aerial battles be chosen carefully. Possessing the patience and the instinctive craftiness of a hunter, Richthofen attacked from a position of advantage. He rarely took unnecessary risks unless he was protecting one of his own men. Richthofen noted in his Air Combat Operations Manual:

One should never obstinately stay with an opponent who, through bad shooting or skilful turning, one has been unable to shoot down, when the battle lasts until it is far on the other side and one is alone and faced by a greater number of opponents. [Richthofen's (MvR) Air Combat Operations Manual; Kilduff, 1993, p. 239]

~

When the author was nearing the end of his tour as an instructor pilot in the Air Force, he was faced with the probability that, should he elect to stay in the service, he would be required to serve a tour as a non-flying Missile Launch Officer (MLO). Although this would allow him to obtain his master's degree during the hours spent in a missile silo on alert, the likelihood of temporary grounding proved unacceptable. He therefore elected to leave the military and seek work as a commercial pilot. Unfortunately, although he interviewed with several major airlines, few were hiring and even scheduled classes were being cancelled. One day, the author noticed a sleek, new Learjet sitting on the ramp where he was doing part-time pilot instructing and commuter airline flying just before separating from the Air Force. Rather than compete for the few jobs available as an airline pilot, he decided on the spot to fly corporate aircraft. In fact, even though the Learjet didn't have afterburners like the T-38, it sported the same high-thrust General Electric engines. Why not take advantage of the best of both worlds!

How determined are you? Are you resolute in pursuing your dream job and unwavering in your plan to "fly the Fokker *Eindecker*," or are you willing to take a *back seat* and hope for the best? To paraphrase one of the sayings of the company chairman for whom the author previously worked, if you can't make a difference, get out of the way of those who will![8] It is important that you avoid those who claim that something can't be done or those negative individuals who find fault with everyone and everything. If you encounter such people, don't argue, but do take up the challenge! If you are a positive individual and you are determined, it is great motivation to prove the naysayers wrong! However, as did Richthofen, pick your battles carefully. You don't have to thumb your nose to get your point across. When you succeed—and you will!—you will have "said" it all!

Somersault Skills May Help (Draw on Your Talents)

It was no trouble at all for him to turn somersaults from a standing position. [Baroness von Richthofen, 1937, p. 79]

Richthofen possessed numerous talents from which to draw. Among them was his ability to flip completely from a standing position, even with his hands tucked at his sides. He was unquestionably agile. Being comfortable upright or inverted was a trait that was easily transferrable to the aerobatics required in air combat.

In addition to his considerable athletic skills, duty and discipline were also ingrained in the Baron's nature, learned from his father, his military training, and his Prussian heritage. In a letter to his mother from the Western Front on February 19, 1915, he wrote that the

French and English were becoming an increasing challenge because they were aware, and taking advantage, of the fact that much of the German fighting contingent was still deployed on the Eastern Front. Nevertheless, the outnumbered German forces refused to give up ground, preferring to be killed rather than to surrender. Richthofen conceded, however, that the English shared the "same blood."[9]

Richthofen was also an excellent hunter. He took great pride in the challenge of the chase as well as the eventual victory over his prey. He was calm, centered, and calculating. His mother noted that her son possessed an appetite for action, coupled with a strong will and focused determination. She also mentioned that he always had definite objectives in mind which he invariably achieved in every area he wished to pursue. However, in spite of his drive, he was not impulsive. She pointed out:

His lifestyle is this: First weigh—then risk. He would correctly recognize the problem, make a plan in his clear head, then nothing else would be able to confuse him. [Baroness von Richthofen, 1937, p. 90]

As related earlier, Richthofen was determined in spite of setbacks. For instance, following a serious mishap, he managed to win the 1913 Imperial cross-country race for army officers:

The last prize I got riding that horse [Blume] was when I rode for the Kaiser Prize in 1913. I was the only one who got over the whole course without a single mistake in direction. In doing so I had an experience which I should not care to repeat. In galloping over a piece of heath land I suddenly stood on my head. The horse had stepped into a rabbit hole, and in my fall I broke my collarbone. Notwithstanding the breakage, I rode another forty miles without making a mistake and arrived keeping good time. [Richthofen, 2005, p. 45]

Richthofen's experiences as a horseman and as a cavalryman also prepared him for his duties as an aerial observer and later as a pilot:

I imagined that, owing to my training as a cavalryman, I might do well as an observer.... Life in the Flying Corps is very much like life in the cavalry. Every day, morning and afternoon, I had to fly and to reconnoiter, and I have brought back valuable information many a time. [Richthofen, 1918, p. 55]

> What are your talents? What strengths do you have that others do not? As we've seen, even the ability to perform *somersaults* can be an advantage. In fact, in today's global, competitive environment, isn't that almost literally what many customers expect? How can you use your talents and those of your employees to achieve your vision? One reason why diversity is such a desirable commodity in organizations is that different backgrounds, strengths, and perspectives bring about accomplishment of company objectives through synergy. Do you empower those who are the most talented in certain areas to perform the needed work? People enjoy and are motivated when empowered to do what they do best. Although Richthofen was by nature humble and somewhat shy, he derived great pride, satisfaction, and pleasure from doing useful work and serving his country.[10]

Chapter 1 Summary

Seek the Blue Max. The *Pour le Merite* was Germany's highest military honor of World War I, awarded for repeated and sustained gallantry. It was equivalent to the Medal of Honor awarded by the United States and the Victoria Cross awarded by England. *Rittmeister* (Cavalry Captain) Manfred von Richthofen sought the coveted award as a symbol of service to his country as well as a trophy attesting to his aviation combat skills.

Pursue your vision, your "Blue Max!" Even if you are only able to seek your vision part time for now, begin today. It's never too early or too late to initiate the actions necessary to realize your dream.

Look to the Sky. "Look to the sky" to that lofty dream you never really felt was obtainable. Your dream should be innovative, conceivable, challenging yet achievable, and even previously unimaginable. It should truly be a passion, and it should provide freedom, challenge, and growth. It should also be fun.

Climb the Steeple. You should be ambitious enough to "climb the steeple" and to take command of your "aircraft." Don't settle for less than the "highest point" or allow others to pilot your "plane" en route to accomplishment of your vision. Expect and insist on the freedom to achieve your dream. Likewise, don't allow walls (or ceilings!) to be built up around your family members or employees. Provide them with the same freedom and support that you expect.

Insist on Flying a Fokker. Be resolute in finding the right tools. "Fly the Fokker *Eindecker*" and refuse to take a "back seat." Avoid those who claim that something can't be done or who find fault with everyone and everything. If you encounter such people, take up the challenge! It's motivating!

Somersault Skills May Help. Bring all of your talents to the table! Utilize the strengths you have that others do not. Exercise your talents and allow your employees to exercise theirs to achieve your personal or corporate vision.

2 SELECT YOUR BOELCKE
(Find a Mentor)

We had a delightful time with our chasing squadron. The spirit of our leader [Boelcke] animated all his pupils. We trusted him blindly. There was no possibility that one of us would be left behind. Such a thought was incomprehensible to us. Animated by that spirit we gaily diminished the number of our enemies. [Richthofen, 2005, p. 95]

As his mother mentioned, Richthofen had considerable courage and forcefulness to realize his ambitions. He recognized and took advantage of the momentous occasion when he met the German hero, *Leutnant* Oswald Boelcke. He did not allow an opportunity to learn from the best slip through his fingers.

~

In Homer's epic poem, "The Odyssey," Odysseus, King of Ithaca, entrusted Mentor with the care of his kingdom when he went off to fight the Trojan War. The goddess Athena took on the appearance of Mentor to serve as guardian to Odysseus's son, Telemachus.

Ask How to Be Victorious

I would have liked so much to find out how Lieutenant Boelcke managed his business. So I asked him: "Tell me, how do you manage it?" He seemed very amused and laughed, although I had asked him quite seriously. Then he replied: "Well it is quite simple. I fly close to my man, aim well and then of course he falls down." [Richthofen, 1918, p. 64]

On October 1, 1915, Richthofen was transferred to the German bomber unit, *Brieftauben-Abteilung-Metz (BAM)*, in Rethel, northeast of Vouziers. While traveling by train to his new assignment, Richthofen met *Leutnant* Oswald Boelcke in the dining car, recognizing him from pictures he had seen in the newspapers. At the time, Oswald had been victorious over four enemy aircraft flying his Fokker *Eindecker*, and he and was rapidly becoming famous throughout Germany.[1]

While Richthofen was somewhat introspective, shy, and reserved by nature, he was also determined not to let such an excellent opportunity get away. He straightforwardly asked Boelcke about his aerial successes. The Baron was fortunate in that he had a captive audience because of the long train ride. They played cards, dined, drank wine, and spent a number of hours discussing their mutual interest in fighter techniques. Richthofen's tenacity fascinated Boelcke and he found himself liking the eager aviator. Boelcke was the son of a schoolmaster and the discussions also fueled his teaching spirit. The mentoring relationship was born! Because Boelcke had been transferred to Rethel to fly barrier patrols, Richthofen would have the added advantage of future contact with his humble new friend and adopted mentor.[2] In the course of their discussions, realizing that Boelcke flew a Fokker while he was an observer on a large battle plane, Richthofen resolved to also fly a Fokker.

～

Mentors are generally older, more experienced individuals or managers who assist less experienced *protégés* (mentees or apprentices) in their careers.[3] Mentors provide their protégés with guidance regarding job skills, career development, and tools to cope with typically dynamic organizational conditions.[4] Mentoring relationships may be primarily job-focused and afford advantages in accelerated learning, visibility, sponsorship, and exposure to challenging assignments. Or they may be of a more social nature and involve counseling, nurturing, and coaching. Mentors themselves benefit from the relationships through job fulfillment and leadership skill enhancement.

Richthofen was determined to be successful as a fighter pilot and was eager to learn all he could from Oswald Boelcke. Even though Boelcke was just under a year older than Richthofen, he had obtained his pilot's certification more than fourteen months earlier than did Richthofen and his first confirmed individual aerial victory some thirteen months earlier. By May 1, 1916, Boelcke had obtained fifteen victories to lead all WWI aces. By all accounts, he indeed was the unquestioned "old" pro! Richthofen was fortunate because Boelcke was detailed, methodical, and a brilliant aerial tactician. Those pilots who were fledgling aviators under Boelcke or those who were later fledglings under Richthofen were also fortunate because failure in the "business" of combat flying was obviously more costly, at least physically, than that of failure in the corporate or social world. For such pilots, leadership under Richthofen or the Master, Boelcke himself, meant survival and recognition far beyond the rates of other country's pilot combatants or, for that matter, other German pilots. It was not by coincidence that *Jasta 2* (later known as *Jasta Boelcke*) and then *Jasta 11* (later known as *Jasta Richthofen*) were the premier German fighter squadrons. In fact, the pilots of these units became arguably some of the best pilots in the world.

~

The author's primary mentor was his father, who taught him the importance of family, integrity, education, and hard work. He stressed honesty and fair-play, but he also encouraged innovation and being proactive in a demanding world—staying "one step ahead of the next guy," as he put it. As far as the author knew, there had been no pilots in the family, and therefore no relatives, or even friends, who had taken to the sky and could provide words of wisdom or practical guidance. However, both the author's father and uncle had enjoyed careers working at the same aerospace firm and they obviously had some influence on his choice of professions.

One Sunday afternoon, at the age of nine, while his parents were *attempting* to rest, this author decided to build an airplane in the back yard out of scrap lumber. The plane became almost large enough to "climb-aboard"—or at least straddle—because the 2x10 inch "fuselage" was too difficult to saw through! Later, the author's father graciously assisted in adding wheels and braces to the unsteady landing struts. Nevertheless, the resulting "machine"—without an engine but sporting a propeller fashioned from a strip of baseboard molding—served no useful purpose, of course, other than to provide an awkward platform for the author's first "solo" (captured as a Kodak moment, courtesy of mom).

Later, when the author entered the world of military and then corporate aviation, he was able to learn from a number of individuals, who assisted him in gaining experience and developing as both a pilot and a person. Over the years, in the relatively small aviation community, he was fortunate to meet and speak with some of aviation's legends such as Neil Armstrong, Eugene Cernan, John Glenn, Bob Hoover, Paul Tibbets, Chuck Yeager, and many others. On May 10, 1997, piloting a Challenger aircraft en route from Oklahoma City to Houston, he was even privileged enough to personally provide George H. W. Bush, the 41st President of the United States, with an airborne tour of his Presidential Library and Museum in College Station, Texas—twenty-nine years after taking his parents for their first-ever airplane ride and excursion. It is amazing how even just a few minutes with some individuals can sometimes alter one's life.

Who is the Oswald Boelcke in your profession? Who is it that epitomizes the success story or the person like whom you would most wish to become? For instance, you may not be successful in securing Phil Mickelson as your personal golf mentor or in acquiring the private tutoring skills of his caddy Jim "Bones" Mackay or America's premier golf teacher Hank Haney. Still, there are countless individuals in most professions who are not only qualified to be excellent mentors but who are more than willing to share what they have learned as they climbed the success ladders in their chosen fields. Although advantageous in many ways, your mentor does not even have to be in your chosen field. In the business world, most management and leadership principles are transferrable. If you find a mentor that you like, especially if he or she serves as a role model in a more social nurturing, counseling context, it may not be so important that the person be specifically in your same profession.

When direct mentoring is not feasible, another approach is to study the person you wish to emulate. Richthofen recognized Boelcke on the train from pictures and articles he had read in the newspapers and military reports. Books, articles, and the Internet are excellent sources of information about your hero or idol. Often, these resources contain valuable anecdotes, experiences, and techniques that can serve as roadmaps for your own journey. When face-to-face contact is not possible, "e-mentoring" using e-mail is an option, as is telecommunication.

Regardless of the medium you select, keep in mind that the mentoring relationship is a joint responsibility. Share your expectations, goals, and your commitment to those objectives with your potential mentor. Be responsive to suggestions and show appreciation for the time he or she provides.

It is important to spend a moment discussing the concept of *networking*. Basically, networking consists of building alliances. For instance, Richthofen often took advantage of his friendship with *Oberleutnant* Fritz von Falkenhayn, staff Technical Officer of the German Air Service (*Kogenluft*), to assist him in getting bureaucracy and logistical problems resolved. In addition to normal channels for acquiring friends and contacts, there are a number of social and business networking sites available on the Internet at little or no cost. They can be supportive and helpful, but they can also be a waste of time for you and for others. Carefully consider each request you make or accept. Be respectful of contacts and followers, especially if you are fortunate to connect with true professionals who are willing to provide their valuable time and suggestions. Be willing to give *more* than you receive from the relationship. Networking should involve genuineness and authenticity, building relationships and trust. Do your best to add to the life and success of others.

Unfortunately, there are some individuals who believe that networking is a free ticket to pick the cherries from the low-hanging branches in another's orchard. Networking should *not* be about making cold-calls and asking favors from strangers. Over the years, the author was visited by a number of pilots or perspective pilots who were looking for a position or were seeking advice regarding their careers. When possible, he would take the time to offer those individuals encouragement and direction. However, occasionally someone would drop by, actually announce that he or she was "networking," and essentially expect to have their career issues or major decisions resolved on the spot, or in short order. The author called this "dumping." Employees sometimes displayed this unfortunate practice by walking into the office and unloading a problem or a we-should-do-this idea. At such times, the author simply turned the tables and asked for that person's solution or how he or she would go about implementing the suggestion. Often, when the individual thought further, the solution was obvious or the "great idea" would prove to have a number of downsides. Take the initiative! Don't expect others to do your work or execute your ideas. Don't forget to always show gratefulness for any assistance you are fortunate to receive.

Be Humble and Appreciative of Your Hero

We had always a wonderful feeling of security when he was with us. After all he was the one and only. [Richthofen, 2005, p. 96]

It is a strange thing that everybody who met Boelcke imagined that he alone was his true friend.... Men whose names were unknown to Boelcke believed that he was particularly fond of them. This is a curious phenomenon which I have never noticed in anyone else. Boelcke had not a personal enemy. He was equally polite to everybody, making no differences. [Richthofen, 1918, p. 101]

I am after all only a combat pilot, but Boelcke, he was a hero. [Richthofen, quoted in Kilduff, 2003; p. 140]

When Richthofen was given command of *Jasta 11* in January 1917, he was sad to leave *Jasta Boelcke*, but, as always, eager to embrace change and a new challenge. He was able to merge his continued drive for personal combat with the requirement of molding his dozen pilots into a team of disciplined, expert aviators with an aggressive hunting spirit. He seriously accepted the responsibility of his new command and began immediately to lead by example, ever conscious of the lessons instilled in him by his mentor and "hero" Oswald Boelcke. As did Boelcke before him, Richthofen drove his men hard to learn and refine tactics, formation flying, and use of armament. He emphasized the requirement for vigilance, attacking at close range, shooting accuracy, and the ineffectiveness of acrobatics that devoured all-important speed and altitude. Finally, he stressed that because the German pilots were outnumbered in the skies (typically by a factor of three), they had to choose their battles carefully, ever conscious of an escape route and a plan to fight another day if conditions were not right for battle.

Richthofen continued to fly training flights with individuals and with groups of his men for at least the first two months after he assumed command of *Jasta 11*. Soon, like his mentor Boelcke, he developed the amazing ability to assimilate essentially everything going on around him, even when engaged personally in a deadly one-on-one battle. This allowed him to effectively evaluate his pilots' performance and suggest improvement. He was challenging with his men, but he never asked them to do anything more than he demanded of himself.

> **Richthofen was just as good a superior officer as a comrade for the officers of his Staffel and his Geschwader. He associated with us off duty as any other comrade [would] … One could go to him with any question and any trouble and find sympathy and help when they were needed….**
>
> **Richthofen is unequalled as an instructor. I have been to different flight training facilities, as well as to the Fighter Pilot School at Valenciennes, and I have never met an instructor who could make the theory of air fighting technique so clear to me as Richthofen does. He especially likes it when his pilots are inquisitive. He does not become impatient when our questions seem to be elementary or silly. Every young pilot who comes here has to fly a few times to the Front alone with Richthofen. After the flight, he and the beginner discuss every aspect thoroughly. [*Leutnant* Friedrich-Wilhelm Lubbert, quoted in Kilduff, 2003; p. 158]**

~

> **He [Army leader and Adjutant-General, von Plessen] stressed over and over how Manfred was so pleasant because of his striking modesty. [Baroness von Richthofen, 1937, p. 165]**

One of the most consistent elements in the life of von Richthofen was his respect, admiration, and appreciation of his mentor, Oswald Boelcke. The most important way he demonstrated his respect for the Master was by becoming in-turn a mentor to his own pilots. He also further honored Boelcke through his dedication to and expansion of *Dicta Boelcke* (Boelcke's aerial tactics). Richthofen later published his own *Air Combat Operations Manual* that expanded and improved upon the aerial combat tactics taught by his mentor.

$\sim$

Sometimes, we pay respect and remind ourselves of the gifts and treasured guidance we have received from our mentors and friends in little ways. The author was once very fortunate to have in his organization an outstanding manager whose position was the Director of Aircraft Maintenance. The author had gone out of his way to recruit the individual not only because of his considerable technical skills but also because he was a great leader. One day that manager revealed that the reason he wore his eyebrows bushy was that he once had had a mentor that he highly respected and after whom he patterned himself. That person had bushy eyebrows!

> Are you humble enough to be subordinate to your mentor, realizing that you probably have a lot to learn? Are you willing to accept the fact that only your mentor knows when you are ready to "fly into combat?" To ultimately be a good leader, you must be a good follower yourself.

How are you showing respect and appreciation to your mentor? Do you sometimes wear "bushy eyebrows" as a self-reminder of your mentor's important and cherished lessons? What are you personally bringing to the mentoring relationship? Are you giving as well as receiving? Are you willing to be a mentor yourself as you gradually develop into one of the experts in your field?

Strive to Gain Experience in Your Machine

**On the previous day we had received our new aeroplanes
[Albatros DIs and DIIs] and the next morning Boelcke was to
fly with us. We were all beginners. None of us had had a success
so far. Consequently everything that Boelcke told us was to us
gospel truth....**
**Before we started Boelcke repeated to us his instructions and
for the first time we flew as a squadron commanded by the great
man whom we followed blindly. [Richthofen, 2005, p. 92]**

On his return from Turkey, Macedonia, and Bulgaria in mid-August
1916, Boelcke made a stop at Kovel to visit his brother, Wilhelm.
There he chose two pilots of *Kagohl 2*, *Leutnants* Erwin Bohme and
Manfred von Richthofen, to join his new unit, *Jasta 2*, at Bertincourt
in northern France.[5]

Richthofen was thrilled that he had been selected by Boelcke and
arrived full of enthusiasm at Bertincourt, on the Somme Front, on
September 1st. While they were waiting for their new Albatros DIs and
DIIs, which didn't arrive until the 16th, Boelcke spent countless hours
teaching his pilots about fighter tactics, formation flying, navigation,
and gunnery. They also began flying the four aircraft they did have
in small group sorties behind German lines to further polish their
developing skills.[6]

Typically before breakfast, Boelcke flew solo patrols in his Fokker
DIII rotary-engine biplane. He scored *Jasta 2's* first victory against a
DH2 that he forced to land on September 2nd, his 20th combat success.
Two weeks later, on September 14th, he forced down another DH2,
this time fully intact. He had it delivered to *Jasta 2* for additional
instruction for his eager fledglings. Boelcke personally generated a total
of seven victories for *Jasta 2* before his pilots would leave the nest.

On September 16th, *Jasta 2* received six new Albatros fighters. Late
in the morning of September 17th, Richthofen flew in tight formation
with the inaugural *Jasta 2* flight of five aircraft with Boelcke in the lead.
Piloting his new Albatros DII, Richthofen selected one of seven FE2b

two-seat fighters of 11 Squadron RFC and attacked it from behind at only ten meters, forcing the pilot to land at the German airfield at Flesquieres. The Baron had achieved his first official aerial combat victory.

Incredibly, on their inaugural flight, the fledgling *Jasta 2* pilots celebrated three other victories by day's end in addition to Richthofen's. Even though he was late getting into the fray because he was watching over his pilots, Boelcke increased his count to twenty-seven, scoring against a FE2 as well.

Jasta 2 closed out a very successful September with 186 combat flights, twenty-one confirmed victories, and four more unconfirmed. Richthofen achieved three victories in September 1916, followed by four in October (plus one more unconfirmed). The Baron's third victory on the last day of September was against a very capable FE2b crew whose gunner, Sergeant Albert Clarkson, had already shot down three German aircraft.

When one has shot down one's first, second or third opponent, then one begins to find out how the trick is done. [Richthofen, 1918, p. 98]

There was a time when Boelcke's bag of machines increased within two months from twenty to forty. We beginners had, at that time, not yet the experience of our master, and we were quite satisfied when we did not get a hiding. It was a beautiful time. Every time we went up we had a fight. Frequently we fought really big battles in the air. There were then from forty to sixty English machines, but unfortunately the Germans were often in the minority. With them quality was more important than quantity. [Richthofen, 2005, p. 95]

By the time Boelcke was killed on October 28, 1916, *Jasta 2* had amassed more than fifty victories, and von Richthofen, Bohme, Kirmaier, and Reimann had all achieved the status of "ace," with five or more victories each.

The celebrated triplanes and Spads were perfectly new machines. However, the quality of the box matters little. Success depends upon the man who sits in it. [Richthofen, 1918, p. 138]

April 1917 was the most successful month of Richthofen's career and also that of his *Staffel*.[7] The Baron downed twenty-one enemy aircraft and his unit claimed a total of ninety, outperforming all other *Jastas*. Bad weather precluded flying on the first day of April, but Richthofen, using his newly refitted Albatros DIII, opened the April scoring with two victories the next day and ended the month on the 29th with an incredible four successes in less than eight hours. He also had additional double victories on April 5th and 8th and a "triple" on the 13th. Major Albrecht von Richthofen proudly witnessed his sons' six-victory day when visiting the aerodrome on April 29th. The two brothers had defeated the equivalent of an entire squadron in a single day! Manfred ended the month with fifty-two total aerial combat successes, surpassing his mentor Oswald Boelcke's total of forty by mid-month. *Jasta 11*, the lowly *Staffel* without a victory just three months earlier, achieved the inconceivable milestone of one hundred victories on April 22nd.

~

Richthofen was in awe of Oswald Boelcke. In spite of the Baron's steadfast determination and self-confidence, his tremendous respect and trust in Boelcke was apparent as he allowed himself to learn gradually and absorb the critical lessons from his mentor. Like Boelcke, Richthofen was detailed and methodical, and he understood that as he gained experience to not let arrogance and exuberance replace humility and cautious energy. He knew that his life and the lives of his fellow pilots were in Boelcke's hands. Richthofen later emphasized this supportive relationship based on trust in his Air Combat Operations Manual:

Everyone must show absolute trust in the leader in the air.... If this trust is lacking, success is impossible from the outset.

> **The *Staffel* gains trust by [the leader's] exemplary daring and the conviction that [he] sees everything and is able to cope with every situation. [MvR Air Combat Operations Manual; Kilduff, 1993, p. 235]**

Are you a good protégé and student? Are you willing to trust your mentor, understanding that any false steps can potentially lead to disaster, if not physically than certainly professionally? Secure in an environment of support and trust, do you permit yourself to learn gradually and consistently from your mentor as you gain experience? Do you show appreciation for the commitment and confidence placed in you? Do you keep up your guard to prevent pride from stepping in as your comfort level increases?

Chapter 2 Summary

Select Your Boelcke. Richthofen had more than sufficiently laid the groundwork (*preparation*) when he had the "lucky" chance encounter (*opportunity*) with his future mentor, German hero *Leutnant* Oswald Boelcke.

Find a mentor, the "Oswald Boelcke" of your profession. He or she should epitomize the success story or the person like whom you would most wish to become. There are countless individuals who are not only qualified to be excellent mentors but who are also more than willing to share what they have learned in their chosen fields. If you find a mentor whom you like, especially if he or she serves as a role model in a more social context, it may not be necessary that the person be in your specific profession. When direct personal mentoring is not feasible, study the individual you wish to emulate. Books, articles, and the Internet are excellent resources containing valuable anecdotes, experiences, and techniques that can serve as roadmaps for your own journey.

Ask How to Be Victorious. Ask your mentor how to reach your goals or "conquer your opponents." Keep in mind that the mentoring relationship is a dual responsibility. Share your expectations, goals, and your commitment to those objectives with your mentor. Be responsive to suggestions and show appreciation for the time he or she provides.

Networking consists of building alliances. Carefully consider each request you make or accept. Be respectful of contacts and followers, especially if you are fortunate to team with true professionals who are willing to provide their valuable time and suggestions. Be willing to give *more* than you receive from the relationship. Networking should involve genuineness and authenticity, and forge relationships and trust. Do your best to add to the life and success of others. Networking is *not* about making cold-calls or asking favors from strangers. Nor is it about dumping your problems or "great ideas" in the laps of others, hoping for resolution or implementation with little or no effort on your part. Be grateful and show appreciation for any assistance you receive.

Be Humble and Appreciative of Your Hero. Richthofen greatly respected, admired, and appreciated his hero and mentor, Oswald Boelcke.

Be humble enough to be subordinate to your mentor, realizing that you most likely have much to learn. Be willing to accept the fact that only your mentor knows when you are truly ready to "fly into combat." To ultimately be a good leader, you must be a good follower yourself. Show appreciation. Make an effort to personally bring something to the mentoring relationship. Be willing to be a mentor yourself as you gradually become one of the experts in your field.

Strive to Gain Experience in Your Machine. Be a dedicated protégé and student. Allow yourself to learn gradually and consistently from your mentor as you gain experience. Trust your mentor, understanding that false steps can potentially lead to disaster. Refuse to let pride intervene as your comfort level improves.

3 BE "FIRST OF THE CHASERS" (Establish Goals)

I had brought down my sixteenth victim, and I had come to the head of the list of all the flying chasers. I had obtained the aim which I had set myself. In the previous years I had said in fun to my friend Lyncker, when we were trained together, and when he asked me: "What is your object? What will you obtain by flying?"—"I would like to be the first of the chasers. That must be very nice." [Richthofen, 2005, p. 102]

Newly-appointed *Kommandeur* Manfred von Richthofen's arrival at La Brayelle on January 15th, 1917, was eagerly awaited by the members of *Jasta 11*. The *Staffel*, formed four months earlier, had not yet scored a single triumph because of lack of direction, inadequate training, and because the unit primarily flew escort missions. *Jasta 11* was one of three *Jastas* assigned to the 6th Army, but it trailed the other two units in both aggressiveness and aerial victories. Even *Flieger-Abteilung 18*, a nearby unit flying two-crew reconnaissance aircraft, had a better victory score than fighter squadron *Jasta 11*. Finally, Richthofen—the true ace of aces with an incredible sixteen aerial combat victories to his credit—landed impressively in his sleek new Albatros DIII, wearing the inspiring and lustrous *Pour le Merite* at his collar.[1] Also, to his *Jasta's* astonishment, Richthofen's Albatros was painted bright red.[2] Parked on the field, Richthofen's red machine stood out in stark contrast with the standard-issue camouflage paint scheme of the other machines, consisting of large irregular patches of green, mauve, and brown on the upper and vertical surfaces.

When Richthofen took command of *Jasta 11*, he was indeed the "first of the chasers" with sixteen combat victories and the recipient of the coveted Blue Max. Carefully following in the footsteps of his mentor, Oswald Boelcke, he had realized his vision of becoming a fighter pilot, mastering the ability to triumph consistently in aerial battles, and then winning the *Pour le Merite*. Although he had also achieved the status of Germany's leading ace, it was bitter-sweet for Richthofen because he had lost his hero Boelcke on October 28, 1916, in a combat-related accident. Nonetheless, Richthofen now stood on the summit of the mountain he had been determined to climb. Like all great explorers before him who had reached the pinnacle of their journeys, the world was further revealed, allowing him to see more of the panorama and the challenging peaks beyond.

As his disillusionment mounted in 1914 with the onset of trench warfare, Richthofen's dream had been to fly ("I joined the Flying Service at the end of May, 1915. My greatest wish was fulfilled."[3]). Even before he met Boelcke in October 1915, he had already understood the necessity of doing battle with more maneuverable aircraft ("Agility is needed and, after all, fighting is my business."[4]). In October 1917 as he was putting the final touches on his autobiography, Richthofen's thoughts reverted to the infantry as they so often did ("Had I not become a professional chaser I should have turned an infantry flier. After all, it must be a very satisfactory feeling to be able to aid those troops whose work is hardest."[5]). In April 1918, he emphasized to journalist *Oberleutnant* Peter Lampel that his primary goal was aerial combat ("Not flying but aerial combat is my main goal in life."[6]). As the vision emerges or changes, so do goals and previous plans to achieve them!

Manfred's brother, Bolko, quoted his oldest brother's response when he queried him about why he had decided to switch to aviation in May 1915:

"I could not devote myself to being only an observer [the primary cavalryman's role in World War I]. I want to be a pilot, and, if so lucky, I want to be the best of them all." And with that, his blue eyes shone and gave proof of the ambition that lived in him. [Bolko von Richthofen, quoted in Richthofen, ed. Stanley Ulanoff, 1969; p. 164.]

~

It is important to note that Richthofen announced to his friend *Leutnant* Bodo *Freiherr* von Lyncker that he wanted to become the "first of the chasers." Remember that earlier he had also informed his mother that he had made plans to "join the fliers." When an individual visualizes his or her goal and announces to family or friends about intentions to do something, it not only solidifies the goal in the mind of that person but it also initiates a powerful psychological force within to assist in making it a reality. Further, it taps into pride and commitment, because typically the person doesn't want to disappoint confidants or to effectively go back on his or her word. Indeed, there was excited resolution in Manfred's voice when he spoke with his mother about his intentions to become an aviator. Once he had conceived, formulated, and then verbalized his plan, there was no second guessing or indecision. He had made up his mind and was determined to see it through.

~

Some months back at a New Year's Eve party with friends, the hostess suggested that we should all write on separate pieces of paper what we wanted to accomplish individually for the upcoming year. Once the anonymous goals were collected, someone read each note aloud and the group was tasked to guess who actually wrote it. This author's note consisted of three words: "Write a book." The fact that the group seemed to easily guess correctly who actually constructed the note made it even more imperative that the author follow through with his resolution. There could now be no turning back!

Understand the Mission

Not flying but aerial combat is my main goal in life. [MvR in interview with journalist Peter Lampel, quoted in Franks & VanWyngarden, 2001; p. 9]

The mission, in my view, can be determined only by a fellow fighter pilot. For that reason we need older, experienced officers in fighter aviation. [MvR Air Combat Operations Manual; Kilduff, 1993, p. 239]

During a defensive battle … it is best that each *Gruppe* [army group] is assigned a *Jagdgruppe* [fighter group]. This *Jagdgruppe* is not bound strictly to the *Gruppe* sector, but its main purpose is to enable the working aircrews to perform their function and, in exceptional cases, to provide them with immediate protection. [MvR Air Combat Operations Manual; Kilduff, 1993, p. 239]

The 1916–1917 winter was one of the most severe on record, but in spite of low clouds and rain in the morning, the afternoon of January 4th was sunny. The Baron's 16th victory that day—against Flight Lieutenant Allan Todd in a Sopwith Pup of 8 Squadron Royal Naval Air Service (RNAS)—would be his last with *Jasta Boelcke* and the one needed, as it turned out, to qualify for the Blue Max.[7] However, Richthofen did not immediately receive the coveted *Pour le Merite*. Instead, on January 10, he was appointed commanding officer of *Jasta 11* based at La Brayelle airfield just outside of Douai, northeast of Arras, on the 6th Army Front. Finally, two days later, von Richthofen received a telegram informing him that he had been awarded the *Orden Pour le Merite*.[8]

In military context, a *mission* consists of a task and its purpose, coupled with specific actions and rationale required to bring about success. Richthofen had been transferred to the 6th Army Sector because the German command believed that the British spring offensive would be staged there, and the aggressive Baron was needed to turn around struggling *Jasta 11*. Germany was faced with a chronic shortage of aggressive combat pilots, and Richthofen was given full-authority to select pilots for his unit that met his discerning criteria. For the same reason, the German government sponsored massive propaganda campaigns that celebrated the accomplishments of its heroes and made certain that they received ample decorations for their efforts. Although it frustrated Richthofen at the time, the Army High Command (*AOK*) had also raised the victory bar even higher for its *Pour le Merite* recipients so that it indeed remained Germany's highest and most prestigious military honor.

Later in the war, Richthofen's mission as a wing commander was to support and protect the army group (*Gruppe*) sector to which his fighter group (*Jagdgruppe*) was attached. He did this effectively by positioning his units close to the Front in the areas of greatest activity and then utilizing Air Defense Officers, a telephone network, and radio-telegraphy to facilitate timely enemy intercepts. Nevertheless, he maintained that the *Jagdgruppe* should not to be tied strictly to the sector, but rather be allowed to perform its primary function of eliminating enemy flight activity—as chartered by the Army High Command—while at the same time providing immediate protection to the sector as necessary. He held that his scarce aerial resources did not allow him and his men to conduct protection, escort, and especially the marginally-productive defensive (barrier) patrols.

Richthofen was an excellent soldier and followed orders. However, he interpreted his mission in the context of the directions of the individual Armies' Officers in Charge of Aviation (*Kofl*) and refused to let the occasional rogue senior officer deflect him and his men from their duty. He did not hesitate to use his determination and influence to suggest tactics and immediately address problems that sometimes arose. Richthofen's wing adjutant, *Oberleutnant* Karl Bodenschatz, pointed out that if the *Rittmeister* encountered some important matter that could be best handled immediately and more effectively through direct interaction with headquarters, he didn't hesitate to climb in his triplane and fly to get the issue resolved at the Air Service's highest levels. Sometimes he did so, regardless of the weather:

He flew to headquarters, laid the stuff on the table, and took care of everything on the spot. On one occasion, during weather so unbelievable that any mouse would have stayed in its hole, he flew to army headquarters, unconcerned, in order to settle some important matter. [Bodenschatz, 1935, p. 84]

∽

The *mission* is the fundamental purpose of a company or an organization—or even an individual!—and it should uphold core values, clarify visionary goals, provide direction, steer actions, and guide decision-making. Most companies have a *mission statement*, and in addition to representing corporate key values, it is sometimes used to resolve conflicts between business stakeholders. Often, companies run into trouble when they stray from their core values, and the mission statement helps them return to what they do best.

Although not all individuals may actually become philosophical, seek out a personal Yoda, and attempt to discover the "meaning of life," there are certainly times when it helps to return to your roots as it were. Life is easier and makes more sense if you have some method of centering yourself when stressed or faced with difficult decisions. Some individuals focus on their religious beliefs, some on family relationships, others simply on returning to their personal core values and integrity of self. Pursuing worthwhile and challenging goals is another great way of re-focusing and getting back into a healthy pattern. This author has found that a combination of all of these seems to be most effective for him. Over the years, he also enjoyed jogging, long walks, playing musical instruments, and exploring nature.

The author once had in his organization an outstanding pilot and good friend who tragically lost a fight—far too early in his life and career—to pancreatic cancer. He not only had a way of celebrating life, but he had his own special reverence for it. A number of years earlier, the organization had lost another pilot to a weekend accident in his small aerobatic aircraft. On Monday morning following the terrible mishap, the pilot who later battled cancer walked into the scheduling room, methodically erased the deceased pilot's name from the board, and then quietly walked out without saying a word to anyone. It wasn't that he was disrespectful, but rather his special way of saying goodbye, letting go, and continuing on with the mission, just as he had done when he lost comrades as a fighter pilot in Vietnam.

> What is your personal mission or your organization's mission? Do you fully understand how the mission relates to you or your team? Do you sometimes take the time to examine your decisions, especially when you stray from your core values and strengths? Are you willing to "fly" the extra mile to discuss strategy and settle disputes in upholding the fundamental purpose of your existence?

Abandon Your Barges (Remove Obstacles)

The gigantic machine made it clear to me that only the smallest aeroplane would be of any use for me in battle. A big aerial barge is too clumsy for fighting. Agility is needed and, after all, fighting is my business. [Richthofen, 1918, p. 95]

When establishing goals, it is sometimes necessary to consider removing obstacles and discarding dead-weight. Although Richthofen recognized that his "giant-plane" offered usefulness as a bomber—it could carry almost as many bombs as a Zeppelin—he soon referred to it as a "barge" because it failed to serve his requirement for speed and maneuverability. Following discussions with his mentor Boelcke in the train en route to his new assignment in October 1915, Richthofen's goals became clear—become a fighter pilot and fly a Fokker single-seat chase plane! Once his unit was installed at Rethel flying in the Albatros CI, Richthofen wasted no time in convincing *Oberleutnant* Georg Zeumer to teach him how to fly in an old two-seater available at the Metz airdrome. Finally, on October 10, 1915, Zeumer sent Richthofen up on his first solo. The aircraft behaved differently with only one pilot aboard and Richthofen hit the ground hard, bounced, and then flipped over on its nose. Two days later aboard the repaired aircraft, the determined Baron made a series of successful landings, and on November 15th found himself on the way to Doberitz, near Berlin, to train as a fighter pilot. Desperately wanting to become a combat pilot, Richthofen applied his Prussian resolve in academics and flying, and on Christmas Day 1915, passed his final examination for pilot certification.[9]

In soloing—as in other activities—it is far easier to start something than to finish it. **Amelia Earhart, 1928**

～

Sometimes the "barge" impeding the way to success is not a physical obstacle or person, but rather an idea, concern, or fear. It was not until the author recognized that his mother was effectively blocking his dream to fly because of her fears about his safety that he was finally able to move forward. His decision to become a pilot, regardless of the ill-conceived concerns of others, brought immediate freedom and renewed determination. Even though he entered the flight instruction program (FIP) offered by the Air Force at his university's adjacent airport several days later than the rest of the group, the author successfully passed his private pilot final check ride when the FAA came to conduct mid-course evaluations.

A *barge* is a large, typically flat-bottomed and unpowered boat that must be towed. What—or who!—are the barges in your life that are slowing you down, reducing your efficiency, and standing in the way of the achievement of your goals and dreams? Are you proactively taking charge of your life? Are there more productive ways of doing things? Are there better tools available? Like Richthofen, perhaps you also need additional training or a better "machine" that will allow you to be more efficient and reach your goals sooner.

Set Your Sights

From Udet I learnt that it is always a great mistake to shoot without first aligning sights and beads precisely, however close to the enemy. [*Oberleutnant* Hans Waldhausen, quoted in VanWyngarden, 2007; p. 47]

One observes the enemy from afar. One has recognized that his squadron is really an enemy formation. One counts the number of the hostile machines and considers whether the conditions are favorable or unfavorable. A factor of enormous importance is whether the wind forces me away from or towards our Front. [Richthofen, 1918, p. 130]

The aggressive spirit, the offensive, is the chief thing everywhere in war, and the air is no exception. [Richthofen, 1918, p. 131]

When he was given command of his own fighter squadron, Richthofen instantly set his sights. He was determined to blend his unrelenting drive for personal combat with the requirement of shaping his dozen pilots into a team of disciplined expert aviators with his aggressive hunting spirit. He embraced the responsibility of his new command and began immediately to lead by example. Richthofen drove his men hard to learn and refine tactics, perfect formation flying, and effectively use their armament. He emphasized the requirement for vigilance, attacking at close range, shooting accuracy, and the ineffectiveness of acrobatics that quickly exhausted critical speed and altitude. Finally, he emphasized that because the German pilots were outnumbered in the skies, they had to choose their battles carefully, be cognizant of an escape route, and have an alternative plan to fight another day if conditions were not favorable.

Richthofen wanted his men to fight as he did, and on the clear afternoon of January 23rd, 1917, led six of his men for the first time to an area over the trenches near Lens. There they came upon two FE8 Scouts that had just shot down two German reconnaissance aircraft. Richthofen charged one FE8 head on, but it promptly dove and sped away. He then attacked the other, flown by the experienced, three-victory British pilot, Second Lieutenant John Hay of 40 Squadron RFC. As his pilots looked on, the Baron quickly dispatched his opponent, following 150 shots from fifty meters, to score *Jasta 11's* first victory.

When he got beneath me I remained on top of him. Everything in the air that is beneath me, especially if it is a one-seater, a chaser, is lost, for it cannot shoot to the rear. [Richthofen, 1918, p. 161]

I started shooting when I was much too far away. That was merely a trick of mine. I did not mean so much to hit him as to frighten him, and I succeeded in catching him. [Richthofen, 1918, p. 161]

～

Goals are objectives generated by individuals, companies, and sometimes even the environment.[10] Examples of the latter occur in a war situation where objectives or missions are often precipitated by the military circumstance itself or, from an operations perspective, by a commanding officer or headquarters as the battle dynamics change. In a military context, *strategy* involves the utilization of all of a country's forces, employing long-range planning, to effect victory. *Tactics*, on the other hand, relates to the actual use and deployment of military personnel in combat. In a corporation setting, strategy involves an overall plan to achieve specific results, while tactics tend to be more operationally-focused.

Goals should be specific (*what*) and achievable. They should also include an appropriate method of attainment (*how*), a method of measuring (*tracking*), and a deadline (*when*). Typically, an individual or organization will have both long-term goals and short-term goals. Larger, more complex goals should be broken down into separate tasks or sub-goals with specific action plans. This is sometimes appropriately called "chunking."

Goals can, and often should, be adjusted, especially if they are longer-range goals. Conditions, demands, and situations can all change over time, and usually do. In World War I, pilots eventually discovered that they were more successful if they set their sights at closer range and when there was little relative motion between the aggressor aircraft and its target.[11] *Setting your sights* (being specific) should be a function of proximity to the "target." It is very important to have a vision and strategic plans. However, getting too detailed regarding far-off objectives can exhaust resources and even result in "shooting down the wrong aircraft" if one obstinately and blindly forges ahead when the environment changes. Remember the sayings: "Ready, fire, aim!" (Good!); and "Having lost sight of our objective, we re-doubled our efforts!" (Not so good!).

Richthofen was not ready to leave *Jasta Boelcke* when the German Air Service gave him command of struggling *Jasta 11*. The Baron found himself in a new (environmental) situation, brought on by orders from the military, and he was faced with the task of establishing a set of goals and tactics to bring his floundering fighter squadron up to his own disciplined and aggressive standards. Richthofen would lead by example, employing his own training and accumulated skills, and he would measure his success in terms of numbers of aerial victories and in competition with his previous organization, *Jasta Boelcke*.

Have you *set your sights* on a goal or a group of goals? Are your goals attainable and specific enough so that when they are reached you will know? Have you found the best methodology to obtain your goals and an efficient way to track progress in reaching them? Further, if your company has given you a set of goals or objectives, remember that there is generally no reason why you can't mesh them with your personal goals. Have you empowered yourself and taken the initiative to employ your own background, training, and creativity to come up with a plan acceptable to management? Are you able to compare your progress and success to other individuals or companies? The company at which the author worked for thirty-one years occasionally provided its employees with various team-building programs and even sponsored an annual Corporate Olympics in which internal teams could compete. Friendly competition, and even more adversarial competition in the aggressive context of business, can be both motivating and rewarding.

Make Yourself Irreplaceable

We have no substitute for your son [MvR] in the whole flying corps. [*General* von Hoeppner, quoted in Fischer, 2001; p. 170]

He was probably the best fighter pilot who ever lived.... He combined excellent eyesight and a certain 'nose' for the hunt with great flying ability. [Bodenschatz, 1935, p. 85]

He [von Richthofen] was worth as much to us as three divisions. [*General* Erich von Ludendorff, quoted in Gibbons, 1927; p. 3]

I had shot down fifty aeroplanes. That was a good number but I would have preferred fifty-two. So I went up one day and had another two, although it was against orders. As a matter of fact

I had been allowed to bag only forty-one. Anyone will be able to guess why the number was fixed at forty-one. Just for that reason I wanted to avoid that figure.... It is some fun to have downed half a hundred aeroplanes. After all, I had succeeded in obtaining permission to bring down fifty machines before going on leave. [Richthofen, 1918, p. 163]

On April 30th, 1917, the Baron received a wire that he was to meet with the Kaiser on May 2nd. Richthofen had been ordered to take leave after surpassing Boelcke's record of forty victories in mid-April. However, Richthofen, refusing to miss the action during the Battle of Arras, protested and was ultimately allowed to remain at the Front until the end of the month. By then, he had recorded fifty-two combat victories!

~

Richthofen was determined to be the best, both as a soldier and as a pilot. His wing adjutant, Karl Bodenschatz, maintained that there were no obstacles that Richthofen could not overcome if it meant an achievement related to his combat success or his *Geschwader*. At twenty-five years of age, Richthofen held the title of *Rittmeister* and the position of *Jagdgeschwader Kommandeur*, a duty for which there was no precedent or criteria. Richthofen was primarily a soldier but, at the same time, the "ultimate" fighter pilot.[12] He refused to become complacent even as his victories and his fame mounted.

Nothing was too difficult for him [MvR], nothing was impossible for him, if it meant achieving something for his combat flying and his Geschwader. [Bodenschatz, 1935, p. 83]

~

This author found that his willingness to add to his formal education and to acquire new skills and job enhancements helped immensely with his work performance and subsequent promotions. His father's advice to "stay one step ahead" translated into never becoming complacent and a continuing, proactive search for innovation and excellence.

> How are you making yourself irreplaceable? Do you have specific abilities or multiple skills that make it difficult, if not impossible, for your company to even consider replacing you? If not, are you making an attempt to add value to yourself as an employee through additional training and diversification of skill sets? Are you continuing to learn and grow in your position and in your profession, not allowing those new to the workplace to bring forth qualities and talents you don't possess or are no longer skilled in using?

Count Your Victories (Measure)

After *Herr Rittmeister* landed, he smacked his hands together and said very happily: "Heavens above, 80 is still a decent number." [*Leutnant* Hans Joachim Wolff, quoted in Kilduff, 2007; p. 215]

April 1917 was the most productive month of Richthofen's career as well as that of his *Staffel*. The Baron defeated twenty-one enemy aircraft and his unit claimed a total of ninety, outperforming all other *Jastas*.[13] Richthofen, using his newly refitted Albatros DIII, opened the April scoring with two victories on the 2nd and ended the month with an incredible four successes in less than eight hours on the 29th. He also had double victories on April 5th and 8th and a "triple" on the 13th. Major Albrecht von Richthofen was on hand to witness the six-victory day registered by Manfred and Lothar when visiting his sons at the airfield on April 29th.[14] Manfred ended his month's work with fifty-two total aerial combat successes, surpassing Boelcke's total of forty by mid-month. *Jasta 11*, scoreless just three months earlier, achieved its one hundred victory milestone on April 22nd. On April 26th, to honor Richthofen and his *Staffel*, the Kaiser ordered the unit to be designated *Jagdstaffel Richthofen*, although after three weeks the humble Baron would not allow the designation to remain in place.

He [MvR] hits him [*Leutnant* Hans Joachim Wolff] on the shoulder and his face breaks out in laughter. "Until you have left your laughable single-digit number of shot-downs behind, 'Little Wolff,' you still won't be a Kanone [literally "cannon" or "big gun," the German equivalent of an ace]." [*Oberleutnant* Peter Lampel, quoted in Franks & VanWyngarden, 2001; p. 49]

Richthofen measured his success by being awarded the *Pour le Merite* and tracking the aerial victories of himself and his men. His admiration and respect for his mentor, *Hauptmann* Oswald Boelcke, seemed to fuel his continual quest to live up to that image. In spite of the fact that he would ultimately double Boelcke's victory total, Richthofen always felt that had Boelcke lived, his hero's successes would have eclipsed those of everyone else.

~

When this author was responsible for the corporate flight department, the organization utilized a number of measurements to track progress and success in reaching its goals. The overall underlying strategy, known as *policy deployment*, was a process to establish, deploy, and implement priorities. It involved alignment of priorities with customers, communication of those priorities throughout the organization, development of plans and tactics to achieve those priorities, appropriate resource allocation to address key issues, and periodic reviews with customers and management. In 1996, the key policy deployment objectives for flight operations included: Safety—zero accidents, incidents, and recordables (lost time injuries); Innovation—100% aircraft readiness; Speed—ability to dispatch worldwide within 1–3 hours; Quality—six-sigma (99.999%) dispatch reliability; and Competitive Advantage—provide company executives (customers) with world-class advantages in terms of time, flexibility, productivity, and comfort. When the author retired at the end of 2004, these metrics were still in place, except that the dispatch reliability goal had been set at 100%. The organization had just received the industry's

Corporate Business Aviation Safety Award for 37 years and 58,767 consecutive flight hours without an accident (nearly 32 million miles). There were zero accidents, incidents, lost time accidents, ground recordable incidents, and occurrences (safety "scares") for the year. Both dispatch reliability and aircraft readiness were steady at 100%. Full credit for these outstanding achievements belongs to the author's dedicated and highly professional employees.

Other statistics tracked included overall budget numbers, flight hours by aircraft, cost per flight hour, number of domestic and international trips, flight hours per pilot, charter hours, training hours, individual development plan (IDP) metrics, and health/fitness metrics including use of the hangar's exercise room. Because safety was the most important priority, organizational bonuses (excluding that of the flight department managers) were tied to meeting and maintaining the safety goals. A safety-related and very important set of statistics included that of the organization's S-A-F-E (Safety Attitude Focus Encounter) and A-C-T-S (Alternative Concepts Toward Safety) programs, which consisted respectively of employees "busting" colleagues for displaying an "attitude" of safety and safety-minded individuals submitting ideas to improve safety. Each person who was "caught" doing something that enhanced safety or who submitted a safety-related improvement idea was given a gift certificate to his or her favorite restaurant or store. Further, the individual who "busted" the safety-conscious colleague was also given a gift certificate. Of course, each S-A-F-E or A-C-T-S 3x5 inch card that was submitted through the program had to be approved by the organization's Safety Council. When the author left the company, the organization had received 159 cards of which 120 were ultimately approved.

Are you diligent in measuring progress towards your goals?—"What gets measured gets done!" Do you typically take a snapshot of where you are initially, determine your ultimate goal, and then measure the milestones en route to your final objective? Do you recognize that in an organization, a little competition between units can have a very positive effect on morale and productivity?

Chapter 3 Summary

Be "First of the Chasers." Richthofen announced to his friend Lyncker that his goal was to become the "first of the chasers." Earlier, he had also informed his mother that he had made plans to "join the fliers." It is a great motivator to announce to family or friends your intention to do something. It not only solidifies the goal in your mind but it also initiates a powerful psychological force within that begins to work to make it a reality.

Understand the Mission. Richthofen's mission was to support and protect the army sectors to which he was attached. He did this effectively by positioning his units close to the Front in the areas of greatest activity and then responding to threats. Richthofen was an excellent soldier and followed orders, but he also understood his mission and refused to let anyone deflect him and his men from their duty. He did not hesitate to use his tenacity and influence to suggest tactics and immediately address problems that sometimes arose.

From a company or organizational perspective, the *mission* is its fundamental purpose and it should uphold core values, clarify visionary goals, provide direction, steer actions, and guide decision-making. Take the time to write a personal, organizational, or company mission statement if it doesn't already exist. Make an effort to fully understand how the mission relates to you or your organization. Be willing to "fly" the extra mile to settle disputes and fight any elements of bureaucracy that stand in the way of upholding the fundamental purpose of your organization's existence.

Abandon Your Barges. When establishing goals, it is sometimes necessary to consider removing obstacles and discarding dead-weight. Although Richthofen recognized that his "giant-plane" offered usefulness as a bomber, he soon referred to it as a "barge" because it failed to provide requisite speed and maneuverability.

Discard the barges in your life that are slowing you down, reducing your efficiency, and standing in the way of achievement of your goals and dreams. Proactively take charge of your life. Find more productive ways of doing things. Search for better tools. Like Richthofen, consider additional training or a better "machine" that will allow you to be more effective and reach your goals easier.

Set Your Sights. Richthofen was not yet ready to leave *Jasta Boelcke* when the German Air Service gave him command of struggling *Jasta 11*, but he was up to the challenge and quickly *set his sights*. He was faced with the task of establishing a set of goals to bring the floundering fighter squadron up to his own disciplined and aggressive standards. Richthofen elected initially to lead by example, employing his own training, accumulated skills, and dedication to engender trust. He measured his success in terms of numbers of aerial victories and in competition with his former organization, *Jasta Boelcke*.

Set your sights on your goals. Your goals should be attainable and specific enough so that you will know when they are reached. Determine the best method to obtain your goals and an effective way to track progress in meeting them. If your company has given you a set of goals or objectives, mesh them with your personal goals if at all possible. Empower yourself and take the initiative to employ your own background, training, experience, and creativity to come up with a plan. Find a way to compare your progress and success with other individuals, organizations, or companies. Competition can be both motivating and rewarding.

Goals can—and often should—be adjusted, especially if they are long-range goals. Conditions, demands, and situations can all easily change over time. "Setting your sights" (being *specific* about goals) should be a function of proximity to the "target." Create your vision and strategic plans, but don't let yourself or your company get so focused on far-off objectives that it exhausts resources or results in scaling the wrong mountain!

Make Yourself Irreplaceable. Richthofen was never content with his current record of total enemy aircraft downed. Even the day after he had recorded 80 official victories and had doubled his mentor's score, he aggressively sought to add to his tally. As Germany's first Wing Commander, he worked to develop high standards where models didn't even exist.

Make an effort to acquire specific abilities and multiple skills that make it difficult or impossible for your company to replace you. Make an attempt to add value to yourself as an employee through additional training and diversification of skill sets. Continue to learn and grow in your position, not allowing those who are new to the workplace to bring in qualities and talents you don't possess or are no longer skilled in using.

Count Your Victories. Richthofen measured his success by being awarded the *Pour le Merite* and tracking the aerial victories of himself and his men.

It is important to measure progress towards your goals. Take a "snapshot" of where you are now. Set your ultimate goal or goals firmly in mind. Be able to "see" where you are going. Find an efficient way to measure progress in reaching your goals. Remember that, especially in organizations, a little competition between units can generally have a very positive effect on morale and productivity.

4 ENVISION YOUR TARGET
(Visualize Victory)

A career in flying was like climbing one of those ancient Babylonian pyramids made up of a dizzy progression of steps and ledges, a ziggurat, a pyramid extraordinarily high and steep; and the idea was to prove at every foot of the way up that pyramid that you were one of the elected and anointed ones who had *the right stuff* and could move higher and higher and even—ultimately, God willing, one day—that you might be able to join that special few at the very top, that elite who had the capacity to bring tears to men's eyes, the very Brotherhood of the Right Stuff itself. [Wolfe, 1979, p. 19]

On the same day we went on the chase for a second time but again we had no success. I felt very sad. I had imagined that things would be very different in a battle squadron. I had always believed that one shot would cause the enemy to fall, but soon I became convinced that a flying machine can stand a great deal of punishment. Finally I felt assured that I should never bring down a hostile aeroplane, however much shooting I did. [Richthofen, 1918, p. 89]

Arriving at home with my squadron, I doubted that I could

bring myself to tell anyone that with a thousand shots I had not scored a single hit! [Lothar von Richthofen, quoted in Richthofen, ed. Stanley Ulanoff, 1969; p. 128]

Earlier in his aviation career as an observer/gunner, Richthofen was surprised and frustrated that he was unable to easily transfer his hunting skills to success with targets in the air. Richthofen indeed had *the right stuff* but soon learned that a "flying machine can stand a great deal of punishment." During WWI, the standard aircraft machine gun bullet utilized by both sides was the .30 caliber, which was also used by the infantry. The bullet provided the foot soldier with the favorable qualities of long range, high hardness, and compactness; but these characteristics didn't prove as effective in bringing down aircraft.[1] Tight groups of hits to the aircraft were sometimes able to tear large enough holes in fabric and structural members to cause vulnerability to subsequent damage from wind and component fatigue. This hazard, however, was not typically a formidable threat because of aiming errors associated with gravity and also motion errors introduced by both target *and* attack aircraft. However, it was indeed cause for alarm if these latter variables were minimized by close proximity and reduced relative motion using the in-trail (usually 6-o'clock) attack position. "Tracer" ammunition proved to be largely ineffectual except at close range because of inherent flaws and illusion issues associated with such rounds.[2] The probability of success was further reduced due to the limited supplies of bullets that could be carried aloft because of weight, reloading problems, and the constant likelihood of machine gun jamming caused by overheat from firing more than short bursts. Even when attacking aircraft were able to inflict multiple hits on their prey, the critical marks—crew, engines, and fuel tanks—were significantly smaller targets than the overall aircraft, additionally restricting success ratios.

As Richthofen would learn from Oswald Boelcke and then later teach his own men, aerial success in World War I depended primarily on the elements of surprise, possessing a highly maneuverable aircraft, and attacking at close range, typically from the in-trail position—directly behind for single-pilot aircraft or from behind and below for an aircraft with a rear gunner. But there were additional ingredients for success that could not easily be taught. The fighter pilot had to be daring, possess aggressive determination, and be highly skilled to attack at such close range. More importantly, he had to have confidence, envision success, and be able to "see" the victory in his mind.

See It in Your Mind

Your nervous system cannot tell the difference between an actual experience and one that is vividly imagined. If we picture ourselves performing in a certain manner, it is nearly the same as the actual performance. Mental practice helps to make perfect. [Maltz, 1960, p. 35]

At that time I had not yet the conviction "He must fall!" which I have now on such occasions, but on the contrary, I was curious to see whether he would fall. There is a great difference between the two feelings. When one has shot down one's first, second or third opponent, then one begins to find out how the trick is done. [Richthofen, 1918, p. 113]

When I had approached the Englishman quite closely, when I had come to a distance of about three hundred feet, I got ready for firing, aimed and gave a few trial shots. The machine guns were in order. The decision would be there before long. In my mind's eye I saw my enemy dropping. [Richthofen, 1918, p. 136]

Richthofen recognized how important it was to "see" his enemies fall in his "mind's eye," to visualize all the elements of a successful air battle. Being able to imagine all stages of the victory before they actually unfolded allowed him to confidently complete the mission successfully. But he also understood that there was no great secret of life, no literal *magic bullets* that he could load into his Parabellum machine gun belts that would ensure success. What he did possess was a positive attitude of success and a total self-belief that propelled both him and his men forward.

~

In his classic book, *Psycho-Cybernetics*, Dr. Maxwell Maltz, discussed a report in *Research Quarterly* concerning the effects of mental practice in improving basketball free throws.[3] In the experiment, three groups of students practiced for twenty straight days with the following results: Group 1 actually practiced throwing the ball for twenty minutes each day and by the end of the experiment had improved 24% over the first day baseline score; Group 2 did not practice and their scores remained the same; Group 3 spent twenty minutes per day *imagining* that they were throwing the ball at the goal, made "corrections" to their aim if they "missed," and their scoring improved 23%!

In the early 1970s when the author was an Air Force instructor pilot (IP), an opportunity presented itself and he was determined to prove that this mental imaging process could be applied to military pilot training as well. One of the students of another IP was having serious problems in the acrobatic ("Contact") phase of training in the USAF T-38 supersonic advanced trainer. As in Richthofen's time, the "washout" (failure) rate for military pilots was somewhere around 50%. This particular student—who had already failed two preliminary evaluations—was to be given two training review flights before he would face his final check with the squadron commander who would determine whether or not he would be forced to leave the program. In addition to his poor flying skills, the student had a tendency to get "check-itis" (fear of check rides) which also lessened his prospects for survival. Review flights prior to students' final checks were given by instructors other than their own, but in light of this student's previous weak performance, none of the other instructors were interested in accepting the task because it appeared hopeless. Further motivated by the challenge, the author volunteered to fly with him but requested an additional training flight because his grade book reflected deficiencies in almost every Contact maneuver. The additional flight was approved and so the author was faced with essentially condensing a very demanding six-week training phase into three one-hour flights. The only way there was any possible hope of success was through the use of *mental* flying. The author insisted that the student "fly" at least two *imaging* flights to each *actual* flight. In theory, because mental flying performed properly is nearly as effective as an actual flight, he would be in effect *tripling* his training exposure. The author convinced him that he could pass the check ride, but only if he listened to everything the author said and that he "ate, drank, and slept" the T-38 for the next three days. The student's imaging flights were to last at least as long as actual flights because it was imperative that he mentally "fly" every minute detail of every maneuver—"holding" the control stick, "seeing" the instrument readings, "checking" outside references, and "feeling" the G forces as the T-38 rolled, looped, and then finally came to a stop in the chocks following a flawless final "landing." Without going into greater detail, the student went on to pass his final check ride with a class-high score of 95%, moving up in his class standing by twelve positions—to the consternation of his fellow students who were his competitors for subsequent unit assignments following graduation!

Most great golfers emphasize the importance of having a clear mental image of the shot and the flight of the ball before actually swinging the club. Can you see yourself making the perfect "shot" and the ball landing in the center of the fairway or right next to the "pin?" Do you recognize the power of your own mind? Are there times when you experience *flow*, when everything comes together and you are operating with effortless control at the peak of your abilities?[4] Have you removed negativity from your thinking? Are you able to visualize your goals? Are you able to use imaging to "see" yourself moving forward through the obstacles en route to those goals? Do you see yourself achieving your dreams and accepting the awards that come from their attainment?

Think Clearly

He [MvR] is always clear, orderly, and prepared. [Baroness von Richthofen, 1937, p. 49]

My philosophy has always been: Take the war calmly. [Lothar von Richthofen, quoted in Richthofen, ed. Stanley Ulanoff, 1969; p. 125]

During an interval in the fighting I convinced myself that we were alone. It followed that the victory [Richthofen's 32nd, April 2, 1917] would accrue to him who was calmest, who shot best and who had the clearest brain in a moment of danger. [Richthofen, 1918, p. 138]

Richthofen maintained orderliness in both his internal and external matters, so much so that he could readily account for every minute of his day. He was frugal with money and had no debts. Manfred's mother often discussed matters of concern with her son because of his ability to see things plainly and objectively. She maintained that his counsel was delivered with calmness and yet conviction that could be measured in experience far beyond his young age. Speaking with him brought security and clarity followed by the wherewithal to handle the particular issue. Even Lothar held the unshakable opinion that his brother was always right.[5] There was no envy—Lothar willingly accepted his place as the younger and adoring brother.

Manfred saw things amazingly clearly. [Baroness von Richthofen, 1937, p. 91]

April 1917 was the most successful month of Richthofen's career and would see the Baron down twenty-one enemy aircraft. Richthofen, flying his Albatros DIII, scored two victories on April 2nd and ended the month with an incredible four successes in less than eight hours on the 29th. He also had additional "double" victories on April 5th and 8th and a "triple" on the 13th. By the end of April, Richthofen had achieved fifty-two total aerial combat victories.

Richthofen had the ability to look at things from a clear and common-sense perspective. Even when he experienced setbacks—such as falling victim to an ambush during a cavalry expedition in August 1914 and his inability to down an enemy aircraft with Zeumer thirteen months later—Richthofen always focused ahead and systematically found ways to overcome every obstacle in his path. At times he was frustrated, but he never faltered in the pursuit of his goals.

He could always understand the essence of difficult questions and give advice with a common sense that scarcely went with his youth. [Baroness von Richthofen, 1937, p. 45]

When Richthofen went up on his first solo flight on October 10, 1915, the aircraft behaved differently with only one pilot aboard and he hit the ground hard, bounced, and then nosed over. Embarrassed but unhurt, Richthofen climbed out of the aircraft, dusted himself off, and then—applying the practical lesson he had just learned—made a series of successful landings two days later aboard the repaired aircraft. Within a month he was on his way to Doberitz, near Berlin, to train as a fighter pilot.

~

Whether you think you can or whether you think you can't, you're right. Henry Ford

Common sense is the ability to make sound decisions. Similarly, *rational thinking* is simply logical, conscious reasoning. As mentioned earlier, having conscious positive, future goals accompanied by strong feelings and desire can become powerful goal-achieving mechanisms within us. However, often we let our past mistakes and failures become who we are because we unwittingly allow irrational beliefs about these disappointments compel us to suffer the "sins" of our past.[6] Indeed, if we let them, our worst nightmares actually *become* our goals because of the strong emotions and fear that typically accompany them. If such false beliefs persist in your life, rationally examine their validity, convince yourself of their absurdity, and then toss them out once and for all. Indignation—and even anger!—often helps in allowing you to move past these false ideas that have been robbing you of your future potential.[7]

When this author enrolled in the program to obtain his doctorate, he studied the curriculum, mapped out a schedule to graduate in three years, and then submitted it to the head of the Industrial/Organizational Psychology Department. He was immediately informed that, even though it was theoretically possible, it had never been done before in such an aggressive time frame, especially in light of the fact that he was a full-time aviation manager and active international pilot. Rather than let this negatively creep into his own thinking, the author took on the warning as a challenge and ultimately accomplished his goal—on schedule.

> Do you view past failures as obstacles to your future or as *opportunities* for learning that serve as stepping stones towards achievement of your goals? Do you focus, think clearly, and use common sense? Do you allow yourself to build confidence even when others appear to be determined to introduce doubt? Do you berate yourself because you "always miss putts from this distance," or do you recognize that you are getting better with practice and will soon be "sinking your putts" on a regular basis?

Nothing was too difficult for him [MvR], nothing was impossible for him, if it meant achieving something for his combat flying and his Geschwader. [Bodenschatz, 1935, p. 83]

Richthofen possessed in large quantities that typically charming self-awareness and self-assurance, which must be innate, which one can never learn. In his face there was a calm,

firm and yet friendly manliness, without any pronounced, determined tenseness, as found in many of our other young heroes. [*Hauptmann* Erich von Salzmann, quoted in Kilduff, 1999; p. 52]

It was the face [MvR's] of someone who was a decent person down to the last corner of his soul. Within his face lay a resilient energy, an energy without restraint, without nervousness, the wonderful energy of youth.... and the look from his clear, sincere eyes was the look of a man at peace with himself, with the world, and with everything in his past. [Bodenschatz, 1935, p. 11]

He wanted to conquer every day anew, at the risk of his life. [Baroness von Richthofen, 1937, p. 126]

On the snowy morning of March 6, 1917, von Richthofen got a taste of his own mortality. He and four members of his *Jasta* attacked a group of Sopwith Strutters of 43 Squadron, but quickly found themselves outnumbered 3-to-1 when 40 Squadron joined in. Richthofen singled out an opponent and closed in, but briefly failing to look aft was suddenly hit in both fuel tanks of his Halberstadt DII by an aircraft that had momentarily moved into firing position behind him. The Baron quickly dived away, switched off the engine to avoid a fire, and landed within the German lines. Just as he did in the days when he was thrown by his horse, von Richthofen took to the air again that same afternoon, this time in *Leutnant* Lubbert's Albatros DIII. Using only one hundred rounds, he secured his 25th victory against a DH2 flown by Lieutenant Arthur Pearson of 29 Squadron RFC, who had been a previous victor and holder of the Military Cross.

Richthofen was not a superstitious person. Many pilots followed rituals and had their own "lucky" items of clothing or fighting gear that accompanied them on their combat flights. When he fell or was knocked down, the Baron simply climbed back on his horse or into another aircraft and charged forward. He was comfortable with himself and confident in his journey.

I think the first one was Richthofen. I recall there wasn't a thing on that machine that wasn't red, and God how he could fly! [Second Lieutenant A.E. Woodbridge, quoted in Franks, Giblin, & McCrery, 1995; p. 150]

Do you have the courage to weigh the consequences of various courses of action and then take calculated risks? Do you have the self-confidence to follow your natural instincts and just "go for it" even if you fall off your horse or "pull it left" after selecting the driver on the narrow fairway? Even the best professional golfers often miss the fairway off the tee. It's the mental courage to take risks and then to manage any "missed shots" that becomes the greatest strength of the "game."[8]

Put Your Change in Your Left Pocket (Don't Overanalyze)

Body and spirit were one in him, a perfect unity. [Baroness von Richthofen, 1937, p. 190]

He [MvR] was the least complicated man I ever knew. Entirely Prussian and the greatest of soldiers. [Ernst Udet, 1935, p. 72]

He [*Leutnant* Oswald Boelcke] seemed very amused and laughed, although I had asked him quite seriously. Then he replied: "Well it is quite simple. I fly close to my man, aim well and then of course he falls down." [Richthofen, 1918, p. 64]

In 1997, Warner Brothers released the movie *Tin Cup*, starring Kevin Costner as golf pro Roy McAvoy. In the movie, psychologist

Molly Griswold (Rene Russo) inspires Roy to join the Professional Golfers' Association tour. Unfortunately, Molly has been dating Roy's nemesis, David Simms (Don Johnson) who is one of the top players on the PGA tour. Roy qualifies for the U.S. Open Championship, but he also falls for Molly. When he learns about her relationship with his arch-rival, he begins to have problems with his characteristically flawless golf swing. At the practice tee the day before the Open, Roy continues to shank the ball, creating an embarrassment for both himself and his friend and caddy, Romeo (Cheech Marin). In desperation, Romeo tells Roy: "Take out all your change and put it in your left-hand pocket … tie your left shoe in a double knot … turn your hat around backwards … take this tee and stick it behind your left ear … now take this little ball and hit it the hell up the fairway, you're ready!" When Roy hits his next shot solidly, he asks Romeo, "How'd I do that?" Romeo explains: "Because you're not thinking about shanking … you're not thinking about the doctor lady … you're not thinking, period! … you're just looking like a fool and you're hitting the ball pure and simple, and that's you're natural [ability]… your brain was getting in the way!"

As a gymnast, Richthofen was a natural. His mind and his body functioned in perfect unison. Every movement was agile and effortless. His grades in the sport were excellent and he received numerous awards in competition. But in spite of his instinct and considerable skills at hunting, he was puzzled with the response when he first queried his mentor Boelcke about how he had successfully shot down four enemy aircraft. The Baron had been trying to overanalyze why he was unable to consistently "bag" his target in the air as he had on the ground. When hunting animal prey, Richthofen was certainly aware of the advantage of getting close enough to his quarry and balancing that benefit with the possibility that the animal might pick up his scent or detect noise. It was through trial and error that Boelcke and Immelmann had learned the "trick" of flying close enough to cancel out the extra ballistic variables not associated with those on the ground. Being an excellent marksman and properly aligning gun sights were important, but it was target proximity that afforded the highest opportunity for success. As in any sport, it is essential to not overanalyze and simply allow yourself to get in the "zone."

~

In general, performance at the expert level is characterized by the accumulation and the automation of skills.[9] However, it has been argued that the ability to control attention is key to the achievement of *peak performance* (the best that one is capable of doing).[10] Further, the direction and organization of attention is a function of *arousal* (brain and the body in a state of readiness). When arousal shifts, attention has a tendency to shift as well. Arousal states that are too low or too high produce inferior results.[11] Sports activities that require high levels of exertion and are relatively less complicated (e.g., shot putting) can be performed at high levels of arousal, while more refined sports activities (e.g., golf) require low arousal levels. Arousal control is central to successful athletic performance, not only because of its effects on focusing, but also because of its direct effects on physical performance. If the levels of cognitive anxiety increase in conjunction with increases in physical anxiety, there is a point beyond which performance deteriorates dramatically.[12]

On most Thursday mornings, this author enjoys an informal round of golf with friends. On one hole—you guessed it, the thirteenth!—he has a tendency to hit the ball too high off the tee. Because he has unintentionally trained himself to expect to hit the ball high on that particular tee box, he often does. Lowering the tee height and/or placing the ball further back in his stance doesn't typically help because his mind still finds a way to instruct his body to alter the mechanics to produce the same results—to lower his head, swing too steeply, or turn his hands too far left on the club. The author has allowed his past errors on the thirteenth tee become who he is on the golf course, or at least on that hole. He has unwittingly allowed irrational beliefs about those bad shots to become a consistent reality. As mentioned earlier, if we let them, our worse fears actually *become* our goals. Alternatively, when the author steps up to that tee with an awareness of the false belief that he can't hit a good shot, but then dismisses the thought as absurd, he delivers a fine shot down the fairway.

> For any particular activity or process, do you sometimes fail to "hit the ball" solidly because of a tendency to overanalyze? Do you sometimes intellectualize too much when you should let yourself settle into your natural rhythm? Do you check your breathing and try to relax, letting your training, knowledge, developed skills, and natural ability take over? Are you aware that too much stress in demanding situations can cause performance to shut down? Have you unconsciously allowed false beliefs suppress progress towards your goals?

Never Enter a "Fight" You Don't Think You Can Win

His lifestyle is this: First weigh—then risk. He would correctly recognize the problem, make a plan in his clear head, then nothing else would be able to confuse him. [Baroness von Richthofen, 1937, p. 90]

Try to secure advantages before attacking. If possible, keep the sun behind you. [*Dicta Boelcke*; English, 2003, p. 62]

One should never obstinately stay with an opponent who, through bad shooting or skilful turning, one has been unable to shoot down, when the battle lasts until it is far on the other side and one is alone and faced by a greater number of opponents. [MvR Air Combat Operations Manual; Kilduff, 1993, p. 239]

Throughout the war, German pilots were significantly outnumbered by their opponents. Undue risk caused loss of life and the valuable expertise of experienced pilots. Both Richthofen and Boelcke cautioned against foolish acts of heroism and failure to secure advantages before attacking the enemy. One such ill-advised episode of heroism involved Werner Voss.

Leutnant Werner Voss was one of the best pilots of World War I. Richthofen recognized the instinctive and natural aviator ability of Voss when they were comrades at *Jasta 2* and appointed him commander of *Jasta 10* on July 30th, 1917. On September 24th—the day he was scheduled to go on leave—Voss was shot down in his Fokker triplane in an epic battle against no less than seven SE5s of 56 Squadron. At the time, Voss was Richthofen's chief rival for aerial victories with forty-eight to his credit. In a similar situation, Richthofen had downed forty-eight aircraft five months earlier and then scored four victories the day before going on his mandated leave. While his father and two brothers waited at the Marckebeke airfield to accompany him on leave, Voss elected to go out alone for one last opportunity to add to his score. Soon he came upon a patrol of SE5s from 60 Squadron and attacked the two trailing aircraft, severely damaging both. However, while he dived to finish off those two aircraft, another patrol of SE5s from 56 Squadron came on the scene. In spite of the huge odds against him, Voss attacked. He was joined briefly by an Albatros—probably six-victory ace Carl Menckhoff of *Jasta 3*—but the Albatros was soon hit and forced to abandon the fight. The SE5s had a 23 mph speed advantage, but the piloting skills of Voss coupled with his more maneuverable triplane allowed him to inflict significant damage on nearly every SE5 in the fray. Unfortunately, Voss was ultimately unable to prevail against the overwhelming number of opponents and their own considerable skills.[13]

~

What Manfred reported in his modest, simple way was like the fighter pilots' 'Song of Songs.' Mutual pride and chivalry ... [Baroness von Richthofen, 1937, p. 116]

Anybody would have been proud to have killed Richthofen in action, but every member of the Royal Flying Corps would also

have been proud to shake his hand had he fallen into captivity alive. [Ace in 56 Squadron RAF, quoted in Wilberg, 2007; p. 85]

In any war, typically there are winners and losers. However, in World War I, aviators generally fought with chivalry on both sides. They showed respect—and even at times admiration—for their opponents.

Often, as we are growing up and later in the business world, we are taught that to be "successful" we must *win* and our competition must *lose*. Sometimes we get so greedy that we only feel like we have "won" if our suppliers—and even our customers—are in essence cheated or deceived as we pad our own coffers. Yet we can achieve a beneficial *win-win* scenario in all or at least most relationships. In team sports, for instance, there are really no "losers." The win-win comes from working together effectively as a team to achieve a successful result or having the opportunity to gauge skills against another team and improve. At this author's alma mater, for instance, the paradigm belief was that we *never lost* a sports event, although sometimes we were *outscored*.

Wolff, my brother and I were flying together. We were three against three. That was as it ought to be. [Richthofen, 1918, p. 174]

At last one of the men plucked up courage and dropped down upon our rear machine. Naturally battle was accepted although our position was unfavorable. If you wish to do business you must, after all, adapt yourself to the desires of your customers. [Richthofen, 1918, p. 182]

Richthofen would not refuse a fight when he was directly challenged. However, when given a choice, there were times when it made more sense to fight another day. He encouraged his pilots to pick their battles carefully for their own safety and for the preservation of precious resources—men and equipment—that were in limited supply.

Do you "first weigh—then risk?" Have you considered any downsides before moving forward with a relationship, task, or negotiation? *Win-win* is when both sides are able to take something positive away from the table. Do you allow for win-win agreements in your dealings with family, friends, customers, and business associates? Do you believe in mutual pride and chivalry? When facing a fragile or weaker opponent, do you allow him or her to "save face?" Do you refuse to "run up the score?" Similarly, do you have the courage to decline a "fight" if your partner or business supplier is insisting on a win-lose at your expense?

Be Able to Control the Outcome

Both of us were in very bad spirits when we reached home. He [Georg Zeumer] reproached me for having shot badly and I reproached him for not having enabled me to shoot well. In short our aeroplanic relations, which previously had been faultless, suffered severely. [Richthofen, 1918, p. 76]

In a well-organized flight there is usually a precise arrangement of individuals. [MvR Air Combat Operations Manual; Kilduff, 1993, p. 232]

With an especially well-coordinated *Staffel* I can also attack a [numerically] superior enemy from above and the other side. [MvR Air Combat Operations Manual; Kilduff, 1993, p. 236]

The *Staffel* must develop diversity, i.e., not become accustomed to one position or the like; rather, individuals must learn to work together, so that each recognizes from the movement of the [next] aeroplane what the man at the joystick wants to do. [MvR Air Combat Operations Manual; Kilduff, 1993, p. 235]

In an earlier air battle, following their unsuccessful attempt to shoot down a British Farman aircraft, Zeumer and Richthofen realized the importance of having control of both the aircraft and the armament for better results. As any good manager knows, it is important to understand and to control the process. Later, however, as *Kommandeur* of his own units, Richthofen also emphasized that teamwork, synergy, and diversity not only meant survival but also greater productivity. It allowed his typically smaller, more-unified fighter squadrons to successfully defeat numerically larger forces.

Do you periodically look at the process that you and your team are using not only to create better products but also to provide greater safety margins and more consistent results? Do you value the diverse cultures and skills of those in your organization? Do you find ways to capitalize on these strengths and leverage even greater results and goal achievements that aren't normally possible with simple individual effort? Do you encourage and even demand teamwork from your employees for the success of the organization and the company?

Use Situation Awareness

He [the fledgling fighter pilot] knows the terrain without a map and the course to and from the Front by heart. He must have practiced many times long orientation flights at home, even during bad weather. [MvR Air Combat Operations Manual; Kilduff, 1993, p. 237]

When over the enemy's lines, never forget your own line of retreat. [*Dicta Boelcke*; English, 2003, p. 62]

Every individual counts the number of opponents at the moment he sights them. At the moment when the offensive begins, everyone must ascertain where all of the enemy aeroplanes are. [MvR Air Combat Operations Manual; Kilduff, 1993, p. 233]

The greatest danger for a single-seater is the surprise attack from behind.... Without fail, everyone must give the highest consideration [to the airspace] behind him. [Richthofen's Air Combat Operations Manual; Kilduff, 1994, p. 237]

Always keep your eye on your opponent, and never let yourself be deceived by ruses. [*Dicta Boelcke*; English, 2003, p. 62]

In another minute, I am back with the formation and continue in the direction of the enemy.... But the captain [Richthofen] has noticed. He seems to have eyes everywhere. His head whips around, and he waves at me. [Udet, 1935, p. 51]

This author defines *situation awareness* as the continuous exploration and integration of all relevant elements of the dynamic environment, including individual credentials, to facilitate anticipation, decision making, and task execution.[14]

One of Richthofen's greatest strengths was his superb situation awareness. His excellent eyesight enabled him to spot enemy aircraft long before others could do so. His lightning-fast reflexes and decision-making gave him the ability to track and later critique the actions of his men even when he was engaged in life-threatening aerial combat of his own.

Situation awareness is arguably as important in the challenges of business and day-to-day living as it is in aviation. Without effective situation awareness, companies can miss changes in market direction or be blindsided by the competition. Similarly, individuals can lose sight of their goals or inadvertently place themselves or others in real physical danger if they fail to maintain vigilance and an attitude of safety. Have you taken the time to study the "terrain?" Do you know the layout of every "fairway" and "green?" What about the hazards? Are you aware of and can you anticipate any "sand traps" or pitfalls? Do you thoroughly understand the environment in which you work or compete? Are you able to make quick decisions in dynamic situations?

Have you studied the strengths and weaknesses of your competition? Do you truly understand yourself, your positive traits and your limitations, and also those of your team?

Chapter 4 Summary

Envision Your Target. Richthofen learned from his mentor Oswald Boelcke and then later taught his own protégés that aerial success depended primarily on the elements of surprise, flying a maneuverable aircraft, and attacking at close range, typically from the in-trail position. But he also stressed additional factors for success that could not easily be taught. The fighter pilot had to be daring, possess aggressive determination, and be highly skilled to attack at such close range. More importantly, he had to have confidence, envision success, and be able to visualize the victory in his "mind's eye."

Identify your goal and then visualize victory! Determine what needs to be done, develop a plan, secure the necessary training and tools, and then boldly attack, watching obstacles progressively fall away, first in your mind and then in reality.

See it in Your Mind. Richthofen recognized how important it was to "see" his enemies fall in his "mind's eye," to visualize all the elements of a successful air battle. Being able to imagine all stages of the victory before they actually unfolded allowed him to confidently complete the mission successfully. But he also understood that there was no great secret of life, no "magic bullets" that would ensure success. What he did possess was a positive attitude of success and a self-belief that propelled both him and his men forward.

Recognize the power of your own mind! Remove negativity from your thinking. Allow yourself to visualize your goals. Use imaging to "see" yourself moving forward through the obstacles en route to those goals. See yourself realizing your dreams and accepting the awards that come from their achievement.

Think Clearly. Richthofen had the ability to look at things from a clear and common-sense perspective.

View past failures as opportunities for learning and stepping stones towards your goals. Focus, think clearly, and use your common sense. Allow yourself to build confidence. Recognize that you are getting better with practice. Muster the courage to weigh the consequences of various courses of action and then take calculated risks. Develop enough self-confidence to at times follow your natural instincts and just "go for it" even if it means that you may occasionally fall off your "horse."

Put Your Change in Your Left Pocket. Don't overanalyze! Richthofen was puzzled with the response when he queried his mentor Boelcke about how he had successfully shot down four enemy aircraft. The Baron had been trying to overanalyze why he was unable to consistently "bag" his prey in the air as he had on the ground when, all along, the answer was to use essentially the very same technique.

As in any sport, it is important to not overanalyze and simply allow yourself to get in the "zone."

Let yourself settle into your natural rhythm. Allow your training, experience, skills, and intuitive ability to take over. Remain calm. Check your breathing and give yourself permission to relax between "shots."

Never Enter a "Fight" You Don't Think You Can Win. Richthofen would not refuse a fight when he was directly challenged. However, there were times when he wisely chose to fight another day.

Consider the downside in any situation. Always "weigh—then risk!" Remember that *win-win* allows both sides to take something positive away from the table. Push for win-win agreements in your dealings with family, friends, customers, and business associates. When facing a weaker opponent, allow him or her to "save face." Refuse to "run up the score!"

Be Able to Control the Outcome. Synergize! Richthofen knew that teamwork, synergy, and diversity not only meant survival but also greater productivity. It allowed his typically smaller units to successfully defeat numerically larger forces.

Take the time to periodically evaluate the process that you and your team are using not only to create better products but also to provide greater safety margins and more consistent results. Value the diverse cultures and skills of those in your organization. Find ways to capitalize on these strengths and leverage them for even greater results and goal achievements. Encourage—better yet, insist on!—teamwork from your employees for the success of your organization and the company.

Use Situation Awareness. One of Richthofen's greatest strengths was his superb situation awareness.

Take the time to study the "terrain." Make an effort to thoroughly understand the environment in which you work or compete. Anticipate and uncover any threats, hazards, or pitfalls. Develop your ability to make quick decisions in dynamic situations. Recognize your own abilities and strengths. Study the strengths and weaknesses of your competition.

5 FLY IN FORMATION
(Grow Your Team)

This morning I'm going to test the *Spirit of St. Louis*.... All our ideas, all our calculations, all our hopes lie there before me, waiting to undergo the acid test of flight. For me, it seems to contain the whole future of aviation. When such planes can be built, there's no limitation to the air.... Today, reality will check the claims of formula and theory on a scale which hope can't stretch a single hair. Today, the reputation of the company, of the designing engineer, of the mechanics, in fact of every man who's had a hand in building the *Spirit of St. Louis*, is at stake. And I'm on trial too, for quick action on my part may counteract an error by someone else, or a faulty move may bring a washout crash. [Lindbergh, 1953, pp. 113–4]

It was a great thing that we could absolutely rely on one another and that was the principal thing. One has to know one's flying partner. [Richthofen, 1918, p. 179]

Richthofen recognized the importance of teamwork, especially in the heat of deadly aerial combat. He emphasized that teamwork in his Air Combat Operations Manual. At times, pilots were expected to attack as a unit ("At the moment the *Kommandeur* goes into a dive to swoop down on the enemy formation, under any circumstances it must be the aim of each and every [pilot] to be the first to engage the opposition."); and at others to hold back in reserve ("The one who is closest to an opponent is the one who alone shall fire."). Richthofen insisted that his *Ketten, Staffel,* or *Geschwader* leaders know their pilots thoroughly and merit absolute trust ("These are the prerequisites: 1. Comradeship; 2. Strict discipline."). The Baron also emphasized teamwork in the context of the dynamics of a battle ("The *Staffel* must develop diversity, i.e., not become accustomed to one position or the like; rather, individuals must learn to work together.").[1]

~

Teamwork exists when separate individuals combine their skills and perspectives in order to produce a single effective team with the ability to share information to perform tasks and sometimes allocate the necessary workload to achieve desired outcomes. Team performance is typically higher when team members are skilled and there is a clear understanding of task roles. Skills and clarity of roles are especially important when teams perform complex tasks and require its members to alter and coordinate behaviors as demands or the environment changes. Such conditions, of course, existed for Richthofen and his men. For complex tasks or unpredictable circumstances, team training under realistic conditions can serve to enhance team performance and effectiveness.

Develop Teamwork

I proposed that our aviation branch [Aircraft Test Establishment at Adlershof Airfield] establish aircraft type tests to select front-line planes. I do not believe that some home-front pilot, especially someone working for one of the manufacturers, should determine the aircraft to be flown at the Front. Now, pilots from many front-line units come to these tests. We fly

the individual types and then agree among ourselves on which types we feel are best suited at the moment. [MvR, quoted in Kilduff, 2003; pp. 162–3]

Richthofen's arrival at La Brayelle on January 15, 1917, to take command of his squadron was a huge event for the men of *Jasta 11*, and the Baron wanted it to be so. The *Staffel* had not scored a single aerial victory, and they were desperate for a true leader. The men were left speechless as the Baron—already a living legend and ace of all aces with sixteen aerial combat successes—shut down his engine and then climbed smartly out of the new, bright-red Albatros DIII, the radiant *Pour le Merite* at his collar flashing with his agile movements. Richthofen's new team, filled with awe, slowly gathered around him.

~

Because Richthofen would be flying with his men in flight, squadron, and ultimately wing strength, he had to be more than a competent and respected commander—he had to be a great leader. Team leaders must first establish the legitimacy of their authority by exhibiting confidence, competency, and dedication to their followers. When leaders are especially effective in image management, they are perceived as possessing extraordinary, charismatic levels of capability and trustworthiness. Charismatic leaders have profound and extraordinary effects on their followers by the sheer force of their personal abilities, and they are able to divert the attention of followers from self-focus to the shared interests of the team.

In the personage of *Rittmeister* von Richthofen ... the *Geschwader* received a *Kommandeur* whose steel hard will in relentlessly pursuing the enemy was infused in every member of the *Geschwader*. His refined lack of pretension, his open, gallant manner; his military skill secured for him amongst the army an unshakeable trust that, despite his young age, was matched with great respect. [*General* von Hoeppner, quoted in Wilberg, 2007; p. 49]

**Everyone must show absolute trust in the leader in the air ...
If this trust is lacking, success is impossible from the outset.
The *Staffel* gains trust by [the leader's] exemplary daring and
the conviction that [he] sees everything and is able to cope
with every situation. [MvR Air Combat Operations Manual;
Kilduff, 1993, p. 235]**

Richthofen was not only an outstanding organization *Kommandeur*
but also a very effective and charismatic leader. In addition to
establishing the legitimacy of his authority by displaying poise,
ability, and credibility, he worked diligently in coaching, guiding, and
supporting his followers in a way that allowed them to maximize their
contribution to the *Staffel's* goals while satisfying their personal needs
and goals.

**On the tenth day I was allowed to go along to the Front. Like
a hen, he watched over me, the 'chick.' All of the beginners
had to fly very closely to him ... every time when we returned
he called us together for criticism. And soon I noticed to my
astonishment that, despite his life-or-death aerial battles, he
didn't let us out of his view for a second. And this gave his *Staffel*
a rock-strong feeling of security. Because each of us knew you
could rely on Richthofen with dead certainty! [*Leutnant* Carl
August von Schoenebeck, quoted in Franks & VanWyngarden,
2001; pp. 23–4]**

~

The author was fortunate to be employed at a company that
encouraged team-building activities—from basic trust exercises, team
problem-solving, and goal achievement to rope courses, cliff repelling,
and even climbing Mt. Elbert, the highest peak in Colorado. These
activities not only helped solidify teams but also allowed individuals to
add confidence and conquer personal fears.

Do you spend time sharpening your leadership abilities and working to develop your team? Are you technically competent and do you continually hone your skills through education and training? Do you strive to establish trust? Do you coach, guide, and develop your personnel to be effective in the dynamic environment? Have you considered taking your group on a team-building outing to promote trust and enhance camaraderie?

Organize (Into Teams of Five or Six)

For the Staffel: In principle, attack in groups of four or six. When the flight breaks up into a series of single combats, take care that several do not go for one opponent. [*Dicta Boelcke*; English, 2003, p. 62]

In a well-organized flight there is usually a precise arrangement of individuals. [MvR Air Combat Operations Manual; Kilduff, 1993, p. 232]

Boelcke divided his twelve pilots into two *Ketten* [flights] in autumn 1916. He made each five to six aeroplanes strong. Six to seven aeroplanes are best led, watched over and maneuvered by one leader. In general, this combat strength is sufficient even today. [Richthofen's Air Combat Operations Manual; Kilduff, 1994, p. 231]

When Richthofen took over his new squadron in January 1917, he merged his drive for personal combat with the task of transforming the *Jasta 11* pilots into an expert team of well-organized and aggressive aviators. The Baron lead by example and drove his men relentlessly to learn and refine tactics, master formation flying, and make effective use of their machine guns. He emphasized vigilance, attacking at close range, target accuracy, and the conservation of all-important speed and altitude. He taught his men to choose their battles and stay on the alert for an escape route if needed.

Richthofen typically divided his squadron into *Ketten* (flights) that flew in formations of five, six, or seven aircraft, depending upon the number of serviceable aircraft and the number of sorties being flown that particular day. When the British began to launch larger units, the Germans were forced to also increase their strength:

> **During very strong British flight operations, however, one is forced to work with stronger *Geschwadern*; I take off with 30 to 40 machines [in a] *Geschwader* flight. (Reason for this; inferior German fighter aircraft or strong [enemy] *Geschwader* activity.) [Richthofen's Air Combat Operations Manual; Kilduff, 1994, p. 231]**

The size of each formation or group of formations was a function of the ability of the *Kommandeur* and his individual *Ketten* (flight) and *Staffeln* (squadron) leaders to maintain effective oversight and control. Mutual cooperation and support were critical. Also of consideration were the experience levels and cohesiveness of the formation members themselves. Strong, aggressive, and well-trained units, such as those under Richthofen's leadership and eagle-like vision, were able to maintain effectiveness as the size of the formations groups grew to *Geschwader* (wing) strength.

~

From a business perspective, communication has a tendency to suffer as the number of individuals in a group or team grows. In meetings with large numbers of participants, there are less opportunities for individuals to speak, factions tend to form, and consensus becomes increasingly difficult.[2] Essentially—just like with Richthofen's fighter units—the ideal team size is five, six, or perhaps seven individuals. Regardless, a team should not be any larger than the number of individuals required to accomplish the task at hand.

Often the best decisions are the outcome of careful, thorough, and synergistic discussions by those involved. Do you make an effort to choose your teams carefully so that they are efficient and generate the greatest results? Are you cautious about size and cohesiveness of the group? Do you value diversity and encourage inputs from everyone? Do you place more emphasis on the successful results generated by the team and not focus too heavily on the contributions of individual members?

Among us there now prevails—at least among most of the *Staffeln*—a spirit that is quite magnificent. Would Boelcke ever be happy about it! This morning I was with von Richthofen, who now has been promoted to *Rittmeister*. It is amazing to what level he has brought his *Staffel* in such a short time. He has nothing but young men around him who would jump through fire for him. [*Oberleutnant* Erwin Bohme, quoted in VanWyngarden, 2007; pp. 28–9]

Chapter 5 Summary

Fly in Formation. *Teamwork* exists when individuals pool their skills and perspectives in order to produce a single effective team with the ability to share information to perform tasks and sometimes allocate the necessary workload to achieve desired results. Richthofen recognized the critical importance of teamwork, especially in the heat of potentially deadly aerial combat.

Develop Teamwork. Richthofen was not only an outstanding organization *Kommandeur* but also a very effective and charismatic leader. In addition to establishing the legitimacy of his authority by exhibiting confidence, competency, and trustworthiness, he worked diligently in coaching, growing, and supporting his followers.

Spend time refining your leadership skills and developing your team. Work to remain technically competent and continually sharpen your skills through education and training. Strive to establish trust from your followers. Coach, support, and develop your personnel to be effective in dynamic environments.

Organize (Into Teams of Five or Six). Richthofen typically divided his squadron into *Ketten* (flights) that flew in formations of five, six, or seven aircraft, depending upon the number of serviceable aircraft and the number of sorties being flown that particular day. The size of each formation or group of formations was a function of the ability of the *Kommandeur* and his individual flight or squadron leaders to maintain effective oversight and control. Mutual cooperation and support were critical.

Generally, the best decisions are the outcome of careful, thorough, and synergistic discussions of those involved. Make an effort to choose your teams carefully so that they are efficient and generate the maximum results. Be cautious about size and cohesiveness of the group. Place value on diversity. Emphasize team results and reward the success generated by the team rather than concentrating on the contributions of individuals.

6 MAKE YOUR FIRST SHOTS COUNT
(Be Aggressive)

When I flew with my brother the first time and watched, I noticed that hardly had my brother begun to fire when the Englishman fell. In general, my brother did not use more than twenty shots. [Lothar von Richthofen, quoted in Richthofen, ed. Stanley Ulanoff, 1969; p. 129]

The commander of Jagdgeschwader I [MvR] doesn't need to add much to this order. It is in keeping with his own view, and his Staffel leaders know him well enough to know that that view is: *Onward! Onward!*—the Prussian Army's curt, cold, harsh word of attack. [Bodenschatz, 1935, p 65]

The continuous attack assures success. [MvR Air Combat Operations Manual; Kilduff, 1993, p. 233]

On the cloudy and overcast late afternoon of April 20, 1918, Richthofen in his all-red Fokker DRI was leading a flight of five other triplanes when they encountered a flight of Sopwith F.1 Camels from No. 3 Squadron RAF, led by Captain D. J. Bell. The Camels were focusing their machine gun fire on the field-grey troops near the old Roman Road. Richthofen abruptly rolled his aircraft in on one of the Camels—flown by Commanding Officer Richard Raymond Barker, a six-victory ace and holder of the Military Cross—when he noted that it was attacking *Leutnant* Hans Weiss from below. After only a few shots, a round punctured Raymond-Barkers's fuel tank, the aircraft caught fire, and then crashed southwest of Hamel Wood. Less than a minute later, the Baron spotted an additional Camel engaged with another triplane below and he dived after it. Richthofen noticed that his second intended victim of the evening and 80th opponent went into a dive, pulled out, and then repeated the tactic several times in an attempt to evade the attack. Unshakable in his maneuverable triplane, the Baron closed the interval from the rear and squeezed off a mere fifty rounds. Most of the Sopwith's fabric-covered fuselage burned away in the air. Nevertheless, the pilot, Second Lieutenant David G. "Tommy" Lewis, managed to land with only minor burns and bruises because the cockpit itself was partially protected by plywood-covered panels. Richthofen made a low pass over the two downed Camels that were only fifty yards apart. He waved to Lewis and then continued over the infantrymen in the trenches and column of men on the roads. The grateful German soldiers waved to the Baron and flung their caps skyward.

On that evening of April 20th, Richthofen had aggressively claimed two victories in the span of three minutes. If there was anything that motivated the Baron to action more than seeing enemy aircraft attacking the basically defenseless field-grey soldiers below it was a fighter attacking one of his men, especially if his pilot was still somewhat inexperienced.

Be Aggressive

Always carry through an attack when you have started it. [*Dicta Boelcke*; English, 2003, p. 62]

If your opponent dives on you, do not try to evade his onslaught,

but fly to meet it. [*Dicta Boelcke*; English, 2003, p. 62]

Turning back by pilots whose engines are misfiring or the like is inappropriate. [MvR Air Combat Operations Manual; Kilduff, 1993, p. 233]

At last I formed a resolution that I also would learn to fly a Fokker. Perhaps then my chances [to shoot down a hostile aircraft] would improve. [Richthofen, 1918, p. 64]

Richthofen recognized early on that to be successful in the air, he and his men had to fly aircraft that delivered both maneuverability and speed in order to aggressively engage their targets. But he also knew that other aspects of maneuverability and speed were critical to being productive—the ability to respond to enemy activity and get to the battle zone quickly. The Baron's "flying circus" concept of locating his bases of operation close to the Front and installing rapid-response telecommunications systems greatly aided in these efforts. Further, Richthofen made sure that he and his men maintained a constant state of readiness to do battle:

Because we always had to be ready for takeoff, we had our flying combinations [overalls] on the whole day—the most some took off were their crash helmets for a short period of time. Hardly had the command to take off come from Richthofen, and he was already sitting in his aeroplane. It was at first [difficult] for me—and later for all new comrades—to first have to get used to this incredible speed. These first days rather exhausted me, even though I was an "old flier"—Richthofen demanded a lot. When the weather was good, there were not fewer than five take-offs [in one day], although I personally participated in as many as seven. [*Leutnant* Richard Wenzl, quoted in Franks & VanWyngarden, 2001; p. 31]

Often organizations and companies that have been very successful in the past begin to lose market share when they are unable to respond quickly to changes in the environment or to competitive companies that are perhaps newer, more flexible, faster in generating new products, or are less burdened with bureaucracy. Sometimes the old "proven" methods of getting the job done are simply no longer productive. Organizations are by necessity becoming more flexible and adaptive in order to survive. For employees, stable careers appear to be less characteristic now than they were in the past. Workforce restructuring, changing operational procedures, and disappearing career-fostering bureaucratic organizations are reasons being offered for the demise of careers.[1] Further, rather than possessing experience based on a career with a single company, workers might need to possess instead a marketable "portfolio" of developed skills.

> Do you and your team sit down occasionally to make certain that you are not only *doing things right* but also *doing the right things*? Are you perhaps straying too far from your core competencies? Have you allowed bureaucracy to get out of hand?

> What about your personal life? Are you willing to cast off old ideas and obstacles that are slowing you down or blocking your success or dreams? Remember the Anthony Robbins quote, "If you do what you've always done, you'll get what you always gotten!"

Durwood J. Heinrich, Ph.D.

Be Willing to Take Calculated Risks

His lifestyle is this: First weigh—then risk. He would correctly recognize the problem, make a plan in his clear head, then nothing else would be able to confuse him. [Baroness von Richthofen, 1937, p. 90]

Richthofen was always logical and calculating in what he did. Possessing the patience and the instinctive craftiness of a hunter, Richthofen attacked from a position of advantage. He was never reckless and rarely took unnecessary risks unless he was protecting or rescuing one of his own men. As did Boelcke before him, Richthofen spent immeasurable hours teaching, coaching, and encouraging his men. He taught his pilots the basics, and then the advanced techniques of combat flying, insisting that they not stray from the sound principles that guaranteed success and provided them with a safety edge. With their exhaustive training, ever-mounting experience, and sense of security under the watchful eye of their leader, Richthofen's pilots proved themselves to be arguably the best aviators of the war.

Generally, the German pilots faced enemy aircraft that were triple their strength. Because the odds were clearly not in their favor, it was critical that they chose their aerial battles carefully. They obviously still took considerable risks, but they also relied on their considerable training, sharpened skills, and the fact that should they be forced to land, it was normally on their own side of the Front because of the typically southwesterly winds in France.

In the characteristic business atmosphere of competitive or economic threats, corporations generally utilize probability and statistical procedures based on various alternatives to minimize risk and potential losses.[2] When the environment provides little or no certainty, risk increases, as does the potential for failure. To move forward in totally uncertain environments, decision makers must often resort to using intuition and instinct and then take calculated risks.

Sometimes election of a *no-decision* is the best decision. However, to move forward, especially when time is limited and action is essential, it is often necessary to take risks. Do you weigh alternatives and then take *calculated* risks as necessary in order to achieve your objectives? Have you invested the time to learn from your mentor, train, and gain valuable experience? Do you then apply all of your skills and credentials to the task at hand? Do you draw on your instinct and intuition as necessary in environmentally-risky situations?

Don't Hesitate to Get Your Chin Dirty

In vain he tried to get out of this poor position; I did not give him the chance. I came so close to him that my machine was smutted by the ensuing explosion of his 'plane. [Oswald Boelcke, 1917, p. 186]

Have I got a black chin? [Boelcke, quoted in Sykes, 2004; p. 56]

When Richthofen reported at Bertincourt, on the Somme Front, on September 1st, 1916, *Jasta 2* only had two Fokker DIIIs and a single Albatros DI. They would receive a fourth—a refurbished Halberstadt—on the 11th. While the unit waited for the new Albatros DIs and DIIs, which didn't arrive until the 16th, Boelcke spent countless hours teaching his pilots about aerial tactics, formation flying, navigation, and gunnery. Boelcke also used the four aircraft he did have to take his men on small group sorties behind German lines to hone their skills. Typically before breakfast, Boelcke flew solo patrols in his Fokker DIII rotary-engine biplane. Upon his return, his fledglings would gather around and ask him if he had been successful, to which he replied: "Is my chin black?"[3] As was often the case, Boelcke's powder-stained face indicated that he had fired his machine guns and downed yet another enemy aircraft. In fact, Boelcke would achieve seven early morning victories before he felt his eager pilots were ready to go into actual battle for themselves.

> **How he [MvR] took care of us beginners was wonderful, and what we learned from him! He himself took the training of each one of his pilots in his own hands. As soon as our duties allowed us, we had to shoot at a target. Everyone received 50 bullets each for both machine guns—and we beginners only made, on the average, from 50–60 hits out of 100. But the 'aces' of the *Staffel* made 80–85. And when Richthofen came back, he almost always had over 90—sometimes he did indeed place all his shots into the target!**
> **On the tenth day I was allowed to go along to the Front. Like a hen, he watched over me, the 'chick.' All of the beginners had to fly very closely to him … every time when we returned he called us together for criticism. And soon I noticed to my astonishment that, despite his life-or-death aerial battles, he didn't let us out of his view for a second. And this gave his *Staffel* a rock-strong feeling of security. Because each of us knew you could rely on Richthofen with dead certainty! [*Leutnant* Carl August von Schoenebeck, quoted in Franks & VanWyngarden, 2001; pp. 23–4]**

As did his mentor Boelcke, Richthofen continued to fly training flights with individuals and with groups of his men several weeks after taking command of *Jasta 11*. Richthofen led by example and demanded as much from himself as he did from his pilots. He insisted on accuracy with machine guns and always led the scorers in training. He kept pace with his younger pilots and often flew five or more missions in a single day, typically the first in his aircraft when an alert was sounded. He possessed the remarkable ability to mentally record essentially everything going on around him, even when personally engaged in a deadly one-on-one battle. This allowed him to effectively evaluate his pilots' performance and suggest improvements. He was challenging with his men, but he never asked them to do anything more than he required of himself.

Are you willing to "get your chin dirty?" Do you understand and discipline yourself enough to just dive into a project and get to work as necessary when the time comes? One of the essential elements of leadership is the willingness to head the "cavalry charge" into battle. Do you demand the same performance from yourself as you do from your employees or team? Are you willing to admit personal mistakes and work to coach and develop the members of your organization?

Chapter 6 Summary

Make Your First Shots Count. Late in the afternoon of April 20th, 1918, Richthofen aggressively claimed two victories in the span of three minutes. If there was anything that motivated the Baron to action more than seeing enemy aircraft attacking the defenseless field-grey soldiers below it was a fighter attacking one of his men, especially if his pilot was still somewhat inexperienced. On that day, the Baron quickly and aggressively positioned his maneuverable aircraft in close behind his victims and added two enemy aircraft to his tally in short order.

Discipline yourself to detect what needs to be done, develop a plan, and make a focused and aggressive attack. If possible, make you first shots count, but if conditions change and the risks are still acceptable, don't hesitate to return for another pass.

Be Aggressive. Richthofen recognized early on that to be successful in the air, he and his men had to fly aircraft that possessed both maneuverability and speed. But he also recognized that other aspects of maneuverability and speed were critical to being productive—the ability to get to the battle zone quickly and to respond aggressively to enemy aircraft activity.

Organizations and companies that have been quite successful in the past often begin to lose ground when they are no longer able to respond rapidly to changes in the environment or to competitive companies that are perhaps newer, more flexible, faster in generating new products, or are less burdened with bureaucracy.

Be aggressive in your business and personal life! Be willing to cast off old ideas and obstacles that are slowing you down or blocking your success or dreams. Don't forget the Anthony Robbins quote, "If you do what you've always done, you'll get what you have always gotten!"

Be Willing to Take Calculated Risks. Richthofen was always logical and calculating in what he did. Possessing the patience and the instinctive craftiness of a hunter, he attacked from a position of strength and advantage. He rarely took unnecessary risks unless he was protecting or rescuing one of his own men.

Weigh alternatives and then take calculated risks as necessary in order to achieve your objectives. Invest time to learn from your mentor, train, and gain experience. Apply your acquired skills and qualifications to the task at hand. Utilize your instinct and intuition as necessary in environmentally risky situations.

Don't be Afraid to Get Your Chin Dirty. Richthofen led by example and demanded as much from himself as he did from his pilots. He insisted on high accuracy with machine guns and always led the scorers in training exercises. He kept pace with his younger pilots and often flew five or more missions in a single day. He was typically the first in his aircraft when an alert was sounded.

Be willing to "get your chin dirty!" Understand that it is often necessary to dive into a project and simply get to work ("Just Do It!"). One of the essential elements of leadership is the willingness to head the "cavalry charge" into battle. Demand the same performance from yourself as you do from your employees or team. Be willing to admit personal mistakes and work to coach and develop the members of your organization.

7 FUNCTION IN "PERFECT UNITY"
(Know Your Strengths and Weaknesses)

Body and spirit were one in him, a perfect unity. [Baroness von Richthofen, 1937, p. 190]

It was a great thing that we could absolutely rely on one another and that was the principal thing. One has to know one's flying partner. [Richthofen, 1918, p. 179]

Always keep your eye on your opponent, and never let yourself be deceived by ruses. [*Dicta Boelcke*; English, 2003, p. 62]

One does not need to be an aerobatic artist or a trick shooter; rather, to have courage to fly right up to the opponent. [Richthofen's Air Combat Operations Manual; Kilduff, 1994, p. 238]

Richthofen's mentor Oswald Boelcke was detailed, methodical, and a brilliant aerial tactician. Richthofen possessed a steadfast determination and self-confidence; and as a skilled hunter, he also shared Boelcke's detailed and methodical approach to flying. Both of these great leaders demanded that their pilots be well-trained, possess an aggressive spirit, and recognize the importance of teamwork and trust. They emphasized proven tactics, supportive formation flying, calculated risk-taking, and fundamental flying skills rather than the use of "tricks."

I place little significant value on the skill of flying itself.... It does not matter whether [or not] one is an aerobatic artist. [Richthofen's Air Combat Operations Manual; Kilduff, 1994, p. 237]

Know Your Strengths and Weaknesses

We had a delightful time with our chasing squadron. The spirit of our leader [Boelcke] animated all his pupils. We trusted him blindly. There was no possibility that one of us would be left behind. Such a thought was incomprehensible to us. Animated by that spirit we gaily diminished the number of our enemies. [Richthofen, 2005, p. 95]

Everyone must show absolute trust in the leader in the air.... If this trust is lacking, success is impossible from the outset. The *Staffel* gains trust by [the leader's] exemplary daring and the conviction that [he] sees everything and is able to cope with every situation. [MvR Air Combat Operations Manual; Kilduff, 1993, p. 235]

Perhaps the greatest strength that was handed down to their pilots by both Boelcke and Richthofen was the confidence to trust their leadership. Boelcke and Richthofen certainly possessed the skills and the self-confidence needed to inspire their men. But they also had the uncanny ability to observe seemingly everything going on during an aerial battle, thereby providing a very important measure of security to their pilots. The trusting protégés felt that should they need help, their leaders would quickly come to their rescue—and they were correct!

Later—especially as more of his men began to paint their aircraft with various combinations of colors accented by a common red— even Richthofen's enemies had the eerie feeling that the Red Baron was everywhere. This was accentuated further when the Fokker DRIs were placed into service because they were so maneuverable, making it appear as though one or just a couple of the triplanes constituted a squadron or squadrons of many more aircraft. Often, enemy aircraft had only to glimpse the red-colored aircraft, and they quickly "turned tail."

Not a single hit was to be found on the whole of the plane.... Now I had to laugh. The Englishman had landed actually out of fear of me! [Lothar von Richthofen, quoted in Richthofen, ed. Stanley Ulanoff, 1969; p. 128]

Another very important practice religiously followed by Richthofen was the pre- and post-flight briefing and evaluation. Individual, flight, squadron, and wing strengths and weaknesses were discussed and resolved. Pilots even had to account for bullet holes sustained to the aft fuselage segments of their aircraft because it meant that they had allowed an enemy to position his aircraft in their vulnerable 6-o'clock position.

Immediately after every *Geschwader* flight a discussion is the most important instructive activity. At this time, everything that happened during the flight from take-off to landing must be discussed. The questioning of individuals can be very useful for clarification. [Richthofen's Air Combat Operations Manual; Kilduff, 1994, p. 234]

The greatest challenges recognized by Richthofen and other *Geschwader Kommandeurs* were the sheer number of the enemy aircraft and, especially later in the war, the superior quality of those machines versus those of German design. The outnumbered German pilots countered by being generally better-trained both as aviators and as masters of their specific fighters. Richthofen understood the leverage that the highly-trained and well-coordinated *Staffels* provided:

> **A *Geschwader* battle on this side of the lines is usually most successful, as I can force an opponent to land.... As long as I can be on the offensive, I can also carry out a *Geschwader* flight far on the other side. With an especially well-coordinated *Staffel* I can also attack a [numerically] superior enemy from above and the other side. [MvR Air Combat Operations Manual; Kilduff, 1993, p. 236]**

~

Companies and organizations sometimes devote too much energy in exploring *what they are not* (weaknesses?) rather than capitalizing on *what they do well* (strengths!). Often companies lose revenue and become less competitive when they compromise their core competencies. They also do this with individual workers by indiscriminately initiating evaluations focused on uncovering employee "weaknesses" and targets for training. Primary job technical training and guidance aimed at sharpening leadership and teamwork skills are critical. Secondary skills and cross-functional training can be productive as well in certain situations, especially in smaller organizations if personnel flexibility is essential. On the other hand, it is not always constructive or economically feasible to attempt to bring everyone up to some pre-determined, all-encompassing skill level. That is what diversity is all about. Not everyone can or should be required to be an expert at everything. Management should work to capitalize on peoples' job-related strengths and at the same time tap into their interests and sources of motivation. Employees should spend the bulk of their time being productive in their principal job positions and should be given opportunities to further their skills and train to be even more valuable in that capacity.

Do you know your personal core strengths and weaknesses and also those of your organization or team? Do you train to maintain and enhance your primary skills and talents rather than to dilute them? Do you—tactfully!—resist attempts by management to unproductively divide your attention and focus if the results are marginal or even detrimental? Do you recognize when others may have special skills and can handle certain tasks more effectively or efficiently than you? Are you willing to delegate, thereby allowing yourself to concentrate on your primary responsibilities and what *you* personally do best?

Count on Ability, not Trickery

The great thing in air fighting is that the decisive factor does not lie in trick flying but solely in the personal ability and energy of the aviator. [Richthofen, 1918, p. 131]

Count Holck was not only a sportsman on land. Flying also was to him a sport which gave him the greatest pleasure. He was a pilot of rare talent and particularity, and that is, after all, the principal thing. [Richthofen, 1918, p. 63]

Only a beginner can be caught and one cannot set traps because an aeroplane cannot hide itself. [Richthofen, 1918, p. 132]

For him [MvR] it [air combat] is the last remnant of an old chivalry in this battle of man against man. He doesn't think highly of stunting in the air. [Baroness von Richthofen, 1937, pp. 106–7]

It's interesting that if one "Googles" the two words "business" and "tricks," the results come in at some 136,000,000 hits! Replacing "tricks" with the word "integrity," on the other hand, only produces results of 12,500,000 (91% fewer hits!). "Business" and "chivalry" brings in a relatively dismal 936,000 matches. Further, if one looks up the word "trick" in any dictionary, it is difficult to find any definition that doesn't contain the word *deception* or *fraudulent*. In contrast, "chivalry" is invariably defined with the words *honor, integrity,* and *courage*.

It seems that in today's world we are bombarded by the idea that we can have anything we want —and have it now!—using some scheme, plot, shortcut, or trick. Perhaps we dress it up a bit, add mystery or glamour, and call it a "secret," but the concept is the same—we expect to get something for nothing or for little or marginal effort. If you are skeptical, Google "success" and "secret" together—the result is some 64,400,000 hits! Why does something have to be mysterious or clandestine for it to appeal to us? Even as youngsters we were taught that if one had to keep something a "secret," he or she probably shouldn't be doing it!

All these tricks may impress people who attend a Sports Meeting, but the public at the battle-front is not as appreciative of these things. It demands higher qualifications than trick flying. [Richthofen, 1918, p. 133]

Richthofen cautioned his pilots about the ineffectiveness and even folly of trickery in combat. Rather he taught the importance of ability, energy, and a strong heart! The Baron also refused to buy into superstition and magical thinking. Rather, he relied on training, skill, dedication, courage, and integrity.

~

When the author's job situation changed in Arizona late in 2007, he and his wife decided to move back to Texas, preferably to the Austin area. Unfortunately, the housing market situation was in a free-fall at the time. The choices were to attempt to ride out the real estate slump in an effort to minimize the loss on the sale of the Arizona home or to sell at a loss and hope to recover the difference on the purchase of a home in Texas. Finally, the decision was made to sell the house and relocate to Austin. However, the market situation was worsening with each day that passed, and in mid-January 2008, the author and his wife put together a very aggressive two-month timeline for the sale of the existing home and move into a new home. The timeline was based on everything falling into place as planned to minimize an inevitable further loss as the market spiraled downward. Even specific closing dates and a move-in date were identified.

Because it was obviously impossible to move into a home in Texas without first selecting one, the author's wife flew to Texas a week later. By that weekend, on Saturday, February 2, 2008, she had purchased a new home that was under construction. That same weekend, the author successfully convinced a real estate agent and his clients—who had already twice toured and shown interest in the Arizona home—to return for a final visit before catching their afternoon flight back home to Illinois. By Monday, February 3rd, the Arizona home was sold.

Without going into further detail, the homes were purchased and sold respectively on schedule and two days late (by the time contract signing was completed). Loss on the old home and the savings on the new home resulted in essentially a "wash." Closings of the existing home and the new home occurred respectively two weeks late—delayed to allow for new home completion—and on the exact date scheduled. In fact, when the agent who was drawing up the contract for the purchase of the new home inquired about the proposed closing date, the author simply gave her the date listed on the timeline. The move-out date was missed (by choice) by one month so that the move-in date would allow for household goods transfer to occur without the need for temporary storage. The last line item on the schedule, the final move-in date, occurred one day ahead of schedule! The author is convinced that all of this happened, not by magic, some secret, or "sending it to the universe," but rather because of careful design, execution, and follow-up. One could argue that a little luck came into play because the new owners of the Arizona home were cash buyers and were willing to put off the closing date to allow for the sellers' Austin home completion. On the other hand, the buyers loved the home, were obviously motivated, and were a perfect match for the pre-determined schedule criteria. The author therefore pursued that particular couple and their agent to agree to a deal and even accepted their initial offer, in spite of the fact that it was slightly lower than desired. At least in this particular case, careful planning, determination, and a willingness to allow for a win-win scenario (no tricks!) resulted in a successful outcome.

> *Chivalry* was the medieval knight's code of honor. Do you decline to engage in spectacular "trick flying" with "smoke on" to impress (or to deceive!) others? Do you refuse to cut corners or provide an inferior product or service in the context of business? Do you generate a reasonable plan and proactively make it happen? Do you work hard in your business or profession and utilize your full ability to achieve excellent results? Do you inspire trust and deliver integrity in your dealings with others? Do you serve as an example to your family and friends?

Seek Quality Rather Than Quantity

There were sometimes from forty to sixty English machines, but unfortunately the Germans were often in the minority. With them [the Germans] quality was more important than quantity. [Richthofen, 2005, p. 95]

The important thing in aeroplanes is that they are speedy. [Richthofen, 1918, p. 151]

In the summer of 1916, the British and French offensives in the Somme and Verdun regions proved to be too much for the single-seat fighter (*Kampfeinsitzer*) squadrons. Recently-promoted air commander *Oberstleutnant* (Lieutenant Colonel) Hermann von der Lieth-Thomsen, implemented Oswald Boelcke's astute recommendation to reorganize the fighter units into pursuit squadrons (*Jagdstaffeln*).[1] Because the Fokker *Eindecker* monoplanes were no longer effective against the latest British fighters, the new *Jastas* received the latest, much faster Halberstadt and Albatros D type aircraft with dual machine guns. Further, the units were staffed with pilots who were carefully selected and given special training at single-seat fighting schools in Germany, advanced training at Valenciennes, and finally squadron training when they arrived at their assigned units. Boelcke, Germany's second highest scoring ace, was given command of *Jasta 2* at Bertincourt, assigned to the 2nd Army. The new strategy proved to be highly successful when Boelcke and five of his pilots, including Manfred von Richthofen, made their maiden hunting mission over Bertincourt on September 16th in their new Albatros DI and DII fighters received only the day before. Amazingly, the fledgling *Jasta 2* pilots celebrated four victories by the end of the day, including Richthofen's first official success over a FE2b. Even though he was late getting into the fray because he was carefully watching over his pilots, Boelcke increased his count to twenty-seven, bagging a FE2 as well. *Jasta 2* went on to have a very successful September flying 186 combat flights, posting twenty-one confirmed victories, plus four more unconfirmed.

Contrary to some beliefs, providing quality does *not* increase cost or compromise productivity if it is built into the process. Do you seek quality rather than quantity, especially when resources are limited? Do you and your company build quality into the manufacturing process so that the resulting products are not only less costly in the long run but are also superior products that meet or exceed the customer's requirements? In pursuit of process improvement and quality, are you careful to always attack problems and not people?

Select the Right Equipment

You are getting new Fokker triplanes. They climb like monkeys and are as maneuverable as the devil. [Manfred von Richthofen, quoted in Bodenschatz, 1935; p. 29]

Early in the day on July 6, 1917, Richthofen led a flight of *Jasta 11* Albatros DVs against six ground-strafing FE2d pusher biplane bombers from 20 Squadron heading for Deulemont. Following a rendezvous with additional German fighters in the area, Richthofen and his formation maneuvered to get behind the enemy aircraft, which then abruptly turned to attack the Albatrosses head-on. Richthofen noted with some surprise that the observer in the FE2d approaching him began firing from very long range when he suddenly felt a blow to the back of his head.[2] The Baron was instantly paralyzed and blinded, but using sheer willpower was able to slowly reclaim his eyesight, restart the engine, and land near Wervicq within German lines. Seriously wounded, Richthofen was taken to Field Hospital No. 76 (St. Nicholas) at Courtrai.

Refusing to remain out of the action, Richthofen continued to fight battles even from his hospital bed. Richthofen was furious about the order that acting Commander *Oberleutnant* von Doring received to utilize the *Geschwader* in squadrons on "barrier flights" to keep British aircraft from crossing German lines. Further, *Hauptmann* Otto Bufe, Commanding General of the German Air Service, had ordered the single German *Staffels* to fly late in the evening and at night against the large British formations that very successfully used the sun behind them to shield their surprise attacks. The inevitable result was that the heavily outnumbered German aircraft could not be as effective and became easy targets. Richthofen used his influence in his letter to his friend *Oberleutnant* Fritz von Falkenhayn, the *Kogenluft* staff's Technical Officer. The Baron also reinforced his appeal for improved fighters to counter the Sopwith Triplane, the SPAD VII, and the Sopwith Camel. The Baron was particularly annoyed that the Albatros DIII and DV aircraft continued to have occasional wing problems.

Despite continuing headaches and periodic procedures to dislodge residual small bone fragments from the wound to his head, Richthofen was determined to get back to his *Geschwader*. When the *Rittmeister* returned to Marckebeke for a brief visit on July 20th, he shook hands with von Doring but said little as he toured the facilities and the flight line with its shot-up and heavily-patched machines. But then he addressed his assembled pilots with some good news: "You are getting new Fokker triplanes. They climb like monkeys and they're as maneuverable as the devil."[3]

Richthofen understood well the importance of having the best, most-effective fighters at the Front, and he spent a considerable amount of his time visiting the aircraft factories and test-flying their latest products. He also valued the input of his colleagues from other units, and together they made recommendations for aircraft selection and suggestions for improvements in aircraft designs:

I proposed that our aviation branch [Aircraft Test Establishment at Adlershof Airfield] establish aircraft type tests to select front-line planes. I do not believe that some home-front pilot, especially someone working for one of the manufacturers, should determine the aircraft to be flown at the Front. Now, pilots from many front-line units come to these tests. We fly the individual types and then agree among ourselves on which types we feel are best suited at the moment. [MvR, quoted in Kilduff, 2003; pp. 162–3]

～

Several years ago as the corporation's business flight demands began to shift increasingly international, the author and his organization carefully analyzed the travel patterns of the top executives. In addition to the requirement to minimize key executive travel time while maximizing their productivity, additional top priorities included the security and safety of those individuals. The recommendation was made, and subsequently accepted, to replace the type of aircraft used for executive transport to more align with their needs. The new longer-range aircraft selected provided faster speeds over greater distances with increased comfort, allowing executives to work effectively and obtain quality sleep en route. This maximized their productivity at the international destinations and also allowed them to minimize their absences from headquarters and from their families. Manufacturer choice, cabin configuration, avionics selection, acquisition, finance, spare parts, training of pilot and maintenance personnel, and logistical issues associated with pre-positioning and crew augmentation were additional issues that were considered and resolved.

Are you and your organization using the right equipment? Do you make certain that your employees have the right tools for their jobs, including appropriate training? Are you continually in search of ways to improve productivity and efficiency? Are you alert for changes in the environment and obstacles that threaten to compromise your effectiveness and business future? Do you place faith in your employees who are the ones actually producing materials, running the processes, and dealing directly with customers? Do you empower those individuals to make suggestions and take ownership of their respective functional areas?

Know Your Equipment

The gigantic machine made it clear to me that only the smallest aeroplane would be of any use for me in battle. A big aerial barge is too clumsy for fighting. Agility is needed and, after all, fighting is my business. [Richthofen, 1918, p. 95]

The main thing for a fighter pilot is the machine gun. He has to master it so that he recognizes the cause of a gun jam…. There is no such thing as a gun jam! When it occurs, I blame only the pilot. A well-firing machine gun is better than a smooth-running engine. [Richthofen's Air Combat Operations Manual; Kilduff, 1994, p. 237]

When the British introduced the Bristol Fighter in the spring of 1917, the aircraft had a significant speed advantage over the German Albatros DIII of some 14 mph. Nonetheless, in addition to minor aircraft technical defects and crew inexperience, the aircraft was initially utilized operationally under the misguided concept that the observer, or machine-gunner, was the primary offensive entity. By the time the pilots realized they could be more effective offensively by employing the forward machine guns in-line with aircraft direction of flight and making the aft gunner defensive, Richthofen had already spread the word that the Bristol was "inferior," thereby reinforcing the confidence and morale of the German pilots.[4] Indeed, Richthofen shot down two Bristol Fighters on April 5, 1917.

Jasta 2 had ventured into battle on September 17, 1916, in new Albatros DI and DII aircraft that they had received just the day before. However, in contrast to the British, they were not only better-trained and led by Oswald Boelcke, but they apparently understood much earlier the criticality of using the forward gun controlled by the pilot who was actually maneuvering the aircraft for attack.

~

When Richthofen was hit in the head by a bullet in an air battle on July 6, 1917, he temporarily lost his eyesight. Although he was momentarily paralyzed as well, he was finally able to muster some motor control and instinctively switched off his engine. Aircraft of World War I were particularly vulnerable to fire if a round penetrated one of the pilot's two fuel tanks, and there were no parachutes available until late in the war. Fortunately, Richthofen was able to recover his vision long enough to make an emergency landing before he passed out.

When the author was flying military aircraft, the Air Force required all pilots—at least the ones in Air Training Command (ATC)—to be competent in blindfold cockpit checks. Although nearly all military aircraft had ejection seats or emergency escape systems of some sort, the possibility always existed of experiencing cockpit smoke, pilot temporary vision loss, or complete electrical failure—at night, of course, according to Murphy's Law! Knowing the exact location of critical switches at such times had obvious value. Ejection was an option, but that too had its own set of drawbacks, and walking back to the base without one's expensive government aircraft was generally frowned upon.

The author, in the context of his job, taught his Air Force students to be experts at finding switches with their eyes closed or covered. Later he taught his civilian pilots the value of this skill as well. Subsequently, in the corporate world, when a flight attendant was a member of the crew, he taught that individual how to shut down the APU (Auxiliary Power Unit) in the event of a ground fire or emergency—yes, blindfolded.

Do you maneuver into precise position for the attack against your competitors, or do you "spray" the environment with test shots, hoping for improbable success? Do you thoroughly understand your operation, your equipment, and the tools used in your business—well enough to perform "blindfolded?" Are there more effective or more efficient ways to operate? Do you adequately train your people? Do you work to encourage your personnel, seek their input, and value and enhance morale?

Be Daring

It is impossible to win the race unless you venture to run, impossible to win the victory unless you dare to battle. Richard M. DeVos

In my opinion the aggressive spirit is everything and that spirit is very strong in us Germans. [Richthofen, 1918, p. 132]

Why do you jeopardize your life in this way every day? "For the man in the trenches," he [Manfred] says simply. "I wish to lighten his hard lot, to keep the enemy fliers away from him." [Baroness von Richthofen, 1937, p. 116]

One should never obstinately stay with an opponent who, through bad shooting or skilful turning, one has been unable to shoot down, when the battle lasts until it is far on the other side and one is alone and faced by a greater number of opponents. [MvR Air Combat Operations Manual; Kilduff, 1993, p. 239]

He [MvR] shall live on within us for all time as a shining example of the boldest spirit of a fighter pilot. [*Hauptmann Reinhard*, quoted in Bodenschatz, 1935; p. 82]

In The Great War, the German Air Service was outnumbered in the skies over France, and Richthofen was faced with the formidable challenge of inflicting the greatest damage to the Allies while incurring minimum losses of his own. Because the British typically brought great numbers of aircraft over German lines, Richthofen was not forced to seek battles in the air and could be selective. When greater wisdom called for it, Richthofen encouraged his pilots to decline or break off a fight. Because Richthofen's "Circus," therefore, typically didn't seek out but rather responded to threats, it was not only extremely operative but elusive as well.[5]

His lifestyle is this: First weigh—then risk. He would correctly recognize the problem, make a plan in his clear head, then nothing else would be able to confuse him. [Baroness von Richthofen, 1937, p. 90]

Richthofen was also very daring and aggressive. He risked his life every day to control the skies and to protect the soldiers in the trenches from enemy aircraft fire. He never backed away from a fight unless the odds were poor that he could win. Nevertheless, he stressed to his pilots the importance of using good judgment to fight another day if appropriate, but—for their own safety—prompted them to take the offensive if backed into a corner:

If a beginner is attacked from behind, however, under no circumstances should he try to escape by slipping away. The best ... method is a sudden, very tight turn and then as quickly as possible take the offensive. [Richthofen's Air Combat Operations Manual; Kilduff, 1994, pp. 237-8]

True leaders should be daring, not because of what they can accomplish, but rather because of the *cause* they believe in. Do you have the perseverance to move forward despite the many obstacles ahead? Do you possess the passion to pave the way as a leader, thereby bringing along others to share the same dream? Are you also willing to adjust your plans if necessary should conditions change or warrant a revised strategy? Are you able to recognize that it is sometimes better to "fight another day" if conditions are not right?

Be Flexible

One fine day a telegram arrived, which stated: "Lieutenant von Richthofen is appointed Commander of the Eleventh Chasing Squadron." I must say I was annoyed. I had learnt to work so well with my comrades of Boelcke's Squadron and now I had to begin all over again working hand in hand with different people.... Besides I should have preferred the *Ordre Pour le Merite*. Two days later, when we were sitting sociably together, we men of Boelcke's Squadron, celebrating my departure, a telegram from Headquarters arrived. It stated that His Majesty had graciously condescended to give me the *Ordre Pour le Merite*. Of course my joy was tremendous. I had never imagined that it would be so delightful to command a chasing squadron. Even in my dreams I had not imagined that there would ever be a Richthofen's squadron of aeroplanes. [Richthofen, 1918, p. 128]

At last one of the men plucked up courage and dropped down upon our rear machine. Naturally battle was accepted although our position was unfavorable. If you wish to do business you must, after all, adapt yourself to the desires of your customers. [Richthofen, 1918, p. 182]

Just a few kilometers behind the lines, often within range of the enemy artillery, we are on fully dressed standby.... Our aircraft, gassed up and ready to go, are right alongside. As soon as an opponent appears on the horizon, we go up—one, two, or an entire *Staffel.* Immediately after the fight we land ... and scour the sky with binoculars, waiting for the next opponent. Standing patrols are not flown.... "This business of standing sentry duty in the air weakens the pilots' will to fight," he maintains. Thus we only go up to fight. [Udet, 1935, p. 50]

Richthofen was ambitious and determined. He was also eager, even sometimes impatient. Once he made up his mind about something, he pursued it with dedication and single-mindedness until he reached his goal. At times, Richthofen was side-tracked by circumstances or by decisions made by his superiors. However, when he felt that the Air Service had issued a command that was not in keeping with his overall mission, he was not hesitant in challenging the order until it was rescinded.

Richthofen could also be flexible and creative. On April 7th, 1917—the same day that he was promoted to *Rittmeister*—Richthofen directed *Jasta 11* to set up seventeen captured English machine guns in the vicinity of the officers' mess in order to counter a second night bombing raid by 100 Squadron RFC.[6] The next morning, the Baron, Schafer, and their comrades were informed by military intelligence that they had forced down three British FE2b aircraft close to the aerodrome by putting their engines out of action using the enemy's own weapons:

The next morning we were extremely surprised and delighted to discover that we had shot down from the ground no fewer than three Englishmen. They had landed not far from our aerodrome and had been made prisoners. [Richthofen, 1918, p. 167]

Organizational flexibility involves modifying processes and procedures in response to the environment, thereby ensuring greater productivity, innovation, and customer satisfaction.

Do you continually "scan the skies" so that you are prepared to respond quickly and appropriately to your customers? When "bombarded" from all sides by your competitors, are you flexible and creative enough to turn the tables and use some of their own weapons against them? Do you remain steadfast in pursuit of your "Blue Max" in spite of setbacks and unseen situations that may cause you to revise your plans to achieve your objectives?

Remain Calm

It's only a hundred yards to the hangars now—solid forms emerging from the night. I'm too high—too fast. Drop wing—left rudder—sideslip --- Careful—mustn't get anywhere near the stall. I've never landed the *Spirit of St. Louis* at night before. It would be better to come in straight. But if I don't sideslip, I'll be too high over the boundary to touch my wheels in the area of light. That would mean circling again --- Still too high. I push the stick over to a steeper slip, leaving the nose down --- Below the hangar roofs now --- straighten out --- A short burst of the engine --- Over the lighted area --- Sod coming up to meet me --- Deceptive high lights and shadows—Careful—easy to bounce when you're tired --- Still too fast --- Tail too high --- Hold off --- Hold off --- Texture of sod is gone --- Ahead, there's nothing but night --- Give her the gun and climb for another try? --- The wheels touch gently—off again—No, I'll keep contact–Ease the stick forward --- Back on the ground—Off—Back—the tail skid too --- Not a bad landing, but I'm beyond the light—can't see anything ahead—Like flying in a fog—Ground loop?—No, still rolling too fast—might blow a tire—The field must be clear—Uncomfortable though, jolting into blackness—Wish I had a wing light—but too heavy on the takeoff --- Slower, now --- slow enough to ground loop safely—left rudder—reverse it—stick over the other way --- *The Spirit of St. Louis* swings around and stops rolling, resting on the solidness of earth, in the center of Le Bourget. [Lindbergh, 1953, pp. 459–60]

'One man's owl is another man's nightingale!' says the Rittmeister.... It is right on, for the exact same fog that is keeping them from taking off is providing the infantry with the possibility of an enormous, unexpected advance. [Bodenschatz, 1935, p. 66]

He could always understand the essence of difficult questions and give advice with a common sense that scarcely went with his youth. [Baroness von Richthofen, 1937, p. 45]

My philosophy has always been: Take the war calmly. [Lothar von Richthofen, quoted in Richthofen, ed. Stanley Ulanoff, 1969; p. 125]

The Red Baron acknowledges his mechanics' reports of hits in his crate with a smile and a shrug. [Udet, 1935, p. 36]

It tickles one's nerves to fly towards the enemy, especially when one can see him from a long distance and when several minutes must elapse before one can start fighting.... I like that feeling for it is a wonderful nerve stimulant. [Richthofen, 1918, pp. 133-4]

Even though Richthofen usually experienced the adrenalin rush during an approaching air battle, he understood the importance of composure and remaining calm. A measure of that calmness came as an outcome of his patience and deliberateness as a hunter. Another reason for the calmness was the fact that, in spite of the enemy's superior numbers, the Baron and his men felt a sense of control in their battles and never doubted their ability to be victorious in the air.

It followed that the victory would accrue to him who was calmest, who shot best and who had the clearest brain in a moment of danger. [Richthofen, 1918, p. 138]

One attacks the two-seater from behind at great speed, in the same direction he is going. The only way to avoid the adroit observer's field of machine-gun fire is to stay calm and put the observer out of action with the first shots. [Richthofen's Air Combat Operations Manual; Kilduff, 1994, p. 238]

He who gets excited in fighting is sure to make mistakes. He will never get his enemy down. Besides calmness is, after all, a matter of habit. [Richthofen, 1918, pp. 136-7]

~

Managed stress (arousal) can be productive and promote well-being and happiness, while *mismanaged* stress can hurt or even prove to be lethal. Both physical and mental types of job stress are among the most important stressors that can aggravate disease. Behavioral responses can serve important "fight-or-flight" mechanisms, but they can also intensify stress consequences. Similarly, physiological stress responses can provide protective and adaptive changes, but they can also promote disease processes, especially when stress encounters are frequent, chronic, or non-adaptive.

Organizational factors that can be helpful in the proactive control of stress include enrichment strategies, employee development, increased autonomy, consistency from management, and personal recognition. Sense of control in the job function is an extremely important element in controlling stress.

In spite of a high casualty rate, for instance, World War II fighter pilots reported the least fear of any U.S. combat aircrew and were particularly receptive to additional tours because of their perceived control.[7] On the other hand, bomber pilots were much less willing to sign up for further combat. Fighter pilots, with their fast and responsive aircraft, could choose to engage the enemy or break off the fight. They perceived themselves as having greater autonomy and freedom of action compared with bomber pilots, who were required to fly their relatively unwieldy aircraft in formations on predetermined routes, regardless of flak or fighter attacks.

Individual proactive strategies to reduce stress include social support; a positive attitude; balance and coping mechanisms; high levels of self-esteem, motivation, and optimism; and personality hardiness. Individuals with *hardiness* typically possess characteristics such as commitment (high level of emotional involvement) to life's activities, a sense of control over events, and a positive attitude toward change.[8] Active, healthy lifestyles contribute significantly to the reduction of personal and occupational stress.

> Have you taught yourself the habit of remaining calm, even under the stress of "battle?" While it is important to take steps to avoid chronic stress, do you recognize that some stress can be productive and keeps you motivated and focused? Do you have the hardiness and enough job control in your position to counter negative stress? Do you allow your employees to enjoy a sense of empowerment and control?

Be Prepared

Luck is what happens when preparation meets opportunity.
Oliver Wendell Holmes

Just a few kilometers behind the lines, often within range of the enemy artillery, we are on fully dressed standby.... Our aircraft, gassed up and ready to go, are right alongside. As soon as an opponent appears on the horizon, we go up—one, two, or an entire *Staffel*. Immediately after the fight we land ... and scour the sky with binoculars, waiting for the next opponent. [Udet, 1935, p. 50]

"Anyone who flies a lot, experiences a lot" was also a maxim of his. "On good days, an average of three take-offs can be made in the morning." Then, of course, he still flew steadily in the afternoons and evenings. The rest of the time he stood with his men on the landing field, pretty much suited-up. [Bodenschatz, 1935, p. 86]

Richthofen was always prepared, both in his professional and in his personal life. His strategy was to position his "Circus" squadrons close to the Front. When enemy aircraft were launched, they were quickly detected either by army personnel or by himself or his men who were constantly scanning the sky with telescopes and binoculars. Because the aircraft and pilots were continually on alert, they were able to launch immediately to intercept the enemy planes. The Baron kept his personal life in perfect order as well, totally prepared financially for the future, whether or not he survived the war:

He is always clear, orderly, and prepared. [Baroness von Richthofen, 1937, p. 49]

~

The motto of both the Boy Scouts and the Girls Scouts of America is *Be Prepared!* Lord Robert Baden-Powell founded the scouting movement in 1907. Like Richthofen, he enjoyed hunting and had joined a cavalry unit (13th Hussars) in 1876 with the rank of Lieutenant. Later, to his Scouts, he emphasized the importance of planning in mind and body for life, preparing for its challenges, meeting them with a strong heart, and living happily without regret, knowing one had done his or her best.

Richthofen was likely never a Boy Scout. When the movement was founded in Germany in 1909, he had already entered the senior school at the Royal Military Academy at Lichterfelde. However, it is interesting that he lived his life much like Baden-Powell had envisioned a life should be lived.

On March 10, 1918, Richthofen wrote a one-sentence note appointing *Oberleutnant* Wilhelm Reinhard of *Jasta 6* his successor should he fall in battle. He handed the envelope containing the note to Bodenschatz on March 15th instructing him to open it should he not return. The Baron was content that the *Geschwader* would be in good hands if something should happen to him. He would not concern himself further:

That is his [MvR's] entire will and bequest. It concerns only and solely his Geschwader. It is the will of a true soldier.... There is nothing in it about his personal concerns, nothing that might perchance, need putting in order. [Bodenschatz, 1935, p. 78]

～

One of the author's organizational policy deployment objectives, mentioned earlier, was to be able to launch at least one of the corporate aircraft anywhere in the world within 1-3 hours. It was not unusual to get a call that an executive was on the way to the airport and needed to be airborne for a domestic destination in twenty to thirty minutes. However, to be able to quickly dispatch an aircraft anywhere in the free world, especially to the Far East, was a huge challenge. To be able to respond, a number of elements had to be in place at all times: on-call standby crews had to be designated; all flight crew members were required to keep standby bags packed at the airport; all passports had to be kept up-to-date with valid visas for any potential destination countries; vaccinations had to be current; aircraft had to have the ability to be launched within two hours, even if they were "down" for progressive maintenance; aircraft international fly-away kits had to be ready to be loaded at any time and kept updated; and operations dispatch had to be available and also have a reliable international routing/clearances supplier standing by at all times to provide assistance.

On at least one occasion, the author's organization received a call that an executive needed to depart for Tokyo in less than two hours. Over-flight, navigation, landing, and parking permits for such destinations typically had to be requested at least a month in advance. Further, proper documents and permit numbers were required to be physically in the hands of the crews. However, dispatch would go to work immediately to secure the appropriate permits using a trusted and responsive service provider while everyone else involved responded to the customer's requirement in their respective areas. The flight would launch on-time for a fuel stop in Alaska where the necessary paperwork and permits for the trip, at least for the Tokyo leg, were waiting! Any remaining permit numbers were relayed to the plane via satellite.

Similarly, the organization had to be prepared for emergencies. For example, on Friday evening (Dallas time), January 7, 2000, one of the organization's aircraft lost its left engine's integrated-drive generator just before landing in Bangalore, India. That aircraft was scheduled to continue its trip the next day. To send a factory team to make the needed repair would take at least a week and it was estimated that the replacement part would be in customs for yet another week. Further, it was late afternoon in Dallas, and the organization's other (identical) aircraft had an important flight scheduled on Monday morning. To address the dilemma, the author and three other pilots, plus two aircraft maintenance technicians, launched Friday evening in the sister aircraft, picked up the only part available (in Montreal) and flew on to Nice, Dubai, and then to Bangalore. Once in Bangalore, the technicians replaced the generator while the pilots captured a couple of hours rest in a hotel. Then they were swiftly on their way back, this time through Singapore, Osaka, Anchorage, and then Dallas, arriving by Sunday afternoon. They had flown around the world in less than two days—41.9 flight hours—to successfully rescue the disabled plane and keep both crucial trips on schedule.

Are you always "clear, orderly, and prepared?" Do you plan and conduct your business and personal life in such a way that when opportunities or challenges present themselves you are ready? Do you stay "suited-up?" Do you continually scan the environment for signs that you should once again take the offensive to avoid disaster and remain competitive?

Learn from Your Mistakes

The greatest danger for a single-seater is the surprise attack from behind.... If a beginner is attacked from behind, however, under no circumstances should he try to escape by slipping away. The best ... method is a sudden, very tight turn and then as quickly as possible take the offensive. [Richthofen's Air Combat Operations Manual; Kilduff, 1994, pp. 237-8]

The most vulnerable spot (in aerial combat) was naturally when one was attacked from behind. It was, therefore, much more important to look to the rear than to the front. This was the only crime that Richthofen knew—a hit from behind! After every aerial flight he went around each machine, and woe to us if he discovered a hit! Then you were really bawled out. [*Leutnant* Carl August von Schoenebeck, quoted in Franks & VanWyngarden, 2001; p. 24]

In a letter to his father in September 1900, Wilbur Wright wrote: "In flying I have learned that carelessness and overconfidence are usually far more dangerous than deliberately accepted risks."[9] However, just as humans are not very successful at determining their own fatigue levels, they are also not especially effective at assessing risk.

Richthofen was determined to live life fully and couldn't resist the urge to occasionally take an ill-conceived risk such as urging his pilot, Georg Zeumer, to make a crash landing or flying through a severe thunderstorm. Fortunately, Richthofen learned from his mistakes and chalked the experiences up as lessons learned. Later, he would lecture his pilots for taking foolish risks.

I had never yet made an attempt to get through thunder clouds but I could not suppress my desire to make the experiment. [Richthofen, 1918, p. 92]

I shall never again fly through a thunderstorm unless the Fatherland should demand this. Now, when I look back, I realize that it was all very beautiful. Notwithstanding the danger during my flight, I experienced glorious moments which I would not care to have missed. [Richthofen, 1918, p. 95]

Manfred always begged me to make a crash landing with him.... It wasn't long at all before I put the machine on its head with an awkward landing. Who was not then happier than Manfred! [*Oberleutnant* Georg Zeumer, quoted in Fischer, 2001; p. 135]

~

On 20–21 May, 1927, Charles Lindbergh flew solo across the Atlantic from New York to Paris, made technically possible by the development of the Wright Whirlwind engine that possessed a reliability, power/weight ratio, and fuel efficiency that was unheard of at that time. "Lucky Lindy" was airborne 33 hours 39 minutes—with little sleep the previous night—battled ice, and survived an involuntary mid-ocean spin.

The old romantic notion that pilots are macho, reckless, daring, devil-may-care, risk-takers is more myth than fact. Like Richthofen, today's pilots are well-trained professionals. They work in concert with other crewmembers to fly aircraft that are technological marvels, some with a non-stop range of seven thousand miles or even more. Just like other professionals and employees in the competitive world economy, today's pilots must be skilled and flexible, physically fit, mentally strong, and competent as managers, team leaders, and players. It also helps to get adequate rest, especially before a grueling task.

> Do you insist on flying through "thunderstorms?" If so, are you aware of the potential consequences? Do you weigh alternatives and then take *calculated* risks as necessary in order to achieve your goals and objectives? In risky situations, do you draw from your training, experience, instinct, and intuition as necessary to minimize the risks involved? Are you willing to admit your mistakes and guide family members and employees away from potential hazards?

Chapter 7 Summary

Function in Perfect Unity. Richthofen possessed a steadfast determination and self-confidence; and as a skilled hunter, he shared Boelcke's detailed and methodical approach to flying. Both of these great leaders required that their pilots be well-trained, possess an aggressive spirit, and recognize the importance of teamwork and trust. Both emphasized proven tactics, *calculated* risk-taking, and fundamental flying skills rather than the use of "tricks."

Know Your Strengths and Weaknesses. Perhaps the greatest strength that was handed down to his pilots by Richthofen was the confidence to trust their leader. The greatest challenges recognized by the *Rittmeister* were the sheer number of the enemy aircraft and, especially later, the superior quality of those machines versus those of German design. The outnumbered German pilots countered by being generally better-trained both as aviators and as masters of their specific fighters.

Make an effort to know your personal core strengths and weaknesses and those of your organization or team. Train to maintain and enhance your primary skills and talents. Resist attempts that unproductively and needlessly divide your attention and focus. Recognize when others may have special skills and can handle certain tasks more effectively or efficiently than you. Be willing to delegate, thereby allowing yourself to concentrate on your primary responsibilities.

Count on Ability, not Trickery. Richthofen cautioned his pilots about the ineffectiveness of trickery in combat. Rather he taught the importance of ability, energy, and a strong heart. The Baron also refused to buy into superstition and magical thinking. Rather, he relied on skill, training, dedication, courage, and integrity.

Chivalry was the knight's code of honor. Refuse to engage in spectacular "trick flying" with "smoke on" to impress others. Reject temptations or opportunities to cut corners or provide an inferior product or service. Work diligently in your business or profession and utilize your ability to achieve results. Inspire trust and maintain integrity in your dealings with others.

Seek Quality Rather Than Quantity. The first *Jasta* fighter units were staffed with pilots who were carefully selected and given special training at single-seat fighting schools in Germany, advanced training at Valenciennes, and finally squadron training when they arrived at their assigned units. The new strategy proved to be highly successful when Boelcke and five of his pilots, including Manfred von Richthofen, made their maiden hunting mission over Bertincourt, even though they had received their new Albatros DI and DII fighters only the day before. Amazingly, the fledgling *Jasta 2* pilots celebrated four victories by day's end, including Richthofen's first official success.

Seek *quality* rather than *quantity*, especially when resources are limited. Contrary to some beliefs, providing quality does *not* increase cost or compromise productivity. Build quality into the process so that the resulting products are not only less costly in the long run but are also superior products that meet or exceed your customers' requirements. In pursuit of process improvement and quality, always attack problems and not people.

Select the Right Equipment. Richthofen understood well the importance of having the best, most-effective fighters at the Front, and he spent a considerable amount of his time visiting the aircraft factories and test-flying their products. He also valued the input of his colleagues from other units, and together they made recommendations for aircraft selection and suggestions for improvements in aircraft designs.

Make certain that you and your organization are using suitable equipment. Provide your employees with the right tools for their jobs, including appropriate training. Search continually for ways to improve productivity and efficiency. Be alert for changes in the environment and obstacles that threaten to compromise your effectiveness and business success. Empower your people to make suggestions and take ownership of their respective functional areas.

Know Your Equipment. The German pilots were generally not only better-trained and guided by the leadership of Boelcke and Richthofen, but they also understood much earlier the criticality of using the forward machine gun controlled by the pilot who was actually maneuvering the aircraft.

Maneuver into precise position for an attack rather than "peppering the skies," hoping for success. Thoroughly understand your operation and the tools used in your business. Look for more effective and more efficient ways to operate. Work to encourage your personnel, seek their input, and value and enhance morale.

Be Daring. Richthofen was very daring and aggressive. He never backed away from a fight unless the odds were poor that he could win. He stressed to his pilots the importance of using good judgment to fight another day if appropriate.

True leaders should be daring, not because of what they can accomplish, but rather because of the cause they believe in. Have the perseverance to move forward despite the potential obstacles ahead. Manifest the passion and pave the way as a leader, thereby urging others along to share the same dream. Be willing to adjust your plans if necessary should conditions change or warrant a revised strategy. Be able to recognize that it is sometimes better to "fight another day" if conditions are not right. Some markets that are profitable to your competition—or even some products that are desired by your existing customers—may not be worth pursuing.

Be Flexible. Richthofen was ambitious and determined. He could also be impatient. Once he made up his mind about something, he typically pursued it with dedication and single-mindedness until he reached his goal. However, the Baron could also be flexible and creative at times in stalking his objectives.

Remain steadfast in pursuit of your "Blue Max" in spite of setbacks and unseen situations that may cause you to revise your plans to achieve your objectives. When "bombarded" from all sides by your competitors, be flexible and creative enough to turn the tables and use some of their own weapons against them.

Organizational flexibility involves modifying processes and procedures in response to the environment, thereby ensuring greater productivity, innovation, and customer response. Continually "scan the skies" so that you are prepared to respond quickly and appropriately to your customers.

Remain Calm. Even though Richthofen usually experienced an adrenalin rush (good stress!) during an approaching air battle, he understood the importance of patience and being calm. Part of that calmness came as a result of his patience and deliberateness as a hunter. Another source of the calmness was the fact that, in spite of the enemy's superior numbers, the Baron and his men felt a sense of control in their battles and never doubted their ability to be victorious in the air.

Teach yourself the habit of remaining calm, even under the pressure of "battle." Recognize that some stress can be productive and keep you motivated and focused. Develop *hardiness* and maintain job control in your position to assist in countering negative stress. Allow your employees to enjoy a sense of empowerment and control.

Be Prepared. Richthofen was always prepared, both in his professional and in his personal life. His strategy was to position his "Circus" squadrons close to the Front. Because his aircraft and pilots were continually on alert, they were able to launch immediately to intercept enemy planes. The Baron kept his personal life in perfect order as well, totally prepared for the future, whether or not he survived the war.

Always be "clear, orderly, and prepared." Plan and conduct your business and personal life in such a way that when opportunities or obstacles present themselves you are ready. Stay "suited-up." Continually scan the environment for signs that you should once again take the offensive to remain competitive or capitalize on certain opportunities.

Learn from Your Mistakes. Richthofen was determined to live life fully and couldn't resist the impulse to occasionally take an ill-conceived risk such as urging his pilot to make a crash landing or flying through a thunderstorm. Fortunately, Richthofen learned from his mistakes and chalked the experiences up as lessons learned. Later, he would reprimand his pilots for taking foolish risks.

Resist the temptation to "fly through thunderstorms." Weigh alternatives and then take *calculated* risks as necessary in order to achieve your goals and objectives. In risky situations, employ your experience, instinct, and intuition as necessary to minimize the risks involved. Be willing to admit your mistakes and guide others away from potential hazards in life and on the job.

8 FIGHT WITH CHIVALRY
(Respect the Competition)

What Manfred reported in his modest, simple way was like the fighter pilots' 'Song of Songs.' Mutual pride and chivalry ... [Baroness von Richthofen, 1937, p. 116]

We waved a hand to the enemy and proceeded with our task. The enemy did likewise. At the time this did not appear to me in any way ridiculous—there is a bond of sympathy between all who fly, even between enemies. [RAF Wing Commander W. S. Douglas, quoted in Jones, 1928; p. 137]

"The German pilots have the highest praise for their opponent who died in an honorable fight." [Note dropped by a German pilot over British lines, quoted in Jones, 1928; p. 141]

Late in the morning of a clear day on the 17th of September, 1916, Richthofen was in close formation with the inaugural *Jasta 2* flight of five aircraft with Oswald Boelcke in the lead. Piloting his new Albatros DII, Richthofen selected one of seven FE2b two-seat fighters of 11 Squadron RFC, suddenly attacked it from behind at only ten meters, forced the pilot to land at the German airfield at Flesquieres, and secured his first official aerial victory. The Baron landed his Albatros next to the FE2b, observed as German soldiers made preparations to transport the injured pilot to a field hospital at Cambrai, and then placed a marker on the observer's grave in nearby Villers Plouich:

I honored the fallen enemy by placing a stone on his beautiful grave. [Richthofen, 2005, p. 94]

Historically, *chivalry* is a term related to the principles and traditions of medieval knighthood and is typically associated with qualities such as courage, courtesy, service, integrity, and honor. Richthofen's Prussian background as well as his military education taught him many of the elements of a knight's code of honor. He was fascinated by the image and challenge of leading his men into battle, defending his country on a horse with his sword drawn. Most of these chivalrous attributes were part of his makeup or were learned. The courteous behavior he displayed around women came as a result of his natural shyness and genuine respect for the ladies. But Richthofen's displays of chivalry—as well as that of many of his comrades—were an integral part of his life and directed towards individuals and even to those against whom he did battle.[1]

"Fight" with Chivalry

The Englishman is a smart fellow. That we must allow. Sometimes the English came down to a very low altitude and visited Boelcke in his quarters, upon which they threw their bombs. They absolutely challenged us to battle and never refused fighting. [Richthofen, 1918, p. 115]

The Boelcke section has an advantage over my squadron of one hundred aeroplanes downed. I must not allow them to retain it. Everything depends on whether we have for opponents those French tricksters or those daring rascals, the English. I prefer the English. [Richthofen, 1918, p. 131]

Richthofen especially admired the English flyers because of their "plucky" courage and daring. The Germans, British, French, and others demonstrated chivalry in the air and on the ground. Especially early in the war, when an esteemed adversary fell or was captured, it was not unusual for one or more pilots of the victorious country to risk their lives to drop small packages containing personal effects or letters from those individuals on the other side of the lines. Downed pilots were often entertained at the adversary's squadron before being escorted to prison camp. The Baron particularly enjoyed a fair battle when both sides possessed the armament and the numerical forces to deliver a formidable fight:[2]

Wolff, my brother, and I were flying together. We were three against three. That was as it ought to be. [Richthofen, 1918, p. 174]

I felt some human pity for my opponent and had resolved not to cause him to fall down but merely to compel him to land. I did so particularly because I had the impression that my opponent was wounded for he did not fire a single shot. [Richthofen, 1918, p. 130]

I've been brought down by [Lothar] Richthofen and am not hurt. I got No.3 stoppages in both my guns and got beaten to the ground. I pretended to land and then went off along the ground hedge-hopping to fool them. All left but R. who followed me and caught me and here I am! ... I am writing this at R's squadron where they are treating me very well. I'm not hurt at all. I was unable to burn my machine as I was caught as soon as I landed.... It is very boring being a prisoner but it is a great consolation to know that it was R. who brought me down. I'm his 40th. [Lieutenant J. K. Summers, quoted in Treadwell & Wood, 1999; p. 117]

When Manfred von Richthofen fought in the air, he demonstrated bravery, courage, integrity, honor, and a servant's heart to his men.

He understood that if he didn't possess and manifest those qualities, trust was impossible. If his men lacked trust and confidence in their *Kommandeur*, the battle was over before it began:

> **Everyone must show absolute trust in the leader in the air.... If this trust is lacking, success is impossible from the outset. The *Staffel* gains trust by [the leader's] exemplary daring and the conviction that [he] sees everything and is able to cope with every situation. [MvR Air Combat Operations Manual; Kilduff, 1993, p. 235]**

> Do you "fight" with chivalry? When you lead your team into "battle," do you do so with skill, bravery, and honor? Do you strive to earn and maintain your team's trust by displaying courage, integrity, faithfulness, and a servant's heart? Even in the midst of battle, do you respect the competition?

Respect the Competition

> **For him [MvR] it [air combat] is the last remnant of an old chivalry in this battle of man against man. [Baroness von Richthofen, 1937, p. 106]**

> **When my opponent has to land on our ground, I am only too pleased to shake hands with him if he has fought fairly and bravely. [*Oberleutnant* Bohme, quoted in Sykes, 2004; p. 62]**

> **Anybody would have been proud to have killed Richthofen in action, but every member of the Royal Flying Corps would also have been proud to shake his hand had he fallen into captivity alive. [Ace in 56 Squadron RAF, quoted in Wilberg, 2007; p. 85]**

With the increasing number of aeroplanes one gains increased opportunities for shooting down one's enemies, but at the same time, the possibility of being shot down one's self increases. [Richthofen, 1918, p. 119]

Richthofen respected his opponents not just because failure to do so could be fatal, but also because they were in the same "business" as he. It was especially gratifying when he faced a worthy adversary with whom he could match wits. One such pilot was seven-victory ace Major Lanoe Hawker of 24 Squadron RFC who might have defeated Richthofen on November 23, 1916, had the rotary engine on his DH2 performed to his expectations:[3]

I was extremely proud when, one fine day, I was informed that the airman whom I had brought down on the twenty-third of November, 1916, was the English Immelmann [Major Lanoe Hawker]. In view of the character of our fight it was clear to me that I had been tackling a flying champion. [Richthofen, 1918, p. 123]

My brother's twenty-second opponent was the celebrated Captain Ball. He was by far the best English flier. Major Hawker, who in his time was as renowned as Captain Ball, I had pressed to my bosom some months previously. It was a particular pleasure to me that it fell to my brother to settle England's second flying champion. [Richthofen, 1918, p. 206]

Do you respect your competition and demonstrate integrity? In a fair "fight," do you extend the same courtesy that you in turn expect? Are you ethical and just in your dealings with others? Do you at times extend a chivalrous hand and show kindness and compassion? Are you sometimes willing to simply "wave" at your opponent and take up the "fight" another day, especially if the interaction or proposed deal borders integrity or ethical grey areas?

Durwood J. Heinrich, Ph.D.

Know When to Leave the "Fight"

One should never obstinately stay with an opponent who, through bad shooting or skilful turning, one has been unable to shoot down, when the battle lasts until it is far on the other side and one is alone and faced by a greater number of opponents. [MvR Air Combat Operations Manual; Kilduff, 1993, p. 239]

Richthofen understood and consistently applied the principles of *Dicta Boelcke*—his mentor Oswald Boelcke's eight rules of aerial combat—to his own flying. Boelcke cautioned against foolish acts of heroism and failure to secure advantages before attacking the enemy. Richthofen passed on these rules to his protégés, as well as a number of his own in his *Air Combat Operations Manual.* He stressed that it was unwise to believe that every mission had to lead to a victory, especially in view of the typically superior forces. In contrast, he noted of his brother Lothar:

If my brother does not have at least one success on every flight he gets tired of the whole thing. [Richthofen, 1918, p. 197]

Do you know when to leave a "fight?" Do you secure advantages before charging ahead at your competition? When conditions are not right or it appears that the situation may force you to compromise your principles or integrity, do you break off the encounter? Do you have the inner strength to stand by your values not only when others are present but also when you are alone? Do you pass on these qualities to members of your family and team?

Don't Be Discouraged

I had imagined that things would be very different in a battle squadron. I had always believed that one shot would cause the enemy to fall, but soon I became convinced that a flying machine can stand a great deal of punishment. Finally I felt assured that I should never bring down a hostile aeroplane, however much shooting I did. [Richthofen, 1918, p. 89]

We did not lack courage. Zeumer was a wonderful flier and I was quite a good shot. We stood before a riddle. We were not the only ones to be puzzled. Many are nowadays in the same position in which we were then. After all the flying business must really be thoroughly understood. [Richthofen, 1918, p. 77]

On his way to becoming a great fighter pilot, Richthofen experienced a number of setbacks. Very early on, his experience as a hunter had given him the feeling that he should be able to dispatch an enemy aircraft with a single bullet. Even after learning more about the resiliency of most basic aircraft materials—and alternatively the vulnerability of other critical elements (e.g., crew, engine, fuel tanks)—he taught his pilots to carefully conserve ammunition and be daring enough to maneuver in close to increase the odds for the victory. To be repeatedly successful, he insisted that his men be proficient in both maintaining and accurately firing their machine guns.

'I approach the enemy until about 50 meters behind him, take aim at him carefully, [and] then the opponent falls.' ... that is the whole secret to shooting down [another airplane]. [Richthofen's Air Combat Operations Manual; Kilduff, 1994, p. 238]

I insist on target practice in flight and at high altitude in tight turns and at full throttle. [Richthofen's Air Combat Operations Manual; Kilduff, 1994, p. 237]

Do you guard yourself against becoming discouraged? Do you accept the fact that it takes time to be successful in any endeavor? Do you view setbacks and failure as part of the learning process and preparation for future triumphs? Do you make an effort to "thoroughly understand" your business and the processes required to be productive and successful?

Be Courageous

Lothar [MvR's brother] and Manfred ... they were models of comradeship and chivalry, models of audacity and fearlessness, models in every sense. [Bodenschatz, 1935, p. 48]

The best thing about being a fighter pilot is that the decisive factor of victory is simply personal courage. [Manfred von Richthofen, quoted in Kilduff, 2003; p. 23]

One does not need to be an aerobatic artist or a trick shooter; rather, to have courage to fly right up to the opponent. [Richthofen's Air Combat Operations Manual; Kilduff, 1994, p. 238]

Although Holck was so young I had never a feeling of insecurity with him. On the contrary he was always a support to me in critical moments. When I looked around and saw his determined face I had always twice as much courage as I had had before. [Richthofen, 1918, pp. 64-5]

Topping the list of the medieval chivalric code of honor's many knightly virtues was *courage*. In the game of chess, the Knight is quite unique in its movements on the chessboard. It is allowed to "jump over" all other pieces of either color in an "L" maneuver—two squares horizontally and one square vertically, or two vertically and one horizontally. Near the center of the board, the Knight can move to or control as many as eight different squares. The classic Knight "fork" is a simultaneous attack on two or more enemy forces. Indeed, Richthofen emphasized the importance of courage and of obtaining and maintaining a position of strength in an air battle, always keeping his options open:

In a well-organized flight there is usually a precise arrangement of individuals. I prefer to lead *Jagdstaffel 11* as if hunting on horseback across a field, then it is no consequence if I turn, push ahead or pull back. [MvR Air Combat Operations Manual; Kilduff, 1993, p. 232]

Are you courageous? Are you willing to attack problems head-on in spite of temporary sacrifices and even the possibility of failure? Do you demonstrate courage to your team and thereby provide them with the confidence to move forward under your leadership? Do you remain in control and "fight" from a position of strength? Do you keep your options open? When conflict is not necessary or even unwise, do you discourage needless displays of aggression and egotism from yourself or your team members?

Chapter 8 Summary

Fight with Chivalry. Historically, *chivalry* is a term related to the principles and traditions of medieval knighthood and is typically associated with qualities such as courage, courtesy, service, integrity, and honor. Richthofen's displays of chivalry, as well as that of many of his comrades, were an integral part of his life and directed towards individuals and even to those against whom he did battle. Richthofen admired the English flyers because of their courage and daring. The Baron particularly enjoyed an even battle when both sides possessed the armament and the numerical forces to deliver a formidable fight.

When Richthofen fought in the air, he demonstrated bravery, courage, integrity, honor, and a servant's heart to his men. He understood that if he didn't possess and manifest those qualities, trust was impossible. If his men lacked trust and confidence in their *Kommandeur*, the battle was over before it began.

"Fight" with chivalry! When you lead your teams into "battle," do so with skill, bravery, and honor. Strive to earn and maintain your team's trust by displaying courage, integrity, faithfulness, and a servant's heart. Even in the midst of "battle," always respect your competitors.

Respect the Competition. Richthofen respected his opponents not just because failure to do so could be fatal, but also because they were in the same "business" as he. To the *Rittmeister*, it was especially gratifying when he faced a worthy adversary with whom he was well-matched.

Respect your competition and demonstrate integrity. In a fair "fight," extend the same courtesy that you in turn expect. Be ethical and just in your dealings with others. Extend a chivalrous hand and show kindness. Be willing to sometimes just "wave" at your opponent and take up the "fight" another day.

Know when to Leave the Fight. Richthofen thoroughly embraced and applied *Dicta Boelcke*—Oswald Boelcke's eight rules of aerial combat—to his personal flying. Boelcke cautioned against foolish acts of heroism and failure to secure advantages before attacking the enemy. Richthofen passed on these rules, along with his own, to his protégés. He stressed that it was unwise to believe that every mission had to lead to success, especially in view of the typically superior enemy forces.

Know when to leave a "fight." Secure advantages before charging ahead at your competition. When conditions are not right or it appears that the situation may force you to compromise your principles or integrity, break off the encounter. Have the inner strength to stand by your values not only when others are present but also when you are alone.

Don't Be Discouraged. On his way to becoming a great fighter pilot, Richthofen experienced a number of setbacks. Very early on, his experience as a hunter had given him the feeling that he should be able to dispatch an enemy aircraft with a single shot. Even after learning more about the resiliency of most basic aircraft materials, and alternatively the vulnerability of other critical elements, he taught his pilots to carefully conserve ammunition and be daring enough to maneuver in close to increase the odds for the victory.

Guard yourself against becoming discouraged. Accept the fact that it takes time to be successful in any endeavor. View setbacks and failure as part of the learning process and preparation for future triumphs. Make an effort to thoroughly understand your business and the processes required to be productive and successful.

Be Courageous. Topping the list of the medieval chivalric code of honor's many knightly virtues was *courage*. Richthofen emphasized the importance of courage and of obtaining and maintaining a position of strength in an air battle.

Be courageous! Be willing to attack problems head-on in spite of setbacks and even the possibility of failure. Demonstrate courage to your team and thereby provide them with the confidence to move forward under your leadership. Remain in control and "fight" from a position of strength. When conflict is not necessary or even unwise, discourage needless displays of aggression and egotism from yourself or your team members.

9 ATTACK OUT OF THE SUN (Secure the Upper Hand)

Try to secure advantages before attacking. If possible, keep the sun behind you. [*Dicta Boelcke*; English, 2003, p. 62]

The most favorable moment for attack against such an artillery-spotting aircraft is when the opponent flies toward the Front from the other side [of the lines]. Then, allowing for the wind factor (east to west), I drop down on him in a steep dive from out of the sun. [Richthofen's Air Combat Operations Manual; Kilduff, 1994, p. 236]

A man surprised is half-beaten. Proverb

On July 6th, 1917, Richthofen was forced to land after suffering a severe head injury. However, he was anxious to get back into battle and on August 16th—in spite of fighting fatigue, headache, and nausea—quickly dispatched a Nieuport 23 of 29 Squadron RFC flown by Second Lieutenant William Williams for his 58th victory. When the exhausted Baron returned to the field, he had to be assisted out of the aircraft and carried to his quarters.

Ten days later on the morning of August 26th, three of Richthofen's *JGI* airfields—Heule, Bisseghem, and Marcke—were attacked by British SPAD VII fighters of 19 Squadron RFC. Interpreting the situation as severe enough to offset the directive that he not fly a combat mission unless "absolutely necessary," the *Rittmeister* launched a counter attack. In less than an hour of the last strafing run, Richthofen was airborne leading the assault with four members of *Jasta 11*. Perhaps even more focused and calculating than usual because of his weakened condition, Richthofen used nature to his advantage and literally dove "out of the sun" on a lone SPAD VII of 19 Squadron flown by Second Lieutenant Coningsby Williams, sending it down for his 59th triumph.

Richthofen taught his men to monitor their targets, maneuver themselves into an advantageous position, and to attack, preferably out of the sun to avoid early detection.

Secure the Upper Hand

In any form of attack, it is essential to assail your opponent from behind. [*Dicta Boelcke*; English, 2003, p. 62]

It happens so quickly, one can hardly speak of a fight. For a moment one thinks the captain [Richthofen] might ram him [Sopwith Camel flown by T.S. Sharpe], he is that close.... Then the Sopwith is shaken by a blow. [Udet, 1935, p. 51]

The German air service recognized early on the importance of proper training and the necessity of preparing combat pilots adequately for battle. Boelcke was successful in arguing that *Jasta* commanders should be allowed to hand-pick the members of their fighter squadrons and to train them further for battle behind the lines. *Dicta Boelcke* emphasized attacking from behind—out of the sun if possible—firing at point-blank range, and turning to face the enemy if attacked from behind, rather than trying to escape. Boelcke's protégé, Richthofen, learned these lessons well and passed them on in turn to his pilots, along with a number of his own successful tactics (*Air Combat Operations Manual*) aimed at securing an advantage.

I started shooting when I was much too far away. That was merely a trick of mine. I did not mean so much to hit him as to frighten him, and I succeeded in catching him. He began flying curves and this enabled me to draw near. [Richthofen, 1918, p. 134]

> Are you and your personnel well-trained in your profession? Do you apply the important lessons learned from your mentor to be a success? Do you pass these lessons on to your protégés and team members? Do you know your competitors? Do you make an effort to study their strategies and tactics and look for weaknesses? Do you truly understand your own strengths and limitations? Do you attempt to secure an advantage and wait for the right opportunity to implement an "attack" or introduce a new product?

Stay on the Offensive

The aggressive spirit, the offensive, is the chief thing everywhere in war, and the air is no exception. [Richthofen, 1918, p. 131]

Infantrymen stand there, rifles pressed to the cheek, and from the ditch a machine gun barks up at us. But the captain [Richthofen] does not come up one single meter because of this, even though his wing planes are taking bullet holes. We are flying and firing close behind him. The entire *Staffel* is a body subject to his will. And this is as it should be. [Udet, 1935, p. 52]

Always carry through an attack when you have started it. [*Dicta Boelcke*; English, 2003, p. 62]

It followed that the victory would accrue to him who was calmest, who shot best and who had the clearest brain in a moment of danger. [Richthofen, 1918, p. 138]

Richthofen taught his men that when they were in the offensive attack mode that they possessed more freedom of action and opportunities to choose their tactics. Unlike a number of aces of both sides who preferred to hunt alone and carefully guard the secrets of their successes, Richthofen was a proponent of training, experience-sharing, formation flying, and teamwork. He recognized the strategic advantage of utilizing the strengths of the individual *Jasta* squadrons combined into collaborative forces, sometimes of wing strength, to overwhelm the enemy.

On the other hand, as in the game of chess, he cautioned his pilots that if they were attacked, their resulting defensive response was often in-effect dictated by their opponents. At such times, he instructed his pilots to remain calm, to be resourceful, and as soon as possible to initiate offensive and counter-attack measures:

The greatest danger for a single-seater is the surprise attack from behind.... If a beginner is attacked from behind, however, under no circumstances should he try to escape by slipping away. The best ... method is a sudden, very tight turn and then as quickly as possible take the offensive. [Richthofen's Air Combat Operations Manual; Kilduff, 1994, pp. 237-8]

If your opponent dives on you, do not try to evade his onslaught, but fly to meet it. [*Dicta Boelcke*; English, 2003, p. 62]

Do you recognize the importance of developing and maintaining internal core strengths as well as being able to tap collaborative external resources for greater strategic leverage? Are you making an effort to remain on the offensive to avoid being forced into a defensive mode that often results in a response dictated by your opponents? Do you and your team remain calm under pressure, meet adversity head-on, and employ appropriate offensive and counter-attack methods and procedures?

Focus

He flew to headquarters, laid the stuff on the table, and took care of everything on the spot. On one occasion, during weather so unbelievable that any mouse would have stayed in its hole, he flew to army headquarters, unconcerned, in order to settle some important matter. [Bodenschatz, 1935, p. 84]

As noted earlier, individuals sometimes experience *flow*, when everything comes together and they are able to operate with effortless control at the peak of their abilities.[1] Richthofen was a very focused and disciplined person not only when he was in the rigors of combat but also when serving as *Kommandeur* of his *Jasta* and *Geschwader*. His focus and determination allowed him to accomplish things when his peers and even his superiors failed. These traits earned him the total respect and trust of his men, which in turn were critical to flight, squadron, and wing successes in battle.

Richthofen was soldier through and through. One noticed this when flying, for he always directed the main focus of his attention on using his troops, and bagging enemy fliers. [*Leutnant* Ernst Udet, quoted in Franks & VanWyngarden, 2001; p. 51]

Are you able to focus on the job at hand, especially when necessary in critical situations? Are you at times able to settle into a *flow* that allows you to work "at the top of your game" almost effortlessly and yet with surprising productivity? Can you put away distractions and interruptions? Do you procrastinate at times? While it is sometimes appropriate and even wise to take a break, do you sometimes allow various disturbances and distractions to get you side-tracked? Do you sometimes put your efforts into activities that, although easier and more enjoyable, may not be the best use of your time? Do you get adequate rest so that you can deliver peak performance, especially when conditions dictate?

Chapter 9 Summary

Attack Out of the Sun. On the morning of August 26ᵗʰ, 1917, three of Richthofen's *JGI* airfields—Heule, Bisseghem, and Marcke— were attacked by British SPAD VII fighters. In less than an hour following the last strafing run, Richthofen was airborne leading a counter assault with four members of *Jasta 11*. Richthofen dove out of the sun on a lone SPAD VII, registering his 59ᵗʰ triumph. Richthofen taught his men to monitor their targets, maneuver themselves into an advantageous position, and to attack, typically out of the sun to avoid early detection.

Secure the Upper Hand. Oswald Boelcke's *Dicta Boelcke* stressed a rear assault, out of the sun if possible, firing at point-blank range, and immediately turning to face the enemy if attacked from behind. Boelcke's protégé, Richthofen, learned these lessons well and passed them on to his pilots, along with a number of his own successful tactics.

Ascertain that you and your personnel are well-trained in your profession. Apply the important lessons learned from your mentor. Pass these lessons on to your protégés and team members. Know your competitors. Study their strategies and tactics and look for weaknesses. Be aware of your own strengths and flaws. Secure an advantage and wait for the right opportunity to implement an "attack" or to introduce a new product or service.

Stay on the Offensive. Richthofen taught his men that when they were in the attack mode that they possessed more freedom of action and opportunities to choose their tactics. He was a proponent of training, shared-expertise, formation flying, and teamwork. He recognized the strategic advantage of utilizing the strengths of individual squadrons combined into collaborative forces, sometimes of wing strength or even greater, to overwhelm the enemy. He cautioned his pilots that if they were attacked, their response was a defensive reaction too often dictated by their opponents. At such times, he instructed his pilots to remain calm, to be resourceful, and to initiate offensive maneuvers and counter-attack measures.

Remain on the offensive to avoid being forced into a defensive mode that often results in a response dictated by your opponents. Recognize the importance of developing and maintaining internal core strengths as well as being able to tap collaborative external resources for greater strategic leverage. Remain calm under pressure, meet adversity head-on, and employ appropriate offensive or counter-attack methods and procedures.

Focus. Richthofen was focused and disciplined, not only as a leader in combat but also when serving as *Kommandeur* of his *Jasta* and *Geschwader*. His focus and determination allowed him to accomplish things when his peers and even his superiors failed. These traits earned him the total respect and trust of his men.

Focus on the job at hand, especially in critical situations. Settle into a *flow* that allows you to work effortlessly and with surprising productivity. Put away distractions and interruptions. Steer clear of procrastination. Although it is sometimes appropriate and even wise to take breaks, do not allow various disturbances to get you side-tracked. Avoid putting your efforts into activities that, although easier and more enjoyable, may not be the best use of your time. Get adequate rest to maintain stamina.

10 COUNT BULLET HOLES
(Be an Efficient Manager)

You cannot manage men into battle. You manage things; you lead people. Grace Hopper

No sooner had he returned from a flight than you would find him already at work in his hut. Nothing went on in the Geschwader that he did not know about. [Bodenschatz, 1935, p. 83]

Management and leadership are *not* the same. One can be an efficient manager, but an ineffective leader; or a charismatic leader and a poor manager. Managers typically concentrate on managing work while leaders *lead* their followers. Managers value rules and stability; leaders innovation and risk.[1] In today's increasingly complex and dynamic environment, both management and leadership are required for successful organizations. Rarely are individuals both strong managers and leaders—but Richthofen was just such a person. He handled management paperwork as efficiently as he led the war in the skies. As an example, he counted bullet holes in his pilots' airplanes (management *control*) while displaying his concern for their safety (leadership *passion*):

The most vulnerable spot (in aerial combat) was naturally when one was attacked from behind. It was, therefore, much more important to look to the rear than to the front. This was the only crime that Richthofen knew—a hit from behind! After every aerial flight he went around each machine, and woe to us if he discovered a hit! Then you were really bawled out. [*Leutnant* Carl August von Schoenebeck, quoted in Franks & VanWyngarden, 2001; p. 24]

This chapter will focus on management, while Chapter 11 will deal with leadership. Bear in mind that some characteristics of managers and leaders are representative of either category. Management and leadership complement each other and are yet uniquely necessary functions for success in business.

Accept Duty and Responsibility

What was reported to us about my uncle [MvR]—his sense of duty, his comradeship, his gallantry and his courage in battle, his devotion to his mission, the necessity of which he was convinced, his patriotism and his moral sense of protecting his own homeland and countrymen—are also today components of responsible thinking civil conduct. [Manfred von Richthofen (nephew and namesake of the ace), quoted in Kilduff, 2007; pp. 10–1]

What a man he was.... he constantly lived beyond those boundaries that we only cross during great moments. His personal life was blotted out when he fought at the front. And he always fought when he was at the front. Food, drink, and sleep was all he was willing to concede to life. Only that which was necessary to keep that machine of flesh and blood going. He was the least complicated man I ever knew. Entirely Prussian and the greatest of soldiers. [Udet, 1935, p. 72]

Duty, discipline, and responsibility were ingrained in Richthofen's nature, learned from his father, his military training, and his Prussian heritage. It was natural for him to not only follow rules but to also make them in the context of being given formal authority. He was a good soldier and therefore expected like results from his subordinates:

His [MvR's] approval will always come in an objective manner without the least trace of sentiment. He serves the idea of the Fatherland with every fiber of his being and expects nothing less from his fliers. He judges a man by what he accomplishes to that end and also, perhaps, by his qualities as a comrade. [Udet, 1935, pp. 52–3]

Richthofen always preferred to be part of the battle. When he was away from the Front and his *Staffel*, he missed the action and his comrades. As a national hero, however, he accepted his duty and the fact that he was thrust into the role of being an ambassador and instrument of motivation and inspiration (traits of leaders) to the German people, factory workers, and potential pilots and soldiers. But leadership characteristics that were even more important to Richthofen were his constant concern and commitment to his pilots and the field-grey soldiers who fought on the battle grounds of the Front. Even though he had a positive impact on the striking workers at the munitions factories and served effectively as an ambassador to many, he remained concerned about the ever-increasing reports of growing English air superiority. He found himself unable to rest as long as enemy air squadrons were pounding German positions.

If I fly out over the trenches and the soldiers cheer me and I look into their faces, gray from hunger, sleeplessness, and battle— then I am glad. [Manfred, quoted in Baroness von Richthofen, 1937; p. 139]

The harder and more difficult the battles became, and the more meaningful the air battle for Germany's destiny, the greater

was Manfred's own sense of responsibility. With it all came the clearness and confidence of the spirit of his unbending will to give his best for the people and for Germany. [Bolko von Richthofen, quoted in Richthofen, ed. Stanley Ulanoff, 1969; p. 166]

> Do you accept duty and responsibility? Are you grateful and respectful of the formal authority granted to you as a manager, father, or mother? Are you willing to work efficiently, utilizing your educational tools and managerial training to plan, problem-solve, and push for results and the bottom line? Do you recognize the importance of the structural elements of organizational stability, rules, and goals and at the same time demonstrate your commitment to values and relationships?

Use Your Common Sense

He could always understand the essence of difficult questions and give advice with a common sense that scarcely went with his youth. [Baroness von Richthofen, 1937, p. 45]

Common sense is the ability to make sound, reasonable, and practical judgments.[2] Such "practical," "successful," or "emotional" intelligence is important as a barometer of success. Traditional IQ (intelligence quotient) and various other intelligence tests tend to be piecemeal and insufficient since measures of the construct of intelligence are typically socio-culturally determined. They simply mirror the ideals and values sacred to the specific designers in any given culture. In other words, an individual's intellectual performance varies "on different occasions, in different domains, as judged by different criteria."[3] Some contend that traditional IQ represents only twenty-five percent of what constitutes true intelligence. They argue that conventional theories and intelligence tests are incomplete and inadequate, and it is time to replace conventional beliefs regarding intelligence, especially the belief in a general factor of intelligence. A "theory of successful intelligence" has been proposed that expands the conventional conception of intelligence to include creative and practical abilities in addition to memory and analytical abilities.[4] The four key aspects of successful intelligence include the following: (a) intelligence is defined as the achievement of success in life in the context of one's personal standards and within one's socio-cultural context; (b) one's ability to achieve success is related to capitalizing on one's strengths and compensating for one's weaknesses; (c) success is achieved through a balance of analytical, creative, and practical abilities; and (d) balancing of abilities is accomplished to adapt to, shape, and select environments.

On the other hand, in a homogeneous culture, intelligence tests for the purposes of academia, for instance, can have some very positive applications. In this context, tests may be indicative of an individual's capacity to learn and successfully function in a particular environment. Similarly, intelligence testing of children for the purpose of educational placement can be a helpful application, as well as the measurement of the intelligence levels of disabled or exceptional individuals in determining overall strengths and deficits so that interventions can be designed. Even so, test scores will likely never be accurately predictive of intelligence or achievement of success because of the subjective nature of the construct.

This author feels that so-called scientific "intelligence" and "high IQ" scores are not what's important because of their questionable validity. If measurements are to be made, they should be structured for specific purposes in the culture and domain of application. What constitutes greater importance is that the individual utilizes his or her physical and cognitive abilities to pursue a lifetime of creative exploration and learning.

~

Richthofen's mentor, Oswald Boelcke, the son of a schoolmaster, was detailed, methodical, and a brilliant aerial tactician. Max Immelmann—Germany's first recipient of the Blue Max along with Boelcke—was a gifted engineer. Richthofen was intelligent, but by his own admission "did just enough work to pass" as a Cadet in Wahlstatt, a school that he disliked because of the "strict discipline."[5] However, he excelled at sports and then worked much harder at the advanced Institution at the Royal Military Academy at Lichterfelde and later when he entered training as an aerial observer and subsequently as a pilot. Because of his determination and application of the knowledge he acquired early as an aviator, Richthofen went on to lead Germany's first Air Wing. As Germany's most-decorated and successful fighter pilot, the *Rittmeister* doubled his mentor's aerial success score (80 vs. 40) and surpassed Immelmann's by a factor of nearly five (80 vs. 17).

In your personal life and in your business, do you apply *common sense*, the sound, practical wisdom that you have acquired over the years through training and experience? Are you sometimes intimidated by those who may have tested as having higher IQs? Do you understand that true intelligence is the achievement of success in the context of one's personal standards and within one's socio-culture? Intelligence is perhaps more accurately defined as one's ability to achieve success by capitalizing on one's strengths and compensating for weaknesses, and achieved through a balance of analytical, creative, and practical abilities.

Establish Priorities / Communicate

He [MvR] is always clear, orderly, and prepared. [Baroness von Richthofen, 1937, p. 49]

He could always understand the essence of difficult questions and give advice with a common sense that scarcely went with his youth. [Baroness von Richthofen, 1937, p. 45]

On June 24, 1917, Richthofen was given command of the first *Jagdgeschwader* (Fighter Wing) comprised of four fighter squadrons, *Jastas 4, 6, 10,* and *11,* and chartered to achieve aerial superiority over critical battle zones, reporting directly to the 4th Army High

Commander. True to form, "Richthofen's Traveling Circus" promptly relocated to Marcke, southwest of Courtrai on July 2nd to stay closer to the Front.[6] That same evening, the new *JGI Kommandeur* assembled his four *Jasta* leaders to the conference room on the second floor of the *Geschwader's* headquarters at Chateau Marckebeke. Richthofen's adjutant, *Oberleutnant* Karl Bodenschatz—recruited from *Jasta Boelcke*—recalled that the *Rittmeister* conveyed an unambiguous and concise message to his men. Richthofen ordered that a direct communications link be established between the *Geschwader* and the Front. He ordered a "circular" phone link to be installed at his four *Jasta* units so that when he picked up the receiver all unit leaders could converse simultaneously. He then brought his staff up-to-date on the ground war, which wasn't good news—increased enemy offensives, heavy bombardment, incessant infantry-support attack aircraft, and relentless clusters of bombing squadrons. Finally, he reiterated *JGI's* air assignment—destruction of the enemy's infantry-support planes, single-seat fighters, and bombers. There was no confusion. He communicated well and made their priorities clear.[7]

~

Every organization has a *culture* which is maintained and conveyed through interaction and communication. Because the number one priority in aviation is safety, communication is a key element in maintaining an environment (culture) of safety.

In modern-day aircraft operations, a simple example of communication and effective feedback is the use of cockpit checklists. For a two-pilot cockpit crew, the process involves a challenge-and-response mechanism that ensures that both pilots are aware of, and acknowledge, each switch movement and operational check.

In this author's corporate flight department, there were several methods used to keep communication lines open. Although he served as both the formal Director of Aviation and the Chief Pilot, the author designated three experienced individuals to serve as Senior Pilots. These pilots had additional key responsibilities in the organization, but they were also members of the Office of the Chief Pilot. All pilots could use the Senior Pilots as sounding boards or they could come to the author directly. Periodic Office of the Chief Pilot meetings were held to discuss issues within flight operations, including employee concerns and suggestions, operational procedures, organizational structure, and promotions—specific salary and pay increase data excluded. Additionally, crew members used their flights with the author as opportunities to discuss various issues. The Office of the Chief Pilot was successful only because of the consistency of the communication messages flowing in and out. The Chief Pilot team members didn't always agree, but they always echoed the decisions of the Office.

Another very important communication process involved the aircraft and efficient maintenance. Because aircraft availability and dispatch reliability were critical to customer service, any aircraft systems problems were immediately relayed to Aircraft Maintenance (e.g., flight phone, satellite, data link). Crews were expected to call in to maintenance to report aircraft status even when the aircraft were functionally perfect. As a result, when the aircraft returned from the flight or trip, any necessary replacement parts or unusual maintenance procedures had already been procured or researched. Similarly, any changes or trip modifications were immediately communicated to or from Dispatch.

Finally, there were a frequent number of standard and ad hoc meetings conducted within the department. Crews (which included flight attendants), maintenance representatives, and dispatch personnel convened religiously before and after every trip. Aircraft Maintenance held an organizational and work-allocation meeting every morning. Pilots and flight attendants met at least once each month for safety and operational issues. All personnel were assembled for a department meeting on at least a quarterly basis. Various team meetings were also held monthly, and generally more often as functional needs dictated. Since flight department members were accustomed to working in teams, it was natural that interpersonal communication was open, ongoing, and consistent.

Because operational communication was critical to a safe and effective flight department, it was accepted as a natural characteristic of the organization. Decentralization of the communication network and a focus on safety and customers served to enhance communication throughout all functions and levels of the organization. Communication openness between employees and management was expected and free-flowing.

Effective communication is critical in any organization. Written communication is also required, especially in larger organizations, as is documentation of processes. Establishing objectives and priorities is vital so that work can be managed and results measured. How well do you communicate? Are you clear and unambiguous when you provide goals and direction? Do you allow for questions and then follow-up as necessary to be sure that your messages are understood? Do you provide your employees with the necessary tools and resources to efficiently accomplish their objectives?

Do It Now

He flew to headquarters, laid the stuff on the table, and took care of everything on the spot. On one occasion, during weather so unbelievable that any mouse would have stayed in its hole, he flew to army headquarters, unconcerned, in order to settle some important matter. [Bodenschatz, 1935, pp. 83–4]

In the summer of 1988, Oregon-based Nike, Inc. released its first "Just Do It" advertisement. *Advertising Age* selected the ad campaign as one of the top five ad slogans of the 20th century, and subsequently the campaign has been enshrined in the Smithsonian Institution. Over the years, the famous slogan has inspired many individuals to realize their potential and strive successfully for goal achievement.

If one were to apply an appropriate time factor to the "Just Do It" slogan, especially in our fast-paced, competitive world, the result might be "Just Do It—Now!" Perhaps better yet is the even more concise and very popular phrase (for good reason!) among managers and time-management gurus—"Do It Now!" This author believes that the mind continually works on issues that are unresolved and projects that are left undone. If one of your problems or projects needs to "simmer," that might be a positive strategy, assuming time is not critical and an immediate resolution is not required. It can allow the mind to digest the issue and often even precipitate a solution or provide further insight. However, outright procrastination tends to breed more procrastination until we occasionally become so stressed out that we can be "frozen in our tracts" from being overwhelmed. The best way to get items off your mental to-do list and avert squandering time is to tackle them now and free up cerebral time and productive physical activity for still greater accomplishments. Keep in mind that it is not essential or even wise to tackle all projects that may come to your attention. Sometimes, it's important to prioritize, simply drop non-critical demands, or to delegate projects. Additionally, don't forget to sometimes just say "No!"

The author once reported to a manager who would not leave the office for the evening until each item on his to-do list, all the day's emails, every article, or new magazine had been addressed, answered, or read. If travel caused the week's workload to accumulate by Friday afternoon, he was in the office bright and early on Saturday mornings. In fact, it was not unusual when the author was at his hangar office on a Saturday to get a call from that manager as if that day was simply a continuation of the week. He would ask a question or make a request as if it was mid-week and the whole world was at work. This policy kept his evenings and most of the weekends free of any office concerns and allowed him to return to work on Mondays with a fresh start, not having to dread the requirement to tackle any previous week's headaches.

Richthofen knew the secret of productivity. He knew that the safety of his men and the success of his operations depended upon his ability to act now, to clear obstacles, and to secure necessary resources. He refused to let things simmer—he did it now!

When something vital needs to be done, do you cite the self-motivator "Do It Now!" to yourself? Do you also encourage the use of this valuable phrase to your family members and those who work for you? In today's dynamic and competitive world, one of the most important methods of reacting—or better yet, *pro-acting!*—now includes *timely* decision-making. Although *rapid* decision-making can also be valuable, it is obviously more imperative to make the *right* decision. Therefore, it is advantageous to have a reasonable number of facts before "plunging in." Be aggressive in your decision-making, but not foolhardy. It is one thing to hit the brakes or steer in an alternative direction approaching a curve while "seeing where the road takes me." It is another to detect that the pool is empty on the way down following a decision to "just go for it" off the high dive (i.e., "Ready, fire, aim!"—powerful! "Leap before you look!"—not so much!)!

Don't Waste Resources

Fire only at close range, and only when the opponent is properly in your sights. [*Dicta Boelcke*; English, 2003, p. 62]

A sure sign of an old hand is that he reserves his ammunition and only fires in short bursts. [Lieutenant J. I .T. "Taffy" Jones, quoted in Franks & VanWyngarden, 2001; p. 72]

One of an executive's greatest responsibilities is managing and leveraging his or her resources, foremost of which are human resources (*human capital* assets). People are *always* the most important assets of an organization and the company. The acquisition, development, and retention of highly competent individuals results in a huge competitive advantage for businesses. In order to be efficient as an organizational leader, it is first necessary to be effective in obtaining and managing the right personnel.

Richthofen was a master at personally choosing the right pilots and staff for his organizations. He spent considerable time visiting flight schools and *Jastas*, studying their operations and evaluating their personnel. He was generally unhappy with the fighter pilots who were previously assigned to him through official channels, and he elected to subsequently reserve the selection process for himself. Once he got new personnel aboard, he made every effort to train, develop, and provide recognition to those individuals. He measured his pilot *return on investment* by their victories and leadership in the skies. If they proved to be unproductive, they were soon reassigned or transferred out:

The Rittmeister selects his people himself.... And if anyone has an eye for faces and behavior, for shooting ability and flying ability, for daredevils and non-daredevils, it's him. [Bodenschatz, 1935, p. 56]

He asks no more from the pilots than he is willing to give himself. But Richthofen is very firm on one point: he keeps only pilots who really accomplish something. He watches each beginner for a time ... then if he feels that the person is not up to the requirements that Richthofen places on a fighter pilot— either in his moral character or technical ability—that man is transferred out. [*Leutnant* Friedrich-Wilhelm Lubbert, quoted in Kilduff, 2003; p. 158]

In The Great War—especially for the Germans—food, supplies, ammunition, as well as resources of almost every other sort were scarce and required careful management and leveraging. Richthofen was not only frugal with his personal possessions but also with the resources used in his profession.

He is always clear, orderly, and prepared. [Baroness von Richthofen, 1937, p. 49]

The great Manfred von Richthofen made a clear distinction between 'hunters' and 'shooters.' The former were very

deliberate, and did not open fire until they knew they could hit their prey; the latter always fired too soon and thereby wasted valuable ammunition that might be needed to save their lives. [*Leutnant* Carl Degelow, quoted in Franks, 2000; p. 61]

One of the keys to being an excellent manager or leader is to be able to effectively orchestrate a workforce or a team. Managers accomplish this through the power of their position, influence, and control; leaders through persuasion, motivation, and passion. Effective managers and leaders must utilize their own skills and abilities, as well as those of their subordinates and followers, in order to accomplish the group's mission. To utilize these resources, the manager/leader must first create a sense of confidence and personal empowerment that allows each team member to demonstrate his or her best efforts. Secondly, the resultant resources must be focused on the task at hand in a manner that provides the best fit between group process and the demands of the environment.[8]

Shortly after Pearl Harbor was attacked on December 7, 1941, Lieutenant Colonel Jimmy Doolittle was recalled to active duty and tasked with planning the first retaliatory raid on Japan. He was subsequently given approval to lead a top-secret attack using sixteen B-25 medium bombers launched from the aircraft carrier USS Hornet. Unfortunately, the normally-equipped aircraft were too heavy to takeoff from the carrier's short deck of only 467 feet and had to be ruthlessly reduced of weight. Accordingly, all loose items and even unnecessary functional pieces of aircraft equipment were dismantled and discarded. Amazingly, despite gale-force winds of 46 mph, 30 feet sea crests, and heavy swells that caused the ship to pitch violently, all sixteen aircraft were successfully launched on April 18th.

In 2002, when the company was experiencing a significant downturn in the economy, the author challenged his staff to find ways to cut spending and reduce operating costs. He posted the following challenge that echoed the spirit of the task the men faced when they reduced weight on Doolittle's B-25s: "Question everything! If it doesn't fill a critical need or produce thrust, throw it overboard. If it must stay on board, make it safer, lighter, smaller, or more efficient!"

Do you refuse to waste scarce and valuable resources? Are you frugal with time and money? Most importantly, if you are a manager and/or leader, do you value, develop, support, and empower your employees and followers?

Train

He [MvR] puts great store in personally trying out each new man. [Udet, 1935, p. 50]

He [the fledgling fighter pilot] knows the terrain without a map and the course to and from the Front by heart. He must have practiced many times long orientation flights at home, even during bad weather. [MvR Air Combat Operations Manual; Kilduff, 1993, p. 237]

How he took care of us beginners was wonderful, and what we learned from him! He himself took the training of each one of his pilots in his own hands. As soon as our duties allowed us, we had to shoot at a target. Everyone received 50 bullets each for both machine guns—and we beginners only made, on the average, from 50–60 hits out of 100. But the 'aces' of the *Staffel* made 80–85. And when Richthofen came back, he almost always had over 90—sometimes he did indeed place all his shots into the target!
On the tenth day I was allowed to go along to the Front. Like a hen, he watched over me, the 'chick.' All of the beginners had to fly very closely to him ... every time when we returned he called us together for criticism. And soon I noticed to my astonishment that, despite his life-or-death aerial battles, he didn't let us out of his view for a second. And this gave his *Staffel* a rock-strong feeling of security. Because each of us knew you

could rely on Richthofen with dead certainty! [*Leutnant* **Carl August von Schoenebeck, quoted in Franks & VanWyngarden, 2001; pp. 23–4**]

In modern fighter combat, tactical mission planning, situation assessment (situation awareness), decision-making, and leadership skills have been found to be critical to the development of competent fighter pilots.[9] Highly-skilled pilots are also more likely to exercise effective flight leadership. As flight leads' skills improve, they are more successful at planning and adjusting their tactics according to the scenario demands. They also progress in their ability to more effectively manage all of the available resources.

Richthofen was an incredible master at selecting the right pilots, providing them with considerable training and coaching, and then watching over them as they developed their decision-making and combat skills. Afterward, he placed them into leadership roles to further hone their situation awareness and tactical abilities. The Baron not only managed his own fighter squadrons and wing extremely well but he also passed on his knowledge to other commanders through his Air Combat Operations Manual. This was critical to the outstanding success rates of his own and corresponding units. But it also ensured that when fighter *Jastas* and *Geschwadern* joined in the air for combat, the actions of the formations and individual pilots could be anticipated and aggregated for maximum success.

Another Richthofen requirement was for training to be conducted so as to simulate actual combat conditions as closely as possible. To ensure this was happening, he routinely visited the other *Staffeln* to standardize training procedures. He personally evaluated every pilot both on the ground and in the air so that he could predict their performance. This system stimulated critical and successful decision-making ability in the adaptive characteristics of the real-world (now known as *naturalistic decision-making*):[10]

"The Staffel will conduct itself in the air just as it conducts itself on the ground." That was his ironclad training principle and he

applied it not only to his own Jasta 11, but extended it to the entire Geschwader as well. [Bodenschatz, 1935, p. 85]

I insist on target practice in flight and at high altitude in tight turns and at full throttle. [Richthofen's Air Combat Operations Manual; Kilduff, 1994, p. 237]

~

The aviation industry has found that pilots generally perform in the real world as they perform in the training environment, especially if the training simulations are realistic—and in today's advanced simulators with full-motion and visual-display capability, they generally are!

An unfortunate example is the Air Florida Flight 90 airline disaster in Washington, D.C., on January 13, 1982. The Boeing 737 crashed into the 14th Street Bridge over the Potomac River on takeoff on a scheduled flight from Washington National Airport to Fort Lauderdale, Florida. The Air Florida jet only reached 352 feet before it lost altitude. The crew had failed to switch on the engine anti-ice protection system and, although they had had the plane de-iced some forty-nine minutes earlier, attempted takeoff with snow buildup on the aircraft flight surfaces. The appropriate course of action would have been to abort the takeoff when the engines failed to deliver the needed acceleration. But there was another very important lesson to be learned from the crash.

Following the disaster, several crews were later given the same scenario in a flight simulator and they "crashed" as well. In fact, none of the subsequent crews were able to keep the aircraft flying under the same set of conditions and existing techniques. The airline's operating procedure for the Boeing 737 was to set the EPR (Exhaust Pressure Ratio) on the engine gauges using the throttles during the takeoff run. Because the engine probes were coated with ice, the "correct" settings were actually incorrect—crews set the EPR at 2.04, but the actual EPR was only 1.70 (75% power) because of the faulty readings.[11] The engines were simply not delivering the required power for takeoff. None of the crews instinctively altered their training procedures and pushed the throttles to maximum, although even a nominal amount of additional power would have allowed the aircraft to miss the bridge and continue its climb!

The author's flight organization operated Learjets for many years. Early on, the procedure taught by the training service provider for loss of an engine, wind shear, or stall was to advance the power levers to maximum power at the onset of the emergency and then immediately retard the levers so that the engine gauge readings would not settle into the red arcs. The reasoning for the procedure was to protect the engines from over-temperature and/or over-speed. However, the procedure required the pilots to either visually verify the reduced power setting or guess at the correct power lever position—which, using "feel," typically resulted in too much power reduction and subsequent dangerous performance loss. Following the Air Florida accident, the author informed the reluctant service provider that his crews would henceforth be applying maximum power (full throttle) under such emergency situations until sufficient altitude and full recovery were reached. A little momentary engine stress—which the engines were very capable of handling—was a small price to pay for avoiding a possible crash.[12]

Although there were a number of poor decisions made by the Air Florida crew, had the pilots simply pushed the throttles forward to maximum thrust or aborted the takeoff when the engines "failed" to deliver the requisite power, they would not have crashed. The purpose of training is to practice procedures and pilot actions so that in actual emergency conditions those responses come naturally and appropriately. Crews should train as they fly and fly as they train. Richthofen knew and taught this important lesson nearly one hundred years ago!

What is your perspective regarding training? Do you make an effort to adapt training scenarios as much as possible to real-world dynamic situations? Do you recognize the criticality of accurate decision-making and understand that such precise assessment ability is only generated following acquisition of considerable skills and experience under actual "combat" conditions? Do you and your employees appreciate the necessity of continuing training over time, especially in today's fast-paced, dynamic environment?

Be Demanding, but Fair

He asks no more from the pilots than he is willing to give himself. But Richthofen is very firm on one point: he keeps only pilots who really accomplish something. He watches each beginner for a time … then if he feels that the person is not up to the requirements that Richthofen places on a fighter pilot— either in his moral character or technical ability—that man is transferred out. [*Leutnant* Friedrich-Wilhelm Lubbert, quoted in Kilduff, 2003; p. 158]

Being *demanding* is a trait typically associated with management because it generally involves formal authority and being in control. It is often linked with *telling* and *pushing* (management) rather than *selling* and *pulling* (leadership). However, there are times (e.g., crisis or military operations) when a more directive approach is appropriate and even necessary. In such situations, the line between effective managers and leaders is even more blurred because of the demands of the moment. In those cases, subordinates react to control and position power (management) and/or commitment and persuasion (leadership). Ideally, individuals respond as followers to the passion and inspiration of their leaders.

Richthofen was both a results-oriented manager and an achievement-focused leader. He was demanding, yet fair. He showed his men both his confidence and appreciation, and they responded with their best efforts. He knew when to be a *manager*—mission, strategy, results, and training/safety of his men—and when to be a *leader*—vision, values, motivation/achievement, and trust. Regardless of his role at the moment, the *Rittmeister* always set an example, demanded the most from himself, and continually demonstrated his passion and commitment to the cause.

~

In February 1997, the Flight Safety Foundation Fatigue Countermeasures Task Force released its Final Report entitled

Principles and Guidelines for Duty and Rest Scheduling in Corporate and Business Aviation.[13] It was based on the recommendations of the NASA Ames Research Center Fatigue Countermeasures Team that had been commissioned by Congress to conduct scientific research regarding crew fatigue, especially in long-haul airline operations. That same year, the author presented the scientific findings and recommendations to his pilots. Because safety was the organization's top priority, its aircraft operated worldwide, and the Foundation's guidelines were based on scientific research over several years, the ensuing mandate was to find a way to incorporate the guidelines effectively into the operation. The problem was that the recommendations consisted of eleven cumbersome pages of principles, guidelines, and tables. In addition to reviewing, endorsing, or slightly modifying the guidelines—at times to be more conservative, at others to be slightly less restrictive for special controlled cases—a simple tool to apply the guidelines had to be found. The result was a one-page PowerPoint chart that included every potential duty-day scenario. The chart was also easily converted to a matrix—preferred by Dispatch—and soon afterward to a slide rule that made it even simpler for the crews to use. Once the slightly-revised guidelines were agreed on, they were presented to the Board and company top management for approval, and subsequently became organizational policy. Dispatch served as the primary gatekeeper because they initially interacted with the customers regarding upcoming trips. Crews were then responsible for remaining within the policy during the course of their trips, but they were allowed a one-hour extension window should weather, unanticipated customer requirements, or emergency situations become factors. The extension—or reduction, in the case of a difficult duty day—was discussed for acceptance or rejection by all affected crewmembers when each situation arose. Planned or anticipated deviations into, or beyond, the window were not allowed. Because of the safety implications, crews that violated the policy were required to report to this author why they did so. Because the author felt strongly that one of the most important aspects of his job as manager of flight operations was to enforce safety, he simply would not allow violations of the policy. Consequently, individuals took it seriously and it was never violated. Passengers and crews remained protected from unsafe extended operations and the accompanying insidious onset of fatigue.

> There are times when team discussions and committee decisions are *not* appropriate. Do you understand the differences between being a manager and being a leader? Are you able to switch roles effectively should conditions dictate? Have you prepared yourself adequately to take on a more directive posture in times of crisis or group indecision? Do you stand firm on the most important issues such as safety? Have you established the relationships necessary so that in such situations your personnel will trust you and follow your direction and leadership?

Brief and Debrief

Before every take-off, without fail, one must discuss what one wants to do (e.g., the direction in which I will fly first). The discussion before take-off is at least just as important as the one after the flight. [Richthofen's Air Combat Operations Manual; Kilduff, 1994, p. 231]

Immediately after every *Geschwader* flight a discussion is the most important instructive activity. At this time, everything that happened during the flight from take-off to landing must be discussed. The questioning of individuals can be very useful for clarification. [Richthofen's Air Combat Operations Manual; Kilduff, 1994, p. 234]

Richthofen is unequalled as an instructor. I have been to different flight training facilities, as well as to the Fighter Pilot School at Valenciennes, and I have never met an instructor who could make the theory of air fighting technique so clear to me as Richthofen does. He especially likes it when his pilots are inquisitive. He does not become impatient when our questions seem to be elementary or silly. Every young pilot who comes

here has to fly a few times to the Front alone with Richthofen. After the flight, he and the beginner discuss every aspect thoroughly. [*Leutnant* Friedrich-Wilhelm Lubbert, quoted in Kilduff, 2003; p. 158]

To Richthofen, communication was absolutely critical. A strategic phone network provided quick response capability to counter enemy threats and a means of simultaneous communication with his squadron commanders and members of his staff. Tactical communications during air combat included hand and flare signaling in addition to machine gun bursts and initiation of certain maneuvers. However, nothing was more important to Richthofen than actual pre- and post-flight briefings so that everyone was always on the same "page" and problems—be they individual or mission-related—could be addressed. Richthofen's men flew as one with their *Kommandeur* because they were well-trained and always appropriately briefed:

We are flying and firing close behind him. The entire *Staffel* is a body subject to his will. And this is as it should be. [Udet, 1935, p. 52]

~

As a manager, planning, coordination, and managing work are important to the success of your operation or endeavor. Even if you are a "team" of one, organization and detailed planning using a process helps ensure that you are able to do things right, especially if the task is complex.

A number of years ago, the author observed that in his corporate flight operations organization there were times when important information was not being disseminated in the pre-flight or post-flight briefings and debriefings. In spite of the fact that such briefings were required according to the Flight Operations Manual and generally did occur, the meetings were typically informal in nature and usually rushed. Often, before flights for example, dispatchers were preoccupied with incorporating last-minute schedule changes to the paperwork, aircraft maintenance technicians were busy getting the aircraft ready for departure, pilots were conducting final pre-flight inspections, and flight attendants were loading catering and commissary items. Similarly, upon arrival at home base, technicians were busy assisting with unloading bags or making preparations to tow the aircraft into the hangar, flight attendants were occupied with removing catering items and dirty dishes, and the pilots were rushing to complete flight logs and depart for home.

To address the pre-flight briefing, the process was formalized. One hour before scheduled takeoffs for domestic flights—one and one-half hours prior for international flights—a representative from Dispatch, the maintenance crew chief for the aircraft (plus quite often the Director of Maintenance), and the flight crew (including the flight attendant) convened in the conference room. First, a dispatcher briefed the crew on destination, flight time, and weather specifics. Next, the technician briefed the team on the status of the aircraft, including any maintenance performed and deferred discrepancies. Armed with the foregoing information, the cockpit crew requested or confirmed the fuel order for the aircraft. Careful consideration was given to weather, alternate airport requirements, cost of fuel at scheduled stops (for "fuel-tankering" decisions), usable runway length, and airport weight-bearing capacity. Once the technician had satisfied any questions and received the fuel order, he or she exited the meeting and readied the aircraft accordingly. Afterwards, dispatch completed the crew briefing, addressing special aspects of the trip and individual passenger catering requirements. Finally, the pilot-in-command briefed his flight crew and all questions and issues were discussed and resolved.

Upon arrival home, a formal post-flight debriefing was conducted. Once the aircraft was parked in the chocks, the main aircraft engines were shut down but the APU (auxiliary power unit) left running. Passengers were de-planed and escorted to their cars with their baggage. Once the passengers departed, a representative from Aircraft Maintenance (plus the specific crew chief for the aircraft if on duty) boarded the aircraft to join the flight crew for a meeting in the aircraft cabin. First, all aircraft discrepancies were discussed. Maintenance error codes were downloaded and recorded when appropriate. Cabin functional problems were pointed out by the flight attendant, including identification of any scratches, pen marks, and spills. When the technicians were briefed and all questions answered, they were excused from the meeting to begin the post-flight of the aircraft. The flight crew then continued the meeting to discuss what went right or what went wrong on the trip. This discussion also included any passenger comments or concerns. Finally, the flight attendant was excused, and the pilots candidly discussed any cockpit procedural or safety issues during the flight or trip. Obviously, an open and trusting atmosphere was necessary for this to be effective.

During a trip when the aircraft was "on the road," the briefings were also held. However, they were typically less formal because ideally most logistical issues were resolved during the planning and preparations stages prior to leaving home base. Typical discussions included trip changes and briefings on upcoming legs, or debriefings on those just flown.

Subsequently, because of the outstanding and dedicated group of professionals in the organization, the implemented solution to the briefing problem rapidly became a best-practice and an industry standard. Subsequent operation safety audits lauded the organization's pre- and post-flight briefing procedure as "one of the most comprehensive the FSF (Flight Safety Foundation) Audit has observed in corporate operations."[14]

Do you take time to establish objectives for your organization or team? Do you involve those individuals in planning, management of activities, and problem-solving? Do you sit down with them to share or develop strategies for coordination and efficient execution? When the task is done, do you thoroughly debrief to discuss what went well or how the process needs to be improved? Finally, do you use the opportunity to praise teams/individuals and celebrate success?

Be Safety Conscious

One of the men asked lightly: "For this short flight you want to buckle up first?—I never do that." Manfred said, "I buckle up before every cross-country flight." [Baroness von Richthofen, 1937, p. 127]

When over the enemy's lines, never forget your own line of retreat. [*Dicta Boelcke*; English, 2003, p. 62]

Losses of loved ones and friends resulting from violent deaths tend to generate reactions similar to post-traumatic stress disorder (PTSD). Sudden or unexpected losses may result in even more severe grief reactions, most likely because they are typically more anxiety-provoking than anticipated losses.[15] Richthofen was keenly aware of the dangers of combat flying to himself and his men. Accordingly, he emphasized the importance of training, teamwork, and strict adherence to policies and procedures. While he didn't allow cowardice, he was lenient with his men when they required time off for important family matters or to recover from personal injuries. He understood the criticality of focus and freedom from distractions in the air. He was strict with his men when it came to safety, but he was deeply affected when one of his men was injured, missing, or killed in action.

~

Humans make errors! Wise and successful managers impress upon their employees that they are human, and as humans they are prone to errors. This acceptance of vulnerability is the critical first step in taking responsibility and avoiding risk-taking behaviors, both on and off the job. Finding ways to *proactively* eliminate human error is the most effective way of improving safety, and adherence to standard operating procedures and safety practices can greatly reduce the opportunities for accidents and incidents. Employees must be trained and given the tools and resources to work safely. Safety is an *attitude* and it should be continually recognized and re-enforced in any organization. Preventing personal injuries is a product of caring, but it is also good business.

In fact, working safely and responsibly should be a condition of employment no matter what the particular business might be.

Safety is obviously critical in aviation, and a number of years ago, the author and his team began to place special emphasis on what they called *safety occurrences*. Routine occurrences can lead to significant events, then to serious incidents, and finally to accidents. Obviously, the team was resolute in maintaining their perfect record of no accidents, but they also felt that if anything occurred that caused a passenger to be frightened or even concerned, then it was something that should be addressed and eliminated. For example, on a flight one day in one of the company's early Learjets, the cockpit handset rang with a message from Dispatch. However, the volume of the ring alarmed one of the passengers, and it was documented as an occurrence. The handset software was subsequently modified so that the volume could be adjusted. Another example of an occurrence was when an aircraft inadvertently ran into clear air turbulence (CAT) while en route. Even when the crew felt that they did everything possible—anticipated and avoided marginal weather conditions, circumvented forecast turbulence and thunderstorms, and pre-briefed the passengers of deteriorating conditions—if someone became alarmed, it still counted as an occurrence. The concept was simple: pay attention to every detail regarding safety! If smaller issues were anticipated and addressed, larger problems were less likely to happen. Because safety was so important, annual department bonuses were tied to achievement of safety goals. Eventually, the organization drove its annual occurrence statistic to an extremely-aggressive "zero."

Do you care enough about your family, friends, and employees to insist on safety? Safety does not depend upon luck—it can be managed. Do you provide your employees with the proper resources to work safely and then hold them responsible for following safety rules and protocols? Do you have an active safety program that emphasizes that both management and employees are jointly responsible for avoiding accidents and incidents? Do you have safety reporting programs in place and are they confidential and non-punitive?

Pay Attention to Your Health

Only a healthy physical constitution like his [MvR's] could be equal to these kinds of demands. [Bodenschatz, 1935, p. 84]

Flying up to seven times per day in the stressful combat arena and in the rarefied air forced Richthofen's and his pilots' stamina to build to some degree. However, the Baron understood that persevering in the face of demanding, stressful work required endurance and strength, and that such stamina was primarily a by-product of thorough training, good health, adequate rest, proper nutrition, and exercise. Consequently, he insisted that he and his men were provided with nutritious food. Although he didn't impose his lifestyle on his men, it was clear to them by example that he encouraged proper rest and moderation in drinking. The *Rittmeister* was also very physically active when he wasn't flying or managing his squadron and wing. In spite of his workload, he always appeared rested and relaxed.[16]

> Maintenance of good health is, or should be, one of your most important goals. Do you give appropriate attention to proper nutrition, exercise, and adequate rest? Do you sleep at least eight hours each night? Do you consider and strive to improve your endurance levels so that in stressful situations you do not become so fatigued that you are ineffectual in your job or in your family?

Chapter 10 Summary

Count Bullet Holes. Management and leadership are *not* the same. One can be an efficient manager, but an ineffective leader; or a charismatic leader and a poor manager. Managers typically concentrate on managing work while leaders *lead* their followers. Managers value rules and stability; leaders innovation and risk. In today's increasingly complex and dynamic environment, both are required for successful organizations. Rarely are individuals both strong managers and leaders—but Richthofen was just such a person.

Accept Duty and Responsibility. Richthofen always preferred to be part of the action. As a national hero, however, he accepted his duty and the fact that he was thrust into the role of being an ambassador and instrument of motivation and inspiration to the German people, factory workers, and potential pilots and soldiers. But leadership responsibilities that were even more important to Richthofen were his constant concern and commitment to his pilots and the field-grey soldiers who fought on the battle grounds of the Front.

Accept duty and responsibility. Be grateful and respectful of the formal authority granted to you as a manager, mother, or father. Be willing to work efficiently, utilizing your educational tools and managerial training to plan, problem-solve, and push for results and the bottom line. Recognize the importance of the structural elements of organizational stability, rules, and goals; and at the same time demonstrate your commitment to values and relationships.

Use Common Sense. Richthofen's mentor, Oswald Boelcke, was detailed, methodical, and a brilliant aerial tactician. Similarly, Max Immelmann was an exceptional engineer. Richthofen was intelligent, but by his own admission "did just enough work to pass" as a Cadet in Wahlstatt. However, he excelled at sports and then worked much harder at the advanced Institution at the Royal Military Academy at Lichterfelde and later when he entered training as an aerial observer and subsequently as a pilot. Because of his determination and application of the knowledge he acquired early as an aviator, Richthofen went on to lead Germany's first Air Wing. As Germany's most-decorated and successful fighter pilot, the *Rittmeister* doubled his mentor's aerial success score and surpassed Immelmann's by a factor of nearly five.

In your personal life and in your business, apply *common sense*—the sound, practical wisdom that you have acquired over the years through training and experience. Recognize that intelligence might be more accurately defined as the achievement of success in the context of one's personal standards and within one's socio-culture. True intelligence is one's ability to achieve success by capitalizing on one's strengths and compensating for weaknesses, and achieved through a balance of analytical, creative, and practical abilities. Don't allow some subjective evaluation or meaningless test derail your effort to reach your goals.

Establish Priorities / Communicate. In June 1917, Richthofen was given command of the first Fighter Wing comprised of four fighter squadrons and chartered to achieve aerial superiority over critical battle zones, reporting directly to the 4th Army High Commander. The new *JGI Kommandeur* assembled his four *Jasta* leaders and delivered an unambiguous and concise message to his men. He painted a short yet intense picture of the situation they faced so that there was no confusion. Richthofen communicated effectively and made the priorities clear.

Make it a point to communicate well. Especially in larger organizations, written communications are required, as are documentation of processes. Establishing objectives and priorities is critical so that work can be managed and results measured. Be clear and unambiguous when you provide goals and direction. Allow for questions and then follow-up as necessary to be sure that your messages are understood and carried out. Provide your employees with the necessary tools and resources to accomplish their objectives.

Do It Now! Richthofen understood the secret of productivity. He knew that the safety of his men and the success of his operations depended upon his ability to act immediately, to clear obstacles, and to secure necessary resources. He refused to let things simmer—he did it now!

When something important needs to be done, cite the self-motivator "Do It Now!" to yourself. Also encourage the use of this valuable phrase to your family members and those who work for you. In today's dynamic and competitive world, one of the most important ways of reacting now includes *timely* decision-making. Although *rapid* decision-making can often be even better, it is more important to have a reasonable number of facts before "plunging in." Be aggressive in your decision-making, but not foolhardy.

Don't Waste Resources. Richthofen was a master at personally choosing the right pilots and staff for his organizations. Once he got them aboard, he made every effort to train, develop, support, and provide recognition to those individuals. He measured his pilot *return on investment* by their victories and leadership in the skies. If they proved to be unproductive, he quickly reassigned them or transferred them out of the organization.

Richthofen was not only frugal with his personal possessions but also with the resources used in his profession. Food, supplies, ammunition, as well as resources of almost every other sort were scarce and required careful management and leveraging.

One of the keys to being an excellent manager or leader is to be able to effectively orchestrate a workforce or a team. Managers accomplish this through the power of their position, influence, and control; leaders through persuasion, motivation, and passion.

Refuse to waste scarce resources. Be frugal with time and money. Most importantly—if you are a manager and/or leader—value, develop, support, and give recognition to your employees and followers.

Train! Richthofen was an incredible master at selecting the right pilots, providing them with considerable training, coaching and watching over them as they developed their decision and combat skills, and then placing them into leadership roles to further sharpen their situation awareness and tactical abilities. The Baron not only managed his own fighter squadrons and wing extremely well but he also passed on his knowledge to other commanders through his Air Combat Operations Manual. This information was critical to the outstanding success rates of his own and that of corresponding units. But it also ensured that when units from various fighter squadrons and wings joined in the air for combat, the actions of the formations and individual pilots could be anticipated and aggregated for maximum success.

Another Richthofen requirement was that training be conducted so as to simulate actual combat conditions as closely as possible. This system generated critical and successful decision-making ability in the adaptive characteristics of the real-world.

Make an effort to adapt training scenarios as much as possible to real-world dynamic conditions. Recognize the importance of accurate decision-making and understand that such precise assessment ability is only generated following acquisition of considerable skills and experience under actual "combat" conditions. Appreciate the necessity of continuing training over time, especially in today's fast-paced, dynamic environment.

Be Demanding, but Fair. Richthofen was both a results-oriented manager and an achievement-focused leader. He knew when to *manage*—mission, strategy, results, and training/safety of his men— and when to *lead*—vision, values, motivation/achievement, and trust. Regardless of his role at the moment, the *Rittmeister* always set an example, demanded the most from himself, and always demonstrated his passion and commitment to the cause.

There are times when team discussions and committee decisions are *not* appropriate. Understand the differences between being a manager and being a leader. Be able to switch roles effectively should conditions dictate. Prepare yourself adequately to take on a more directive posture in times of crisis or group indecision that causes stagnation. Establish the relationships necessary so that in such situations your personnel will trust you and follow your requisite direction and leadership.

Brief and Debrief. To Richthofen, communication was absolutely critical. However, nothing was more important to him than actual pre- and post-flight briefings so that everyone was always informed and problems—whether they were individual or mission-related—could be addressed. Richthofen's men flew as "one" with their *Kommandeur* because they were well-trained and always appropriately briefed.

As a manager, planning, coordination, and managing work are important to the success of your operation or endeavor. Even if you are a "team" of one, organization and detailed planning using a process helps ensure that you are able to do things accurately and efficiently, especially if the task is complex.

Take time to establish objectives for your organization or team. Involve those individuals in planning, management of activities, and problem-solving. Sit down with them to share or develop strategies for coordination and efficient execution. When the task is done, debrief to discuss what went well—to hold the gains!—or how the process needs to be improved. Finally, use the opportunity to praise individuals and celebrate success.

Be Safety Conscious. Richthofen was completely aware of the dangers of combat flying to himself and his men. Accordingly, he emphasized the importance of training, teamwork, and strict adherence to policies and procedures. While he didn't allow cowardice, he was lenient with his men when they required time off for important family matters or to recover from personal injuries. He understood the criticality of focus and the absence of any personal distractions in the air.

Care enough about your family, friends, and employees to insist on safety. Safety does not depend upon luck—it can be managed. Give your employees the proper resources to work safely and then hold them responsible for following safety rules and protocols. Develop an active safety program that emphasizes that both management and employees are *jointly* responsible for avoiding accidents and incidents. Implement safety reporting programs and make sure they are confidential and non-punitive.

Pay Attention to Your Health. Richthofen understood that persevering in the face of demanding, stressful work required endurance and stamina, and that stamina was a by-product of good health, adequate rest, proper nutrition, and exercise. He insisted that he and his men were provided with nutritious food. Although he didn't impose his lifestyle on his men, it was clear to them by example that he encouraged proper rest and moderation in drinking.

Maintenance of good health is—or should be—one of your most important goals. Give appropriate attention to proper nutrition, exercise, and adequate rest. Get at least eight hours of sleep each night. Strive to improve your endurance levels so that in stressful situations you do not become so fatigued that you are ineffectual as an employee or as a family member.

11 MOUNT A GUN TO YOUR MACHINE
(Be an Effective Leader)

Everyone must show absolute trust in the leader in the air. If this trust is lacking, success is impossible from the outset. The *Staffel* gains trust by [the leader's] exemplary daring and the conviction that [he] sees everything and is able to cope with every situation. [MvR Air Combat Operations Manual; Kilduff, 1993, p. 235]

Richthofen was a born leader. Sharp as a razor in service matters; at all times fair, especially in the air over the Front. He saw everything. He gave new men in the *Jasta* every chance to score a victory. He gave away victories, if by doing so the young pilot was able to score his first kill. He protected every member of the flight [as much as] possible, but there was no pardon if a pilot sneaked away from a fight. That pilot would be transferred immediately. [*Leutnant* Wilhelm-Gisbert Groos, quoted in Kilduff, 2007; pp. 154–5]

Oberleutnant Rudolf Lang was the original Commanding Officer of *Jasta 11* which reached operational readiness at Douai airbase at La Brayelle on October 11, 1916. The missions flown by *Jasta 11* were typically reconnaissance and escort in nature, all flown according to proper protocol. Lang was likely selected because of his military and management skills. However, he apparently possessed neither the leadership skills nor the aggressiveness necessary to secure aerial victories for himself or his squadron. When Richthofen arrived to assume command on January 15, 1917, the *Staffel* had not yet achieved a single victory—but that would change quickly!

Manfred von Richthofen's arrival at La Brayelle as new *Kommandeur* of *Jasta 11* was a monumental and, as it turned out, inspiring event for its eager members. Richthofen, with an incredible sixteen aerial combat victories to his credit, landed impressively in his sleek Albatros DIII. He climbed out of the new and latest-model aircraft, wearing the striking *Pour le Merite* at his collar—the living ace of aces. It was also impossible for the *Jasta* to overlook the fact that Richthofen's DIII was painted a bold bright red!

Richthofen knew that in spite of his obvious resume of being an outstanding technically-competent fighter pilot, he would also have to earn the trust and respect of his new organization as their leader. He would begin by displaying incredible piloting skill, self-confidence, initiative, courage, and strict dedication to the mission. Further, because his pilots had been so far unsuccessful in combat, he would initially be more *directive* in his leadership style and would concentrate on training and coaching his men.

Seven months later, Richthofen would again display his leadership but use a slightly different approach to motivate his men. On July 20, 1917, when Richthofen briefly visited his *Geschwader* following the severe injury to his head, he said little at first. After he toured the facilities and took note of the shot-up fighters with their numerous patched surfaces, he suddenly turned to his men and announced, "almost fiercely," that they would soon be getting the new Fokker aircraft:[1]

You are getting new Fokker triplanes. They climb like monkeys and they are as maneuverable as the devil. [Richthofen, quoted in Bodenschatz, 1935; p. 29]

Be a Leader

During the battle the leader should not lose the overall view of his *Kette* and the enemy formation. This [state of precision] is achieved only after numerous *Geschwader* battles. This vision is a basic necessity and the most important point for a *Kette* leader. [Richthofen's Air Combat Operations Manual; Kilduff, 1994, p. 236]

It is a strange thing that everybody who met Boelcke imagined that he alone was his true friend.... Men whose names were unknown to Boelcke believed that he was particularly fond of them. This is a curious phenomenon which I have never noticed in anyone else. Boelcke had not a personal enemy. He was equally polite to everybody, making no differences. [Richthofen, 1918, p. 101]

Manfred is idolized by the troops. [Baroness von Richthofen, 1937, p. 161]

He [MvR] would ... visit to this or that *Staffel*, and fly with them against the enemy. [Baroness von Richthofen, 1937, p. 175]

From *Ketten-, Staffel-, or Geschwader* leaders I require the following: He knows his pilots thoroughly. The way the Staffel [performs] on the ground is the way it will be in the air. Therefore, these are the prerequisites:
1. **Comradeship**
2. **Strict discipline.** [MvR Air Combat Operations Manual; Kilduff, 1993, p. 235]

It is difficult to guess exactly what Richthofen knew about the psychology of leadership. What he did know was what he learned from his father, his military training and experience, his mentor Boelcke, and from his own logical mind. First and foremost, he knew that one could not lead men into battle without what he referred to as "strict discipline." He was referring not to a harsh, autocratic management style, but rather an environment of trust created from following a competent, self-confident leader who carried the banner of the vision and emphasized the critical importance of comradeship, teamwork, and adherence to technical maneuvers and procedures. He enhanced the level of trust by not only being the best at military protocols and combat skills, but also by demonstrating his uncanny ability to observe everything transpiring in the air. Most importantly, Richthofen supported his people—with a passion!

This belief in his [MvR's] own ability, coupled with an inner strength and obvious modesty, I believe, truly made him a leader to a special degree. His Uhlans, when he was a lieutenant, and later all of his subordinates in the *Jagdgeschwader* Richthofen, had unshakable faith in him. He did not flatter them, but he defended them and kept his word, and service under him was made easier through his cheerfulness and brightness; indeed, they often thrived on the high spirits he showed in the face of the most difficult tasks. In the bravery of his spirit, in his absolute lack of fear, he was an example to all who followed him in war. Indeed, despite the complete impossibility of it all, he could demonstrate a new aerial procedure or undertake an unpleasant task that would have given anyone else a feeling of anxiety. [Bolko von Richthofen, quoted in Richthofen, ed. Stanley Ulanoff, 1969; p. 165]

As a superior, Richthofen is loved by all. You can talk to any of the enlisted men, especially the mechanics, with whom the pilots are very close ... and they will tell you that they love and respect him above all others. So it is only natural that such a superior gets on so well with his officers, too. It is truly remarkable how calmly he deals with all his subordinates even at times when, inwardly, we know that he must be very upset. Richthofen is an ideal leader. [*Leutnant* Friedrich-Wilhelm Lubbert, quoted in Kilduff, 2003; pp. 158–9]

> Are you a true leader? Do you refuse to compromise when it comes to integrity and adherence to your vision and mission? Do you maintain highly-developed technical skills and serve as an example in espousing values? Are you unfaltering when it comes to self-confidence, decision-making, and courage in "battle?" Do you go out of your way to show support for your family members, friends, team, or organization?

Be Innovative

I had had built into my machine a machine gun [mounted over the upper wing], which I had arranged very much in the way in which it is done in the Nieuport machines. [Richthofen, 1918, p. 80]

Suddenly his [Lothar's] machine turned a somersault and plunged perpendicularly, turning round and round. It was not an intended plunge, but a regular fall. That is not a nice thing to look at, especially if the falling airman is one's own brother. Gradually I had to accustom myself to that sight for it was one of my brother's tricks. As soon as he felt sure that the Englishman was his superior he acted as if he had been shot. [Richthofen, 1918, p. 144]

Following his pilot certification on Christmas day 1915, Manfred von Richthofen reported on March 16, 1916, to No. 2 Combat Wing, Battle Squadron 8 based at Metz, flying the Albatros CIII. The Baron was disappointed that he was not yet able to fly the faster, more maneuverable Fokker, and also that he was now the pilot of a two-seat aircraft of which only the observer had a machine gun to fire at the enemy. However, this did not deter Richthofen. Using the French Nieuport aircraft as a template, he attached a machine gun to the upper wing of his reconnaissance aircraft so that it could be fired over the propeller arc. His fellow pilots, who had laughed at the clumsy installation, were silenced on April 26, 1916, when the German official communiqué noted that two hostile aircraft had been shot down in aerial combat above Fleury, southwest of Douaumont. One of these was a French Nieuport II scout pursued and shot down by Richthofen himself.

~

On July 19, 1989, a United Airlines DC-10 made a controlled crash-landing at Sioux City, Iowa. Captain Al Haynes and his crew used their creativity to save 184 people aboard an aircraft that had lost all hydraulic power—an engine core disintegration knocked out three completely independent systems—and had no aileron, elevator, or rudder (roll, pitch, yaw) controls. They were able to maneuver the aircraft that had lost all flight controls—"couldn't happen," according to the manufacturer—and landed the aircraft using only differential thrust on the engines, controlled by a DC-10 flight instructor that just happened to be flying as a passenger on the aircraft!

Some converging factors that contribute to creativity such as that demonstrated by Captain Haynes and his crew include: a domain, consisting of a set of procedures and practices; an individual, who introduces a novel variation to the domain; and a field, composed of experts who serve as gatekeepers to the domain and make decisions regarding which novel variations should be incorporated.[2]

For a creative environment to exist, the organization's structure should consist of intelligent individuals who are all considered to be valuable to the organization's success. They must be trained well in their particular domains, be able to think "outside the box," and be encouraged and rewarded for utilizing creativity. They must be sensitive to all types of environmental stimuli.

Creative individuals often possess traits such as "openness to experience, impulsivity, self-confidence, introversion, aloofness, and rebelliousness."[3] However, remarkably, depending on the particular situation, they can be playful or diligent, introverted or extroverted, aloof or sociable, conservative or rowdy.

> As a leader in your organization and company, do you exercise *possibility thinking*, innovation, and creativity? Do you cultivate these traits in your organization? Are you typically careful to use existing roads or do you sometimes take calculated risks based on experience and intuition and set off in new directions? Do you tend to be *reactive* when it is often too late and problems have already occurred, or are you *proactive* and prepare for and anticipate situations that lead to exciting opportunities?

Establish Trust

The spirit of our leader [Boelcke] animated all his pupils. We trusted him blindly. There was no possibility that one of us would be left behind. Such a thought was incomprehensible to us. Animated by that spirit we gaily diminished the number of our enemies. [Richthofen, 2005, p. 95]

Everyone must show absolute trust in the leader in the air. If this trust is lacking, success is impossible from the outset. The Staffel gains trust by [the leader's] exemplary daring and the conviction that [he] sees everything and is able to cope with every situation. [MvR Air Combat Operations Manual; Kilduff, 1993, p. 235]

According to Greek legend, Pythias and his friend Damon—followers of the philosopher Pythagoras—journeyed to the Italian city of Syracuse around 4th century BC where Pythias was subsequently accused of plotting against Syracuse's tyrant, Dionysius I. Pythias was sentenced to death, but pleaded that he be allowed to return home briefly to settle his estate and say goodbye to his family. When Pythias asked his friend Damon to take his place while he was absent, Dionysius agreed with the arrangement but with the condition that Damon would be put to death in the place of Pythias should he not keep his pledge. Dionysius was convinced that Pythias would not come back, yet Damon accepted the terms. When the day that Pythias promised to return passed, Dionysius prepared to execute Damon. At the moment the executioner was about to kill Damon, Pythias arrived, apologizing to his friend for his delay, telling him about his ship being captured by pirates. Pythias had been thrown overboard but managed to swim to shore and make his way back to Syracuse. Dionysius was so impressed with the display of trust and faithfulness that he freed both men and made them counsels to his court.

~

The trust that Richthofen's men placed in him was not a product of close friendship but rather his charisma, combat skills, and unshakeable dedication to the cause. The Baron had learned from Boelcke that men were motivated by the "spirit," character, strength, and courage of their leader. Richthofen also realized and taught the importance of "absolute trust in the leader in the air." This came from his self-confidence, steadfastness, absolute attention to procedures, and fierce support of his men. With training and trust as the foundation, Richthofen's men worked together to achieve the near impossible.

Gen von Hoeppner would write in his memoirs: "In the personage of Rittmeister von Richthofen ... the Geschwader received a Kommandeur whose steel hard will in relentlessly pursuing the enemy was infused in every member of the Geschwader. His refined lack of pretension, his open, gallant manner; his military skill secured for him amongst the army an unshakeable trust that, despite his young age, was matched with great respect." [Wilberg, 2007, p. 49]

> Do you have integrity? Are your behaviors in harmony with your adopted principles? Are you honest and ethical in dealing with others? Do you keep your promises? Are you worthy of and do you value the trust that your family and others place in you? Do you project confidence, determination, and dedication to your mission? Do you support your personnel and put their welfare ahead of your own?

Handpick Your Staff

I had never imagined that he [Boelcke] came to look me up in order to ask me to become his pupil. I almost fell upon his neck when he inquired whether I cared to go with him to the Somme. Three days later I sat in the railway train and traveled through the whole of Germany straight away to the new field of my activity. At last my greatest wish was fulfilled. [Richthofen, 1918, p. 96]

The Rittmeister selects his people himself.... And if anyone has an eye for faces and behavior, for shooting ability and flying ability, for daredevils and non-daredevils, it's him. [Bodenschatz, 1935, p. 56]

There are many good squadrons in the Army, and Jasta 37 is far from the worst. But there is only one Richthofen group. [Udet, 1935, p. 49]

It was a great thing that we could absolutely rely on one another and that was the principal thing. One has to know one's flying partner. [Richthofen, 1918, p. 179]

When *Oberleutnant* Karl Bodenschatz reported to *Jasta 2* on October 28, 1916, as its new adjutant, he was informed that *Hauptmann* Oswald Boelcke had been killed in the tragic mid-air collision with

Leutnant Erwin Bohme just that morning. Less than three months later, Richthofen was given command of *Jasta 11*, but not before Richthofen and Bodenschatz had become good friends at the re-designated *Jasta Boelcke*. Five months later, almost immediately after Richthofen became *Kommandeur* of Germany's first *Jagdgeschwader* (fighter wing), he called Bodenschatz to ask him to be his adjutant. Even though Bodenschatz had been offered the position of adjutant of an infantry regiment, he quickly jumped at the opportunity to be on Richthofen's staff. In fact, he arrived for duty even before the paperwork was completed.

As a leader, Richthofen understood the importance of recruiting and attracting the right talent for his *Jasta* and later *Geschwader*. He was also aware of the important dynamics of this process. First, the Baron very successfully ensured that his organization was the best not only in terms of combat successes and leadership but also in pride and esprit de corps. Everyone wanted to fly with Richthofen. Second, with essentially an endless list of strong, eager candidates, the Baron was able to select the best of the best. Finally, he carefully trained and groomed his recruits as aggressive fighter pilots and potential leaders under his own personal supervision.

He asks no more from the pilots than he is willing to give himself. But Richthofen is very firm on one point: he keeps only pilots who really accomplish something. He watches each beginner for a time ... then if he feels that the person is not up to the requirements that Richthofen places on a fighter pilot—either in his moral character or technical ability—that man is transferred out. [*Leutnant* Friedrich-Wilhelm Lubbert, quoted in Kilduff, 2003; p. 158]

~

In a military setting, the commander has somewhat more latitude regarding the selection of personnel for certain duties and critical assignments then does a manager or leader in today's business world. Richthofen was able to transfer out individuals who proved to be technically or morally weak. Still, today's savvy managers and leaders carefully identify, train, and grow their personnel in their respective job functions. Individuals who fail to develop in certain positions can be given additional training or assistance in developing in other areas in which they have greater interests and/or aptitude. Every individual is different and progresses at his or her own pace.

Richthofen recognized this truth regarding individual differences when he patiently waited for *Leutnant* Hans Joachim Wolff to develop as a combat pilot. "Wolfchen" ("Little Wolff") had been with the *Geschwader* for quite some time. However, during that period, he managed to get both himself and his machine shot up several times. Consequently, he was ineffectual as a fighter pilot for more than eight months with *Jasta 11*. Nevertheless, Richthofen sensed the youngster's ability and allowed him to remain with the unit. Under the *Rittmeister's* guidance, Wolff finally developed the knack, tore into the enemy squadrons, and was able to dispatch ten opponents in a relatively short time.[4]

> Do you make every effort to effectively lead and develop your organization into one in which talented potential employees want to be members? Do you carefully recruit the right individuals the first time so that training and development time is not wasted? Do you recognize that all employees are different, bring important diversity to your group, but sometimes need varying levels of training, coaching, and support? Do you attempt to place your employees not only into productive positions but also ones that they themselves feel most utilize their natural talents and abilities?

Inspire Others

I see Manfred, how he occupies himself with the children; how they hang on him, how it makes him happy to look into so many young faces glowing with enthusiasm. [Baroness von Richthofen, 1937, p. 124]

Manfred is idolized by the troops. [Baroness von Richthofen, 1937, p. 161]

At the time Richthofen was just at the beginning of his glorious rise, perhaps only one among many. Despite that, he caught my attention immediately. There was something in his bearing that created an especially pleasant impression. Richthofen possessed in large quantities that typically charming self-awareness and self-assurance, which must be innate, which one can never learn. In his face there was a calm, firm and yet friendly manliness, without any pronounced, determined tenseness, as found in many of our other young heroes. [*Hauptmann* Erich von Salzmann, quoted in Kilduff, 1999; p. 52]

Lothar [MvR's brother] and Manfred … they were models of comradeship and chivalry, models of audacity and fearlessness, models in every sense. [Bodenschatz, 1935, p. 48]

A German fighter pilot shoots over the forward lines … Blood red is its fuselage. It strikes deep over the German trenches … before it again fades away … But those below … follow the red flier with their eyes as long as they can; from their half-opened lips comes the cry of enthusiasm. [Baroness von Richthofen, 1937, p. 117]

On July 6, 1917, Richthofen sustained his severe head injury and wasn't able to visit his *Geschwader* until July 20th. On that date, Bodenschatz drove the *Rittmeister*, Major von Richthofen, Kurt Wolff, and Manfred's nurse, Katie Otersdorf, to *JGI's* airfield at Marckebeke. During the fifteen minute car journey, an infantryman spotted the *Rittmeister* with his *Pour le Merite* and head bandage as the automobile passed a long column of soldiers. The excited soldier cried out "Richthofen!!!" Like wildfire, the beloved name roared down the long column of grateful infantrymen. The men recalled their defenselessness in their dugouts as they were showered with artillery fire and as enemy infantry-support aircraft and bombers rained terror on their vulnerable positions. But then they recalled how Richthofen and his red machines had so often roared into action overhead, scattering the enemy aircraft and ending the hellish bombardments. "Richthofen!!!"[5]

~

Richthofen knew what it was like to serve in the trenches and to be a fledgling pilot. Out of his passion to be the best evolved his drive and determination. From this strength of mind grew his innate ability to attract followers and instill enthusiasm and courage.

There is now a splendid aerial operation here. The English come over in huge swarms with new, very fast aircraft. However, among us there now prevails—at least among most of the *Staffeln*—a spirit that is quite magnificent. Would Boelcke ever be happy about it! This morning I was with von Richthofen, who now has been promoted to *Rittmeister*. It is amazing to what level he has brought his *Staffel* in such a short time. He has nothing but young men around him who would jump through fire for him…. Von Richthofen himself is full of vigor. Even if on some days he flies five sorties, one does not notice a trace of fatigue in him. [*Oberleutnant* Erwin Bohme, quoted in Van Wyngarden, 2007; pp. 28–9]

Richthofen was the master of inspiration and motivation, not because he particularly worked at it but rather because he believed so passionately in service to his country. In addition to giving audience to numerous dignitaries and organizations, he spent a great deal of his leave time with children. He enjoyed looking into the faces of the many enthusiastic young individuals, inspiring them and patiently answering their endless questions.

Are you able to inspire others? Do you demonstrate the dedication to a cause or vision such that your steadfast determination blazes the path for all to follow? As a spouse, parent, friend, mentor, or leader do you recognize the power of your position to influence the lives of others? Through your knowledge, skills, and courage in the face of obstacles do you understand and humbly respect your ability to inspire and motivate? Do you recognize your obligation to positively influence and set an example for the next generation?

Support Your Personnel

Richthofen was just as good a superior officer as a comrade for the officers of his Staffel and his Geschwader. He associated with us off duty as any other comrade (would) … One could go to him with any question and any trouble and find sympathy and help when they were needed. [*Leutnant* Friedrich-Wilhelm Lubbert, quoted in Kilduff, 2003; p. 158]

In flying with others I have never had the same feeling of superiority as when I flew with my brother. [Lothar von Richthofen, quoted in Richthofen, ed. Stanley Ulanoff, 1969; p. 123]

In the winter of 1917 while Richthofen's *Jagdgeschwader I* was headquartered at Chateau Marckebeke in northern France, a soldier discovered by accident a sizable stash of fine Burgundy and Bordeaux wines hidden in the garden beneath a group of shrubs. When the two-thousand bottle find was reported to the *Kommandeur*, he elected to keep the wine for his men rather than send it to headquarters. Accordingly, he immediately distributed six hundred bottles to his mechanics. He sent the rest to the *Geschwader* officers' mess where each bottle was subsequently sold for one mark. This especially thrilled Bodenschatz because the arrangement offset the financial headaches regarding how the officers' mess was to be sustained as the war lingered on.[6]

Individuals appreciate and respond to support, encouragement, and appreciation. Richthofen was concerned about the comfort of his men and went out of his way to grant them leave and down-time when it was needed, especially if they received unfortunate news from home. He understood the importance of placing them under his watchful care. He patiently mentored, taught, coached, and counseled. He never allowed his men to enter into overly dangerous situations without being there to protect them:

> **We knew we could depend on him [MvR] like a rock. If things were going badly, if we were ever in a hole, he'd notice and pull us out ... One could not help but feel and be touched daily by his extraordinary energy and will power. He shone with calm in the most critical moments which quite naturally exercised the most salutary influence on all of us. [*Leutnant* Carl August von Schoenebeck, quoted in Wilberg, 2007; p. 46]**

Do you support the members of your family and organization? Do you make an effort to listen and understand their problems? Do you provide leadership through example, training, mentoring, and coaching? Are you there for them unconditionally when they are struggling or in danger of being defeated? Do you give them time to grieve or work through significant issues?

Encourage Others

In another minute, I am back with the formation and continue in the direction of the enemy.... But the captain [MvR] has noticed. He seems to have eyes everywhere. His head whips around, and he waves at me. [Udet, 1935, p. 51]

A German fighter pilot shoots over the forward lines ... Blood red is its fuselage. It strikes deep over the German trenches ... before it again fades away.... But those below ... follow the red flier with their eyes as long as they can; from their half-opened lips comes the cry of enthusiasm. [Baroness von Richthofen, 1937, p. 117]

They had often seen his red airplane flying over their trenches ... in complete disregard for their own danger, they had deserted the shooting ramparts and observed his aerial battles. [Baroness von Richthofen, 1937, p. 190]

If I fly out over the trenches and the soldiers cheer me and I look into their faces, gray from hunger, sleeplessness, and battle— then I am glad. [Manfred, quoted in Baroness von Richthofen, 1937; p. 139]

Fight on and fly on to the last drop of blood and the last drop of fuel, to the last beat of the heart. [Richthofen, drinking a toast to his fellow pilots]

A significant component of leadership and support of others is providing encouragement. Sometimes a situation may be serious or seem insurmountable, yet a good leader inspires his or her team and urges them onward. Richthofen went out of his way to provide encouragement, whether it was to his mother who was concerned for his safety or to his men who were exhausted and frustrated with the course of the war. He was also the first to offer congratulations and recognition for the successful missions flown by his men.

Do you encourage members of your family and organization? Do you boost and comfort them when they are down or discouraged? Do you reassure them and rally their spirits when they struggle? Do you applaud their efforts and share their excitement and triumphs when they are successful?

Give Credit to Others

He [Army leader and Adjutant-General, von Plessen] stressed over and over how Manfred was so pleasant because of his striking modesty. [Baroness von Richthofen, 1937, p. 165]

Richthofen understood the value of inputs from other fighter pilots regarding the best aircraft to utilize at the Front. He knew that the experienced aviators were highly qualified to not only evaluate new aircraft but also to make constructive suggestions concerning optimal performance enhancements to existing and future designs:

I proposed that our aviation branch [Aircraft Test Establishment at Adlershof Airfield] establish aircraft type tests to select front-line planes.... Now, pilots from many front-line units come to these tests. We fly the individual types and then agree among ourselves on which types we feel are best suited at the moment. [Richthofen, quoted in Kilduff, 2003; pp. 162–3]

On March 18, 1918, *Oberleutnant* Bodenschatz documented an example of Richthofen's determination to give his men credit for victories in contrast to rumors among English and French airmen that he often transferred the victories of his comrades to his own tally. Bodenschatz referenced Richthofen's actual combat report of the two successes that occurred late that morning during a ten minute interval. In the account, Richthofen described the mission in which he and *Leutnant* Gussmann of *Jasta 11* attacked a Bristol Fighter and then he and *Leutnant* Loewenhardt of *Jasta 10* fired on a Breguet. The *Kommandeur* certified that Gussmann and Loewenhardt brought their aircraft down respectively near Joncourt and south of Le Cateau.[7]

He [*Oberleutnant* Loewenhardt] knew much to say of Manfred, he often flew under his leadership; he spoke with deep veneration of the pure character of his dead captain, how Manfred in selfless camaraderie immediately withdrew if another of his men had a chance at the enemy. [Baroness von Richthofen, 1937, p. 178]

Richthofen kept a tally of his combat successes. It was a means of measurement. As was the case with all pilot victories of The Great War, visual confirmations were made, reports filed, documentation completed, and decorations and honors awarded. The Baron desired to be "the first of the chasers," but he wanted that distinction to be realized in the service of his country. As a leader, he also wanted his men to be successful. Their victories meant not only higher personal totals and increased motivation but also increased organizational statistics. These, in turn, translated into progress towards accomplishment of the mission of protecting the skies and the field-grey soldiers who fought below from bombing, strafing, and reconnaissance havoc.

Richthofen never exaggerated under any circumstances. [Bodenschatz, 1935, p. 51]

It never crossed Richthofen's mind to claim a victory he didn't earn. He was victorious over several aircraft that crashed on the other side of the Front and could not be confirmed by German observers. On more than one occasion, he simply didn't claim a legitimate victory. Often he backed off to allow his pilots to move in on the enemy while he served as observer and protector. He even attempted, albeit unsuccessfully, to revise policy so that his later victories—all those following his 63rd victory—would be awarded to the squadron and wing. Regardless, he fought for his men to guarantee that they received appropriate well-deserved credit for their combat successes.

The fastest way to lose the respect and loyalty of your followers is to take credit for their accomplishments. Do you give credit to others? Do you go out of your way to ascertain that your personnel receive the rewards to which they are entitled? As did Richthofen, do you involve your key personnel in decision-making that will serve the entire group?

Durwood J. Heinrich, Ph.D.

Encourage Healthy Competition

I was trying to compete with Boelcke's squadron. Every evening we compared our bags. However, Boelcke's pupils are smart rascals. I cannot get ahead of them. The utmost one can do is to draw level with them. The Boelcke section has an advantage over my squadron of one hundred aeroplanes downed. I must not allow them to retain it. [Richthofen, 1918, p. 131]

In the evening we were able to send off the proud report: 'Six German machines have destroyed thirteen hostile aeroplanes.' Boelcke's Squadron had only once been able to make a similar report. [Richthofen, 1918, p. 119]

Richthofen knew the value of stimulating healthy competition. When he took command of *Jasta 11*, he appealed to the heretofore unsuccessful pilots to take up the challenge to excel—and to even surpass—the incredible victory record of *Jasta Boelcke*, a record that Richthofen himself had helped establish. Indeed, in both March and April, 1917, *Jasta 11* would outscore all other *Jastas*. The lowly *Staffel* without a single victory just three months earlier achieved its one hundred victory milestone on April 22nd.

~

There were a number of ways in which the author's corporate flight organization competed, both externally and internally. In general, corporate flight department safety records were on a par with those of the airlines, but they were not perfect. Obviously, the author's organization was absolutely determined to maintain its flawless accident safety record, and it was fortunately able to do so through its proactive safety programs. A remarkable world-class leadership advantage was also enjoyed by the organization's Aircraft Maintenance department, which consistently surpassed both the corporate and the commercial aircraft availability and dispatch reliability records. That was no small accomplishment considering the company operated three, then four, and finally two business aircraft world-wide during the author's last ten years at the company. Less aircraft meant fewer opportunities to substitute another aircraft or its parts should an aircraft experience a maintenance problem. The efficient progressive aircraft maintenance program, coupled with the fact that it was the industry's first corporate organization authorized to perform in-house warranty maintenance, was the key to their incredible one hundred percent standard over several years.

Another industry benchmark was the S-A-F-E/A-C-T-S program mentioned in Chapter 3.[8] It was employed internally as a methodology to promote and enhance the all-important safety culture. It also became an excellent vehicle to uniquely encourage healthy internal competition while simultaneously fostering support between departments. Organizational team safety bonuses were tied to the success in reaching and maintaining overall safety program goals. At the same time, even though individual awards were annually presented in the S-A-F-E/A-C-T-S program, it was to everyone's advantage to proactively "catch" individuals with safety "attitudes" and to submit safety suggestions for *any* internal organization or process—i.e., "a rising tide lifts all the boats."[9] In the organization's annual Safety Awards Banquet, individuals were recognized for the number of approved "busts" (catching someone with a safety attitude) or safety improvement suggestions. However, emphasis was placed on the results posted by teams and the entire organization. It was interesting and inspiring that if the banquet was drawing near and a particular employee had not yet contributed individually, his or her colleagues always provided their assistance to bring the participation up to one hundred percent. Every person and every team were consistently honorees and/or award winners at the banquet!

> Do you recognize the tremendous motivational power of the ability to excel and to compete in a healthy rivalry? Have you provided a challenge for your team, organization, or company? Do you encourage, support, and celebrate success and the will to win?

Durwood J. Heinrich, Ph.D.

Be a Good Teacher

How he [MvR] took care of us beginners was wonderful, and what we learned from him! He himself took the training of each one of his pilots in his own hands.... On the tenth day I was allowed to go along to the Front. Like a hen, he watched over me, the 'chick.' All of the beginners had to fly very closely to him ... every time when we returned he called us together for criticism. And soon I noticed to my astonishment that, despite his life-or-death aerial battles, he didn't let us out of his view for a second. And this gave his *Staffel* a rock-strong feeling of security. Because each of us knew you could rely on Richthofen with dead certainty! [*Leutnant* Carl August von Schoenebeck, quoted in Franks & VanWyngarden, 2001; pp. 23–4]

Richthofen is unequalled as an instructor. I have been to different flight training facilities, as well as to the Fighter Pilot School at Valenciennes, and I have never met an instructor who could make the theory of air fighting technique so clear to me as Richthofen does. He especially likes it when his pilots are inquisitive. He does not become impatient when our questions seem to be elementary or silly. Every young pilot who comes here has to fly a few times to the Front alone with Richthofen. After the flight, he and the beginner discuss every aspect thoroughly. [*Leutnant* Friedrich-Wilhelm Lubbert, quoted in Kilduff, 2003; p. 158]

Richthofen loved his country, and he was confident that he could make a difference in the war. He also cared deeply about the safety of his men and did everything he could to adequately prepare them for battle in the skies. The Baron used his influence to secure the most-advanced aircraft, but he also knew that the right machine was only effective in the hands of a capable and well-trained pilot and if it was maintained by the best technicians. He was convinced that extensive training, coaching, and leadership oversight were key ingredients not only in enhancing safety but also in creating an advantage strategically in the air war. He was a tough taskmaster and demanded excellence. He therefore took the time to patiently train his personnel and to also be a role model to other leaders so that they might replicate his training methods. Further, he passed on his knowledge formally to other commanders through his *Air Combat Operations Manual*.

~

Being a good teacher is about more than simply mastering the material. A good teacher must know his or her pupils and understand their particular needs. Each person is different and learns at a slightly dissimilar pace. Even more important than patience is the willingness to take the time to make the subject matter interesting and clear.

A good teacher is like a candle—it consumes itself to light the way for others. **Author Unknown**

Are you a good teacher or mentor? Do you thoroughly understand the material and are yourself the master? Are you willing to spend the time and energy in making the subject matter interesting and understandable? Do you challenge your trainees and demand excellence? Are you patient? Do you recognize that individuals advance at different paces and learn more effectively from different approaches? Do you invest the time to answer all questions and use scenarios as examples to facilitate learning? Do you encourage and celebrate success?

Be Willing to Adapt

The *Staffel* must develop diversity, i.e., not become accustomed to one position or the like; rather, individuals must learn to work together, so that each recognizes from the movement of the [other] aeroplane what the man at the joystick wants to do, especially when the leader proceeds to attack or a tight turn

indicates an enemy attack from above to his fellow flyers. [MvR Air Combat Operations Manual; Kilduff, 1993, p. 235]

We are flying and firing close behind him. The entire *Staffel* is a body subject to his [MvR's] will. And this is as it should be. [Udet, 1935, p. 52]

Richthofen recognized that it was not possible to train for every scenario. The Allied Powers changed their tactical, and even their strategic plans, frequently. However, the Baron did understand the criticality of training consistency—and yet with enough training diversity—so that his pilots flew as though they were one entity, regardless of the situation. In Richthofen's mind, training, discipline, and experience would translate into an integrated group of pilots, flexible enough and intuitive enough to adapt and make the right decisions in unusual circumstances.

It was a great thing that we could absolutely rely on one another and that was the principal thing. One has to know one's flying partner. [Richthofen, 1918, p. 179]

Are you and your organization flexible, willing, and able to adapt? Have you trained your personnel in methodology targeting how to respond under both normal and projected unusual circumstances? In addition to adequate and appropriate training, do you enforce the discipline necessary for team members to act consistently and dependably under unforeseen situations? Do you insist that your personnel obtain sufficient experience under a broad range of scenarios so that they are able to respond intuitively and appropriately under most unusual conditions?

Be Willing to See Opportunity

One fine day a telegram arrived, which stated: "Lieutenant von Richthofen is appointed commander of the Eleventh Chasing Squadron." I must say I was annoyed. I had learnt to work so well with my comrades of Boelcke's Squadron [*Jasta Boelcke*] and now I had to begin all over again working hand in hand with different people. It was a beastly nuisance. Besides I should have preferred the *Ordre Pour le Merite*.

Two days later, when we were sitting sociably together, we men of Boelcke's Squadron, celebrating my departure, a telegram from Headquarters arrived. It stated that His Majesty had graciously condescended to give me the Ordre Pour le Merite. Of course my joy was tremendous.

I had never imagined that it would be so delightful to command a chasing squadron. Even in my dreams I had not imagined that there would ever be a Richthofen's squadron of aeroplanes. [Richthofen, 1918, p. 128]

Richthofen was typically enthusiastic in taking on new challenges. However, when he was given command of *Jasta 11*, he was understandably sad to leave *Jasta Boelcke* and also disappointed that he did not immediately receive the Blue Max following his sixteenth victory. Nonetheless, ever the faithful soldier, he quickly recognized that his background, combat pilot skills, and leadership had prepared him for just such an assignment. He then eagerly embraced the task, especially when he was in fact awarded the *Pour le Merite* just two days later. He realized that his new command represented a tremendous opportunity to integrate his drive for personal combat with the appealing prospect of successfully molding his dozen previously-ineffective pilots into a team of disciplined expert aviators with his own aggressive hunting spirit.

Luck is what happens when preparation meets opportunity.
Oliver Wendell Holmes

"Gluck muss man haben." ["One has to be lucky," old German saying, quoted in Kilduff, 1993, p. 35]

~

After separating from the Air Force in 1973, the author obtained his Learjet type rating (certification) and then worked several months for a Learjet charter company based in Dallas. However, because he traveled extensively and the future of the charter company itself looked questionable, he decided to take a position as a production supervisor at the company at which he would subsequently spend the next thirty-one years. At the time, the company owned a Learjet 24B, and because the author missed flying, he sought out the Flight Department Manager and was soon able to assist when a full-time pilot was either on vacation or ill. In late 1974, the weak economy forced the company to dismiss a huge number of employees. Although the author would have been unquestionably caught up in the layoffs because of low seniority, the company Flight Department Manager went to upper management and requested that the author be reassigned to the aviation department in view of his credentials and the fact that the company was to soon take delivery of a new longer-range Learjet 36. Less than eight years later, the author was the company's Director of Aviation, responsible for thirty-six pilots, technicians, and staff, along with $40M of aviation-related assets, with eight business and flight-test aircraft. Luck? Perhaps. But more likely, *preparation* meeting *opportunity*.

Are you willing and able to recognize opportunity when it knocks? Are you aware—better yet, do you eagerly anticipate!—that your education, training, background, and experience have actually prepared you for opportunities that may come your way? Even if you are not looking for a change, are you open to possibilities and new challenges? Are you able to visualize and embrace a potentially better future?

Consider the Greater Good

[MvR, when asked by his mother to give up flying following his head injury] **Who should fight the war then, if we thought that way? The soldier alone in the trenches?! [Manfred, quoted in Baroness von Richthofen, 1937; p. 139]**

If I fly out over the trenches and the soldiers cheer me and I look into their faces, gray from hunger, sleeplessness, and battle—then I am glad. [Manfred, quoted in Baroness von Richthofen, 1937; p. 139]

Richthofen felt strongly that what he was doing was morally right and for the greater good. He felt particularly duty-bound to do all he could for the men in the trenches and the German people at home sacrificing greatly for the war effort:

Higher authority has suggested that I should quit flying before it catches up with me. But I should despise myself if, now that I am famous and heavily decorated, I consented to live on as a pensioner of my honor, preserving my precious life for the nation while every poor fellow in the trenches, who is doing his duty no less that I am doing mine, has to stick it out. [MvR, *Reflections in a Dugout,* **quoted in McGuire, 2001]**

Self-sacrifice is necessary to be a successful leader. Are you willing to sacrifice for the greater good? Are you sympathetic and appreciative of those in your charge? Are you willing to show the necessary courage and resolve in "battle" to motivate and inspire your team?

Compare Notes

My enemy with his burning machine landed smoothly while I, his conqueror, came down next to him in the barbed wire of our trenches and my machine overturned.
The two Englishmen, who were not a little surprised at my collapse, greeted me like sportsmen. As mentioned before, they had not fired a shot and they could not understand why I had landed so clumsily. They were the first two Englishmen whom I had brought down alive. Consequently, it gave me particular pleasure to talk to them. I asked them whether they had previously seen my machine in the air, and one of them replied, "Oh, yes. I know your machine very well. We call it 'Le Petit Rouge.'" [Richthofen, 1918, p. 104]

I proposed that our aviation branch [Aircraft Test Establishment at Adlershof Airfield] establish aircraft type tests to select front-line planes. I do not believe that some home-front pilot, especially someone working for one of the manufacturers, should determine the aircraft to be flown at the Front. Now, pilots from many front-line units come to these tests. We fly the individual types and then agree among ourselves on which types we feel are best suited at the moment. [Richthofen, quoted in Kilduff, 2003; pp. 162–3]

Richthofen respected his opponents not just because to do otherwise could prove to be fatal, but also because they were in the same "business." He especially admired the English pilots because of their "plucky" courage and daring. The *Rittmeister* particularly enjoyed a fair battle when both sides possessed the armament and the numerical forces to deliver a formidable fight. The Germans, British, and French aviators demonstrated chivalry in the air and on the ground, especially early in the war. Downed pilots were often entertained at the adversary's squadron before being taken to prison camp. In such instances, it was not unusual for pilots to exchange general comments concerning air battles. At times, valuable pieces of information could thus be acquired.

Richthofen also recognized the value of obtaining the views of his fellow pilots concerning appropriate aircraft to be used at the Front. By comparing notes, more information became available for accurate decision-making and therefore resulted in delivery of better equipment.

> Do you compare notes? Even with competitors, there are times when ethical broad discussions regarding customer service, for instance, can be beneficial to all. Do you seek out the opinions and expertise of your staff and those actually providing services at the "Front?" More data equates to more information, resulting in better decision-making. Implementation of the good ideas of others typically increases motivation and encourages subsequent contribution.

Don't Be a Base Hog

I am a restless spirit. Consequently my activity in front of Verdun can only be described as boresome. At the beginning I was in the trenches at a spot where nothing happened. Then I became a dispatch bearer and hoped to have some adventures. But there I was mistaken. The fighting men immediately degraded me and considered me a Base-hog. I was not really at the Base but I was not allowed to advance further than within 1500 yards behind the front trenches. There, below the ground, I had a bomb-proof, heated habitation. Now and then I had to go to the front trenches. That meant great physical exertion, for one had to trudge uphill and downhill, crisscross, through an unending number of trenches and mire-holes until at last one arrived at a place where men were firing. After having paid a short visit to the fighting men, my position seemed to me a very stupid one. [Richthofen, 1918, pp. 58-9]

He wanted to conquer every day anew, at the risk of his life.
[Baroness von Richthofen, 1937, p. 126]

Richthofen experienced some cavalry action on the Eastern Front in August of 1914 and was awarded the prestigious Prussian Iron Cross the following month. However, following his unit's transfer to the Western Front, his vision of leading horse-mounted charges against the enemy soon died away with the reality of the trench and barbed-wire standoffs of the war. His subsequent service as a communications officer in the Signal Corps, *Ordonnanzoffizier* (assistant adjutant), and finally supply officer proved unacceptable to the young *Uhlan*. Visualizing possibilities flying with the "cavalry of the air," he applied and was accepted to aircraft observer school at Cologne in May 1915:

One fine day, our division became busy. We intended a small attack. I was delighted, for now at last I should be able to do something as a connecting link! But there came another disappointment! I was given quite a different job and now I had enough of it. I sent a letter to my Commanding General and evil tongues report that I told him: "My dear Excellency! I have not gone to war in order to collect cheese and eggs, but for another purpose." At first, the people above wanted to snarl at me. But then they fulfilled my wish. Thus I joined the Flying Service at the end of May, 1915. My greatest wish was fulfilled. [Richthofen, 1918, p. 56]

While an officer of the General Staff was considered by the various armies to hold an honorable and valuable position, Richthofen and the German soldiers felt a measure of contempt for an individual who they considered to be a "base-hog." Similarly, the British referred to a young and capable officer who avoided actual combat as being "Something on the Staff." The last thing Richthofen wanted was to be placed in a position that he considered to be unproductive in the war effort.

Are you a "base-hog?" Or are you willing to leave your office, get out "on the floor" with your personnel, and help them fight the "war" in the "trenches?" It is impossible to fully comprehend and appreciate the circumstances surrounding your workers unless you observe first-hand their constraints and needs.

Chapter 11 Summary

Mount a Gun to Your Machine. When he took over as commander of *Jasta 11*, Richthofen knew that in spite of his obvious resume of being an outstanding technically-competent fighter pilot, he would also have to earn the trust and respect of his new organization as its leader. He would begin by displaying incredible piloting skill, self-confidence, initiative, courage, creativity, and strict dedication to the mission. Because his pilots had been so far unsuccessful in combat, his initial plan also included being more directive in his leadership style, and he concentrated on training and coaching of his men.

Be a Leader. Richthofen understood that one could not lead men into battle without "strict discipline." He was referring not to a harsh, autocratic management style. Rather, he would build an environment of trust created from following a competent, self-confident leader who carried a guidon of the vision and emphasized the critical importance of comradeship, teamwork, and adherence to technical maneuvers and procedures. He would enhance the level of trust by not only being the best at military protocols and combat skills, but also by demonstrating his uncanny ability to observe everything in the air. Most importantly, Richthofen would support his people—with a passion!

Be a true leader! Refuse to compromise when it comes to integrity and adherence to your vision and mission. Maintain highly-developed technical skills and serve as an example in espousing values. Be unfaltering when it comes to self-confidence, decision-making, and courage in "battle." Go out of your way to show support for your team or organization.

Be Innovative. Early in his career as a pilot, using the French Nieuport aircraft as a template, Richthofen attached a machine gun to the upper wing of his reconnaissance aircraft so that it could be fired over the propeller arc. His fellow pilots, who had laughed at the awkward installation, were silenced on April 26, 1916, when the German official communiqué noted that two hostile aircraft had been shot down in aerial combat above Fleury, southwest of Douaumont. One of these was a French Nieuport II scout pursued and shot down by the Baron himself.

As a leader in your organization and company, exercise possibility thinking and innovation! Cultivate those characteristics in your organization as well. Take calculated risks based on experience and intuition and set off in new directions. Don't be *reactive* when it is often too late and problems have already occurred. Choose instead to be *proactive* and prepare for and anticipate situations that lead to opportunities.

Establish Trust. The trust that Richthofen's men placed in him was not a product of close friendship but rather his charisma, combat skills, and unshakeable dedication to the cause. The Baron had learned from Boelcke that men were motivated by the "spirit," character, strength, and courage of their leader. Richthofen also realized the importance of "absolute trust in the leader in the air." This came from his self-confidence, steadfastness, absolute attention to procedures, and fierce support of his men. With training and trust as the foundation, Richthofen's men worked together to achieve the near impossible.

Show integrity! Make certain that your behaviors are in harmony with your adopted principles. Be honest and ethical in dealing with others. Be worthy of and value the trust that your family and others place in you. Display confidence, determination, and dedication to your mission. Support your personnel and put their welfare ahead of your own.

Handpick Your Staff. As a leader, Richthofen understood the importance of recruiting and attracting the right talent for his *Jasta* and later *Geschwader.* First, the Baron very successfully ensured that his organization was the best not only in terms of combat successes and leadership but also in pride and esprit de corps. Consequently, everyone wanted to fly with Richthofen. Second, with essentially an endless list of strong, eager candidates, Richthofen was able to select the best of the best. Finally, he carefully trained and groomed them as aggressive fighter pilots and potential leaders under his own supervision.

Today's savvy managers and leaders carefully identify, train, and grow their personnel in their respective job functions. Individuals who fail to develop in certain positions can be given additional training or assisted in developing in other areas in which they have greater interests and/or aptitude.

Make every effort to effectively lead and develop your organization into one in which talented potential employees want to be members. Carefully recruit the right individuals the first time so that training and development time is not wasted. Recognize that all employees are different, bring important diversity to your group, but sometimes need varying levels of training, coaching, and support. Place your employees not only into productive positions but also ones that they themselves feel most utilize their natural talents and abilities.

Inspire Others. Richthofen was the master of inspiration and motivation, not because he particularly worked at it but rather because he believed so passionately in service to his country. He knew what it was like to serve in the trenches and to be a fledgling pilot. Out of his passion to be the best, his drive and determination evolved. From this strength of mind came his innate ability to attract followers and instill enthusiasm and courage.

Inspire others! Demonstrate the dedication to a cause or vision such that your steadfast determination establishes the path for all to follow. As a spouse, parent, friend, teacher, mentor, or leader recognize the power of your position to influence the lives of others. Through your knowledge, skills, and courage in the face of obstacles, understand and humbly respect your ability and responsibility to inspire and motivate.

Support Your Personnel. Individuals appreciate and respond to support, encouragement, and appreciation. Richthofen was concerned about the comfort of his men and went out of his way to grant them leave and down-time when it was needed. He understood the importance of placing them under his watchful care. He patiently mentored, taught, coached, and counseled. He never allowed his men to enter into dangerous situations without leading them and being there to protect them.

Support your family members and organization. Make an effort to listen and understand their problems. Provide leadership through example, training, mentoring, and coaching. Be there for them unconditionally when they are struggling or in danger of being "defeated."

Encourage Others. A large component of leadership and support for others is providing encouragement. Sometimes a situation may be serious or seem insurmountable, yet an outstanding leader inspires his or her team and urges them onward. Richthofen went out of his way to provide encouragement, whether it was to his mother who was concerned for his safety or to his men who were exhausted and frustrated with the course of the war. He was also the first to offer congratulations and recognition for the heroics and successful missions flown by his men.

Encourage members of your family and organization. Uplift and comfort them when they are down or discouraged. Reassure and rally their spirits when they struggle. Applaud their efforts and share their excitement when they are successful.

Give Credit to Others. The Baron desired to be "the first of the chasers," but he wanted that distinction in the service of his country. As a leader, he also wanted his men to be successful. Their victories meant not only higher personal totals and increased motivation but also increased organizational numbers. These, in turn, meant greater success in protecting the skies and the field-grey soldiers who fought below from bombing, strafing, and reconnaissance havoc. Often Richthofen backed off to allow his pilots to move in on the enemy while he served as observer and protector. He even attempted to revise policy so that some of his later victories could be awarded to the squadron and wing. Regardless, he fought for his men to guarantee that they received appropriate credit for their combat successes.

Give credit to others! The fastest way to lose the respect and loyalty of your followers is to take credit for their accomplishments. Go out of your way to ascertain that your personnel receive the rewards to which they are entitled. As did Richthofen, involve your key personnel in decision-making that will serve the entire group and motivate them even further.

Encourage Healthy Competition. Richthofen knew the value of stimulating healthy competition. When he took command of *Jasta 11*, he appealed to the heretofore unsuccessful pilots to take up the challenge to excel and to even surpass the incredible victory record of *Jasta Boelcke*. Consequently, in both March and April, 1917, *Jasta 11* would indeed outscore all other *Jastas*. The lowly *Staffel* without a single victory just three months earlier achieved its one hundred victory milestone on April 22nd.

Recognize the tremendous motivational power of the capability to excel and compete in a healthy rivalry. Provide a challenge for your family members, team, organization, or company. Encourage, support, and celebrate success and the will to win.

Be a Good Teacher. Richthofen loved his country, and he was convinced that he could make a difference in the war. He also cared deeply about the safety of his men and did everything he could to adequately prepare them for battle in the skies. The Baron used his influence to secure the most-advanced aircraft, but he also knew that the right machine was only effective in the hands of a capable and well-trained pilot. He was convinced that extensive training, coaching, and oversight were key ingredients not only in enhancing safety but also in creating an advantage strategically in the air war. He was a tough taskmaster and demanded excellence. He therefore took the time to patiently train his personnel and to also be a role model to other leaders so that they might replicate his training methods. Further, he passed on his knowledge formally to other commanders through his Air Combat Operations Manual.

Be a good teacher or mentor! Thoroughly understand the material and make yourself the master. Be willing to spend the time and energy in making the subject matter interesting and understandable. Challenge your people and demand excellence. Be patient! Recognize that individuals advance at different paces and learn better from varying approaches. Invest the time to answer all questions and use scenarios as examples to facilitate learning.

Be Willing to Adapt. Richthofen recognized that it was not possible to train for every scenario. However, he did understand the importance of training consistency—and yet with enough training diversity—so that his pilots flew as though they were one entity, regardless of the situation. In Richthofen's mind, training, discipline, and experience would translate into an integrated group of pilots, flexible enough and intuitive enough to make the right decisions in unusual circumstances.

Make certain that you and your organization are flexible, willing, and able to adapt. Train your personnel so that they are capable of responding appropriately under both normal and projected unusual circumstances. In addition to adequate and timely training, enforce the discipline necessary for team members to act consistently and dependably under unforeseen situations. Insist that your personnel obtain sufficient experience under a broad range of scenarios so that they are able to respond intuitively and correctly under most unusual conditions.

Be Willing to See Opportunity. Richthofen was typically eager to take on new challenges. However, when he was given command of *Jasta 11*, he was understandably sad to leave *Jasta Boelcke* and also disappointed that he did not immediately receive the Blue Max following his sixteenth victory. Nonetheless, ever the faithful soldier, he was quickly able to recognize that his background, combat pilot skills, and leadership had prepared him for just such an assignment. He realized that his new command represented a tremendous opportunity to integrate his drive for personal combat with the appealing prospect of successfully molding his dozen previously-ineffective pilots into a team of disciplined expert aviators with his aggressive hunting spirit.

Be able to recognize opportunity when it knocks. Be aware—better yet, eagerly anticipate!—that your education, training, background, and experience have actually prepared you for opportunities that may come your way. Even if you are not looking for a change, be open to possibilities. Be able to visualize and embrace a potentially better future if it seems right.

Consider the Greater Good. Richthofen felt strongly that what he was doing was morally right and for the greater good. He felt duty-bound to do all he could for the men in the trenches and the German people at home sacrificing for the war effort.

Self-sacrifice is a necessary trait of successful leaders. Be willing to sacrifice for the greater good. Show empathy and appreciation to those in your charge. Demonstrate the courage and resolve in "battle" to motivate and inspire your team.

Compare Notes. Richthofen respected his opponents not just because to do otherwise could prove to be fatal, but also because they were in the same "business." The Baron particularly enjoyed a fair battle when both sides possessed the armament and the numerical forces to deliver a formidable fight. The Germans, British, and French demonstrated chivalry in the air and on the ground, especially early in the war. Downed pilots were often entertained at the adversary's squadron before being taken to prison camp. In such instances, it was not unusual for pilots to exchange general comments concerning air battles. At times, valuable bits of information could thus be acquired.

Richthofen also recognized the value of obtaining the views of his fellow pilots concerning appropriate aircraft to be used at the Front. By comparing notes, more information became available for accurate decision-making and resulted in delivery of better equipment.

Compare notes! Even with competitors, there are times when ethical general discussions regarding customer service, for instance, can be beneficial to all. Seek out the opinions and expertise of your staff and those actually providing the services at the "Front." More information results in better decision-making, and implementation of the good ideas of others typically increases motivation and encourages subsequent contribution.

Don't Be a Base Hog. Richthofen's brief tours of service as a communications officer in the Signal Corps, *Ordonnanzoffizier* (assistant adjutant), and finally supply officer proved unacceptable to the energetic young cavalryman. Visualizing possibilities flying with the "cavalry of the air," he applied and was accepted to aircraft observer school at Cologne in May 1915.

Although an officer of the General Staff was considered by the various armies to hold an honorable and valuable position, Richthofen and the German soldiers felt a measure of contempt for an individual who they considered to be a "base-hog." Similarly, the British referred to a young and capable officer who avoided actual combat as being "Something on the Staff." Richthofen refused to be placed in a staff position where he felt he would be unproductive in the war effort.

Don't be a "base-hog!" Be willing to venture out of your office, get out "on the floor" with your personnel, and help them fight the "war" in the "trenches." It is impossible to fully comprehend and appreciate the needs of your workers unless you observe first-hand their constraints and job requirements.

12 PAINT YOUR MACHINE RED
(Make Your Product Stand Out)

It occurred to me to have my packing case painted all over in staring red. The result was that everyone got to know my red bird. My opponents also seemed to have heard of the color transformation. [Richthofen, 1918, p. 129]

A German fighter pilot shoots over the forward lines ... Blood red is its fuselage. It strikes deep over the German trenches ... before it again fades away.... But those below ... follow the red flier with their eyes as long as they can; from their half-opened lips comes the cry of enthusiasm. [Baroness von Richthofen, 1937, p. 117]

They had often seen his red airplane flying over their trenches ... in complete disregard for their own danger, they had deserted the shooting ramparts and observed his aerial battles. [Baroness von Richthofen, 1937, p. 190]

Richthofen chose to paint his Albatros DIII red, possibly because it was the color of his *Uhlan* Regiment. It had also been the color chosen by his mentor, Oswald Boelcke, who had elected to paint the spinners of *Jasta 2's* aircraft red to facilitate *Staffel* identification. Regardless, previous attempts made by the Baron and other pilots to use various camouflage schemes proved futile, and Richthofen boldly wanted his aircraft to stand out, not only to his pilots, but also to his opponents.[1] He sought to challenge his opponents and blatantly did so using his strikingly-colored aircraft as his calling card.

> **One can certainly not make oneself invisible in the air, and so at least ours recognize me. [Manfred, quoted in Baroness von Richthofen, 1937; p. 116]**

There is evidence that the Baron had painted his Albatros red in December 1916 while still at *Jasta Boelcke*, and even as early as October. Before the end of January, Richthofen would become known as The Red Baron, *Le Petit Rouge* (The Little Red One), and *Le Diable Rouge* (The Red Devil). The presence of the dazzling red machine served as an inspiration to his comrades and a challenging warning to his adversaries.

Make Your Product Stand Out

> **I recall there wasn't a thing on that machine that wasn't red, and God how he could fly! [Second Lieutenant A.E. Woodbridge, 20 Squadron RFC, quoted in Franks, Giblin, & McCrery, 1995; p. 150]**

> **At last one of the men plucked up courage and dropped down upon our rear machine. Naturally battle was accepted although our position was unfavorable. If you wish to do business you must, after all, adapt yourself to the desires of your customers. [Richthofen, 1918, p. 182]**

> **Every flyer on the other side knew him, for at the time he alone flew a red-painted aeroplane. For that reason ... [his pilots wanted] to have all *Staffel* aeroplanes painted red and implored my brother to allow it so he would not be so especially conspicuous. The request was granted; for ... everyone knew**

... it attracted attention.... My brother's crate was glaring red. Each of the rest ... had some additional markings in other colors ... as recognition symbols. [Lothar von Richthofen, quoted in Kilduff, 2007; p. 109]

Pilots on both sides of the Front were often grounded during the typical rainy and snowy weather in northern France and Belgium in February and March 1917. Richthofen used the time to further develop his men, refine *Boelcke's Dicta*, and write a series of reports to the Chief of Field Operations that would later become the basis of his own *Air Combat Operations Manual*. It was during this time that the members of *Jasta 11* began to paint their aircraft. They had heard rumors that their leader's all-red machine had become the target of a special "anti-Richthofen" squadron, and they implored him to allow them to paint their aircraft with red markings as well. Richthofen agreed but reserved the all-red paint scheme as his own. Individual colors allowed the pilots to identify each other during swirling dogfights and made confirmations of victories easier for ground observers. By mid-April, as his men completed painting their aircraft with various combinations of bright colors accented by a common red, Richthofen's enemies had the eerie feeling that the Red Baron was everywhere. Later, this was punctuated even further when the Fokker DRIs were placed into service because they were so maneuverable, making it appear as though one or just a couple of the triplanes constituted a whole squadron or squadrons containing many more aircraft than normal.

I would say that all the machines of the squadron had been painted red because our English friends had by-and-by perceived that I was sitting in a blood-red band-box. Suddenly there were quite a lot of red machines and the English opened their eyes wide when one fine day they saw a dozen red barges steaming along instead of a single one. [Richthofen, 1918, pp. 173-4]

When they observed the tremendous success of Richthofen's squadron during March and April 1917, other *Jasta* units soon also adopted primary and subsidiary color schemes. Later, Richthofen, in his Air Combat Operations Manual, urged all *Staffels* to paint their aircraft for easier identification:

So that the *Staffeln* do not come together in disorder, it is advisable that each *Staffel* has its own emblem marking. The *Kommandeur's* aircraft must be very conspicuously painted. [MvR Air Combat Operations Manual; Kilduff, 1993, p. 232]

Within the *Staffel*, each [pilot] has a special distinguishing emblem on his machine, best [applied] on the rear part of the tail above and below. [Richthofen's Air Combat Operations Manual; Kilduff, 1994, p. 235]

Richthofen knew what he was doing when he chose red as the color for his aircraft. Red was the choice of his *Uhlan* Regiment and also the color of *Jasta Boelcke's* aircraft nose spinners. However, he most likely chose red because the color historically symbolized combat, aggression, danger, energy, boldness, courage, and leadership. Richthofen well understood that once he began to mount victories in his red Albatros, he would be specifically targeted by every Allied fighter pilot in the skies. Yet he had the courage and confidence in his ability to defeat all challengers. Further, he wanted to energize his own men. Indeed, the invincible Baron in his all-red aircraft was as much a legend to the German and Central Power pilots as he was to those of the Allied Powers. Additionally, when the *Jasta 11* pilots began to paint their aircraft red coupled with their own individual markings, the resulting identification system enhanced communication and teamwork dramatically. It also allowed observers on the ground to more easily confirm victories. Richthofen's pilots, sporting their leader's color, also had to step up their performance. They were not about to disgrace the color of their leader or their squadron. Lothar mentioned that the pilots looked at their newly painted red aircraft "proudly." The red color denoted "insolence" and drew attention:[2]

It had long been our wish to have all aeroplanes of our *Staffel* painted red, and we implored my brother to allow it. The request

was granted, for we had shown ourselves worthy of the red color by our many aerial kills. The red color signified a certain insolence. Everyone knew that. It attracted attention. Proudly, we looked at our red birds. My brother's crate was glaring red. Each of the rest of us had some additional markings in other colors—we chose these colors as recognition symbols. Schafer, for example, had his elevator, rudder and most of the back part of the fuselage painted black, Allmenroder used white, Wolff used green and I had yellow. As a yellow dragooner, that was the appropriate color for me. In the air and from the ground, as well as from the enemy's view, we all looked to be red, as only small parts were painted in another color. [Lothar von Richthofen, quoted in VanWyngarden, 2004; p. 13]

In July 1917 after *Jagdgeschwader I* was formed, Bodenschatz described *JGI's* aircraft on the airfield at Marckebeke. When the Albatros DVs and Pfalz DIIIs were lined up in groups of twelve behind their respective *Staffel* leaders, the result was colorful and dramatic. *Jasta 11's* machines were red, *Jasta 10's* yellow, *Jasta 6's* black with zebra stripes, and *Jasta 4's* sported black wavy lines on the fuselages. The colors allowed the pilots—and ground observers—to differentiate the *Staffeln* in the air. In addition, since each pilot added individual aircraft markings as well, it was possible to detect immediately who was at the controls of a particular machine.[3]

~

To be continually successful, a company must sustain competitive advantage. Similarly, it is critical that its key executives maintain an edge by being more productive than their counterparts at competing companies. The author's organization—a corporate flight department— was responsible for not only providing transportation for the company's key executives, but also guaranteeing that it did so in the safest, most efficient, and cost-effective way possible.

First of all, the organization had to "paint" its aircraft so that they attracted attention from its customers. Entities within the company were naturally concerned with the bottom line and organizational business profits, and aircraft flight hours were charged out to the users. When the rate was set too high or when entity revenues were poor, usage suffered, in turn mandating a rate escalation and triggering a subsequent utilization death-spiral. The flight department's job was to "sell" the advantages of corporate aviation—safety, security, comfort, and enhanced productivity—and convince the corporation itself to shoulder all or a greater portion of the fixed cost. Organizations could then fly the corporate aircraft when it made business sense to do so.

The flight department also had to make certain that the aircraft appropriately served the needs of its customers. When it placed new longer-range aircraft into the fleet in 1994, flight activity jumped dramatically—some 56%. In 1996, because of increased flight demands and the fact that aircraft down for maintenance are not only non-productive but also continue to generate fixed cost, the author set of goal of both 100% reliability and 100% dispatch availability. This was a particular challenge to the aircraft maintenance department because ultimately all inspections—with the exception of major engine overhauls—were channeled in-house and had to be accomplished progressively (i.e., on-going inspections performed piecemeal following flights). By the time the author retired in 2004, the aircraft maintenance department had achieved a remarkable six-year span of perfect dispatch availability and reliability!

Finally, the organization was increasingly pressured to fly more hours, with less staff, and do so with a flawless safety record and world class scheduling (dispatch) team. In 1997, an outside safety audit of the flight department by the Flight Safety Foundation (FSF) stated that the organization "exhibited a high regard for safety and has the most active and effective safety program which FSF has observed during over 40 years of conducting such audits." They further affirmed that the organization's "dispatch is among the best dispatch facilities FSF has observed in the corporate aviation community." When the author retired at the end of 2004, the organization had just received the results of its most recent FSF audit. It noted it their executive summary that the organization was "rated as outstanding in most areas. This is an exceptional rating that is not usually granted by the FSF Audit Team and places this flight operation in the top five percent of those firms audited." The outstanding group of employees that the author had been privileged to lead had indeed made their products stand out!

Have you "painted your aircraft red" to cause apprehension in the minds of your competitors? Are you making your product or products stand out from the crowd? Do you take the "safe," easy road and create commonplace products that require extraordinary marketing efforts to sell them? Or do you attempt to make quality products that are unique, remarkable, and beyond customer expectations? Are you and your team insolent and brazen enough to be the best?

Chapter 12 Summary

Paint Your Machine Red. Richthofen chose to paint his Albatros DIII red, possibly because it was the color of his *Uhlan* Regiment. It had also been the color chosen by his mentor, Boelcke, who had elected to paint the spinners of *Jasta 2's* aircraft red for identification. But primarily, Richthofen wanted his aircraft to be distinctive, not only to his pilots, but also to his opponents. It is likely that the Baron had painted his Albatros red in December 1916 while still at *Jasta Boelcke*, and even as early as October. Before the end of January, 1917, Richthofen would become known as The Red Baron, *Le Petit Rouge* (The Little Red One), and *Le Diable Rouge* (The Red Devil). The presence of the stunning red machine served as an inspiration to his comrades and a challenging warning to his adversaries.

Make Your Product Stand Out. Richthofen knew exactly what he was doing when he chose to paint his aircraft bright red. He most likely selected red because the color historically symbolized combat, aggression, danger, energy, boldness, courage, and leadership. Richthofen was well aware that once he began to add to his victories in his red Albatros, he would be specifically targeted by every Allied fighter pilot in the skies. Yet he had the courage and confidence in his ability to defeat all challengers. The invincible Baron in his all-red aircraft was as much a legend to the German and Central Power pilots as he was to those of the Allied Powers. Further, Richthofen wanted to strengthen his own fighting force of pilots. When the *Jasta 11* pilots began to paint their aircraft red coupled with their own individual markings, the resulting identification system enhanced communication and teamwork dramatically. It also made it easier for ground observers to confirm victories. Richthofen's pilots, sporting their leader's color, also had to take their performance to a higher level. They refused to disgrace the color of their *Kommandeur* or their squadron. Lothar mentioned that the pilots looked at their newly painted red aircraft "proudly" and the red color "signified a certain insolence."

Paint your "aircraft red" to cause anxiety in the minds of your competition! Make your product or products stand out from the crowd. Reject the "safe," easy road creating commonplace products that require extraordinary marketing efforts to sell them. Develop quality products that are unique, remarkable, and beyond customer expectations. Work to demonstrate that you and your team are insolent and brazen enough to be different!

13 TAKE YOUR CIRCUS ON THE ROAD
(Stay Close to Your Customers)

Just a few kilometers behind the lines, often within range of the enemy artillery, we are on fully dressed standby.... Our aircraft, gassed up and ready to go, are right alongside. As soon as an opponent appears on the horizon, we go up—one, two, or an entire *Staffel*. Immediately after the fight we land ... and scour the sky with binoculars, waiting for the next opponent. Standing patrols are not flown.... "This business of standing sentry duty in the air weakens the pilots' will to fight," he maintains. Thus we only go up to fight. [Udet, 1935, p. 50]

On June 24, 1917, the day of his 55th aerial victory, Richthofen received an official telegram designating him as the commander of the newly formed fighter wing, *Jagdgeschwader I*, consisting of *Jagdstaffeln* units 4, 6, 10, and 11. The new wing was commissioned to be situated at appropriate hot spots along the Front to destroy enemy single-seat fighters, infantry support aircraft, and bombing squadrons in those crucial combat sectors. As a result, Richthofen could launch as many as 50–60 aircraft at a time to spoil the onslaught of increasing numbers of enemy aircraft in the combat zones.

There were some members of the Army Staff who felt that a constant curtain of "barrier" flights that patrolled up and down the Front was the best strategy to protect the combat soldiers below. However, Richthofen knew that such a policy wasted valuable men, machines, and fuel. He also knew that those preventive flights would likely be in the wrong place anyway when an assault was initiated. By positioning his mobile operations directly in the battle zone less than 20 kilometers behind the front lines, establishing direct communications to the forward most Front, and then maintaining the ability to be airborne in literally less than a minute, Richthofen and his men could deal directly and immediately to any threats that had just been launched. Because of its mobility and colorful aircraft, the British immediately dubbed the Baron's *Geschwader* "Richthofen's Circus."

Stay Close to Your Customers

Other squadrons live in castles or small towns, twenty or thirty kilometers behind the front-lines. The Richthofen group dwells in corrugated shacks ... They are rarely more than twenty kilometers behind the foremost outposts. Other squadrons go up two or three times a day; Richthofen and his men fly five times a day. Others close down operations in bad weather; here they fly under almost any condition.... The biggest surprise for me is the forward combat airstrips. [Udet, 1935, pp. 49–50]

"Anyone who flies a lot, experiences a lot" was also a maxim of his. "On good days, an average of three take-offs can be made in the morning." Then, of course, he still flew steadily in the afternoons and evenings. The rest of the time he stood with his men on the landing field, pretty much suited-up. [Bodenschatz, 1935, p. 86]

At last one of the men plucked up courage and dropped down upon our rear machine. Naturally battle was accepted although our position was unfavorable. If you wish to do business you

must, after all, adapt yourself to the desires of your customers. [Richthofen, 1918, p. 182]

Richthofen's "Flying Circus" was the unquestioned elite aerial fighting division of the entire German Air Service. The famed and colorful unit traveled by train, lived and stored their aircraft in tents, and, most importantly of all, positioned themselves where they could find the most "customers." Often, Richthofen lost patience with the observations of others and continually searched personally for locations from which his wing could best serve the German infantry.[1]

The word *customer* is derived from the word "custom" and referred to someone who frequently visited a particular shop that provided a certain line of goods or services. In turn, the store keeper sought to maintain a relationship with the buyer so that this "custom" of purchases could be anticipated in the future.

Richthofen often referred to his opponents as "customers" because they frequently returned to the skies where the ensuing "business transaction" consisted of the interchange of hardware (machine gun fire!). The Baron's opponents were in fact his competitors who relentlessly pushed for control of the skies and destruction in the battlefields below. Richthofen well understood that his true customers were the field-grey soldiers who fought beneath the skies in the saw tooth ground trenches and alternatively in "no-man's land"—often in hand-to-hand combat in conjunction with the latest offensive. Richthofen knew personally what the soldiers experienced and he wanted to ease their burden as best he could. He felt that if he could stay close to the combat zone, he could at least assist in keeping the Allied aircraft from raining havoc on the German troops. He would respond to the threats of his opponents, but his focus would be on protection of the German soldiers.

A German fighter pilot shoots over the forward lines ... Blood red is its fuselage. It strikes deep over the German trenches ... before it again fades away ... But those below ... follow the red flier with their eyes as long as they can; from their half-opened lips comes the cry of enthusiasm. [Baroness von Richthofen, 1937, p. 117]

Higher authority has suggested that I should quit flying before it catches up with me. But I should despise myself if, now that I am famous and heavily decorated, I consented to live on as a pensioner of my honor, preserving my precious life for the nation while every poor fellow in the trenches, who is doing his duty no less that I am doing mine, has to stick it out. [MvR, *Reflections in a Dugout*, quoted in McGuire, 2001]

~

In 2000, the author and his flight operations organization completed a new hangar facility and relocated from an airport in the heart of Dallas to one on the northeast outskirts of the Metroplex. The decision was made in order to build a world-class facility more suited to the company's aviation needs, take advantage of tax breaks, and benefit from less congestion (fewer takeoff and landing delays). However, the biggest advantage afforded by the move was that the new facility was significantly closer to the organization's two primary customers—the chairman and the president of the company. For a company to remain successful, its executives must be more productive than their counterparts at competing companies. To reach and maintain that competitive edge, a company executive's time must be valued and maximized. The proximity of the hangar also removed the stresses associated with driving the highways from the equation for these satisfied passengers.

Do you know who your *primary* (not necessarily *ultimate*) customers are? For a particular organization, the primary customers may be the end users of products or services, or they may be internal company recipients of sub-assemblies, services, technical support, or training. As an individual, your primary customer could just as easily be person sitting next to you in the production process. Do you place your major focus on the needs and concerns of your customers rather than spending your time constantly worrying about what your competitors are doing? Richthofen respected his competitors in the air, but he had no fear of them. He was concerned with protecting his comrades on the ground and in the air, and he was constantly developing more efficient and effective ways to do just that. He reminded his mother that she need not worry, especially when he was in the air. He explained that he and his pilots could handle their adversaries, even though they were outnumbered.[2]

> Are you and your team willing to go closer to the "Front" to thoroughly understand first-hand the conditions under which your customers battle each day? Do you listen to their needs and work to make their jobs easier? Do you understand how your products are being utilized and whether or not there are better solutions? Do you frequently "fly over the trenches" to let your customers know that you are there providing your support?

Chapter 13 Summary

Take Your Circus on the Road. On June 24, 1917, Richthofen was placed in command of the newly formed fighter wing, *Jagdgeschwader I. JG1* was commissioned to be situated at appropriate hot spots along the Front to destroy single-seat fighters, infantry support aircraft, and bombing squadrons. By positioning his mobile operations directly in the battle zone less than 20 kilometers behind the front lines, establishing direct communications to the forward most Front, and then maintaining the ability to be airborne in literally less than a minute, Richthofen and his men could deal directly and immediately to any threats that had just been launched. Because of its mobility and colorful aircraft, the British dubbed the Baron's *Geschwader* "Richthofen's Circus."

Stay Close to Your Customers. Richthofen often referred to his opponents as "customers" because they frequently returned to the skies where the ensuing "business transaction" consisted of interchange of hardware (machine gun fire!). The Baron's opponents were in reality his competitors who relentlessly pushed for control of the skies and destruction in the battlefields below. Richthofen well understood that his true customers were the field-grey soldiers who fought beneath the skies in the ground trenches and alternatively in "no-man's land," often in hand-to-hand combat in conjunction with the latest offensive. Richthofen knew personally what the soldiers experienced and he wanted to ease their burden as best he could. He felt that if he could stay close to the combat zone, he could at least assist in keeping the Allied aircraft from raining havoc on the German troops. He would respect and respond to the threats of his opponents, but his focus would be on protection of the German soldiers.

Know who your customers really are! Place your primary focus on the needs and desires of your customers rather than spending all of your time worrying about what your competitors are doing. Be conscientious about frequently visiting the "Front" to thoroughly understand first-hand the conditions under which your customers battle each day. Listen! Understand how your products are being utilized and whether or not there are better solutions. Don't forget to "fly over the trenches" often to let your customers know that you are there providing your support.

14 BE MODEST IN YOUR VICTORIES
(Be True to Yourself)

He [Army leader and Adjutant-General, von Plessen] stressed over and over how Manfred was so pleasant because of his striking modesty. [Baroness von Richthofen, 1937, p. 165]

Richthofen never exaggerated under any circumstances. [Bodenschatz, 1935, p. 51]

Manfred was extremely truthful. Even today my mother cannot praise enough the extent to which they, as parents, could consistently rely on him. He gave precise and clear answers to every question, without regard for what the consequences to himself could be. [Bolko von Richthofen, quoted in Richthofen, ed. Stanley Ulanoff, 1969; pp. 164-5]

The chief thing is to bring a fellow down. It does not matter at all whether one is credited for it or not. [Richthofen, 1918, p. 79]

Boelcke might have shot down a hundred aeroplanes [had it not been] for his accident, and many others of our dear dead comrades might have vastly increased their bag but for their sudden death. [Richthofen, 1918, p. 185]

Richthofen measured his service to his country and his success as a pilot by earning the coveted *Pour le Merite* and tracking the aerial victories of himself and his men. His admiration and respect for his mentor Boelcke seemed to kindle his continual quest to live up to that image. In spite of the fact that he would ultimately double Boelcke's victory total, Richthofen always felt that had Boelcke lived, his hero's successes would have eclipsed those of everyone else. Unlike several very prominent pilots in the war, the Baron's integrity kept him from padding his victory log, taking credit for the successes of others, or boasting about his accomplishments. It never occurred to Richthofen to claim a victory he didn't earn, even when he was victorious over several aircraft that crashed on the other side of the Front and could not be confirmed by German observers. On more than one occasion, he simply didn't claim a legitimate victory. Often he backed off to allow his pilots to move in on the enemy while he served as an airborne observer and protector. He even attempted to revise policy so that some of his later personal victories could be awarded to his squadron and wing. Many claim that Richthofen's true victory total was closer to one hundred.

As mentioned earlier in Chapter 11, in March of 1918, *Oberleutnant* Bodenschatz offered an example of Richthofen's resolve to give his men due credit for their victories. There were sometimes rumors among English and French pilots that he often took credit for the victories of his comrades. Bodenschatz referenced Richthofen's actual combat report in which he described flying with *Leutnant* Gussmann of *Jasta 11* in an attack on a Bristol Fighter and then ten minutes later with *Leutnant* Loewenhardt of *Jasta 10* when they fired on a Breguet. The *Kommandeur* certified that Gussmann and Loewenhardt brought those respective aircraft down.[1]

Be Humble

I had never imagined that it would be so delightful to command a chasing squadron. Even in my dreams I had not imagined that there would ever be a Richthofen's squadron of aeroplanes. [Richthofen, 1918, p. 128]

It is under these extremely difficult and doubtful circumstances that I, fortunately, find myself one of these [aviation observer] selectees. [Richthofen, quoted in Kilduff, 1993; p. 33]

I am after all only a combat pilot, but Boelcke, he was a hero. [MvR, Sept 1917]

I always used to salute him [MvR] at first. He refused to tolerate that. [Menzke, quoted in Baroness von Richthofen, 1937; p. 152]

He [MvR] was the least complicated man I ever knew. Entirely Prussian and the greatest of soldiers. [Udet, 1935, p. 72]

Richthofen was somewhat introspective, shy, and reserved. The courteous behavior he displayed around women came as a result of his natural shyness and genuine respect for the ladies. Although he was naturally humble, he derived great pride, satisfaction, and pleasure from serving his country. At the same time, he was never arrogant. Even though he was obviously extremely successful as a combat pilot, he always felt that there were others, especially the great Oswald Boelcke, who had aviation skills that surpassed his own. Like Boelcke, Richthofen was detailed and methodical; and he was vigilant that as he became more and more experienced to not let arrogance and exuberance replace humility and cautious energy.

The Baron's adjutant, Bodenschatz, noted that Richthofen sought comfort only when it was not an expense or didn't detract from operations. Typically, his everyday clothing was simple—a knit sweater and deerskin trousers, with the *Pour le Merite* around his neck. If it was cold, he would add a leather jacket. On festive occasions of if guests were expected, he would be in uniform. He enjoyed good food and used mustard generously. He didn't have "prima donna" moods, and if good food supplies were limited, he tended to be exceedingly satisfied nonetheless. He took pleasure in a glass or two of good wine but always remained sober, even when others around him apparently over-indulged.[2]

In spite of your achievements, do you remain humble? Are you thankful and take pride in what you have accomplished, but do so without overconfidence, conceit, and arrogance? Are you secure in yourself so that you don't feel you have to brag about you talents and blessings? Are you willing to admit that many aspects of the person that you have become and the skills that you possess are likely the result of what your parents, mentors, and teachers have passed on to you? Are you willing to respect others and appreciate their talents, even when they eclipse those of your own?

Beware of Pride

When I read [my] book, I smile at my own insolence. No longer am I so insolent in spirit. Not because I can imagine how it would be one day when death is breathing down my neck; surely not for that reason, although I have thought about it often enough that it can happen. I have been told by [people in] high places that I should give up flying, for one day it will catch up with me. I would be miserable with myself if now, burdened with glory and decorations, I were to become a pensioner of my own dignity in order to save my precious life for the nation, while every poor fellow in the trenches endures his duty as I do mine. [MvR, *Der rote Kampfflieger*, 1933; quoted in Kilduff, 2007, p. 213]

Pride, when seen as a virtue, is a reasonable or justifiable self-respect.[3] It can also manifest itself as a high opinion of one's country, such as national pride. When viewed as a vice, it is often termed vanity, inordinate self-esteem, arrogance, or hubris. In this latter sense, pride is the opposite of humility.

What Manfred reported in his modest, simple way was like the fighter pilots' 'Song of Songs.' Mutual pride and chivalry... [Baroness von Richthofen, 1937, p. 116]

Richthofen was determined to live life fully and couldn't resist the urge to occasionally take an ill-conceived risk such as urging his pilot to make a crash landing or flying through a thunderstorm. Such actions were probably more the result of exuberance rather than overconfidence and pride. Fortunately, Richthofen learned from his mistakes and chalked the experiences up as lessons learned. Later, he would caution and reprimand his pilots for taking foolish risks.

Manfred always begged me to make a crash landing with him.... It wasn't long at all before I put the machine on its head with an awkward landing. Who was not then happier than Manfred! [*Oberleutnant* Georg Zeumer, quoted in Fischer, 2001; p. 135]

When I pulled my machine out of the hangar the first signs of an approaching thunderstorm became noticeable. Clouds which looked like a gigantic pitch-black wall approached from the north. Old experienced pilots urged me not to fly. However, I had promised to return and I should have considered myself a coward if I had failed to come back because of a silly thunderstorm. Therefore I meant to try. [Richthofen, 1918, p. 93]

I shall never again fly through a thunderstorm unless the Fatherland should demand this. Now, when I look back, I realize

that it was all very beautiful. Notwithstanding the danger during my flight, I experienced glorious moments which I would not care to have missed. [Richthofen, 1918, p. 95]

There is a definite difference between pride in your personal or team accomplishments and arrogant pride based on a feeling of superiority and vanity. Positive pride can motivate and boost creativity. On the other hand, an attitude of superiority and arrogance can alienate and undermine good leadership. Do you manifest virtuous pride in the celebration of the accomplishments of family members, employees, and a personal job well-done? Do you strive to retain humility and avoid becoming conceited and arrogant?

Laugh *with* Yourself

Manfred could be quite amusing, even boisterous. [Baroness von Richthofen, 1937, p. 90]

One of the Englishmen whom we had shot down and whom we had made a prisoner was talking with us. Of course he inquired after the Red Aeroplane. It is not unknown even among the troops in the trenches and is called by them 'le diable rouge.' In the Squadron to which he belonged there was a rumor that the Red Machine was occupied by a girl, by a kind of Jeanne d'Arc. He was intensely surprised when I assured him that the supposed girl was standing in front of him. He did not intend to make a joke. He was actually convinced that only a girl could sit in the extravagantly painted machine. [Richthofen, 1918, pp. 156-7]

One day, Richthofen received a letter from a novice who was preparing to become a nun. She indicated that she had hung a picture of him on her convent wall. However, when the abbess saw the picture, the young novice said she was severely reprimanded and reminded that nuns were not allowed to hang pictures of men on their walls, even if this particular one was that of a famous fighter pilot. When she was forced to remove the picture, the novice explained in her correspondence to the Baron that she found a way around her dilemma. Richthofen noted:

She did something that perhaps flatters, if not misrepresents, me. She wrote to a friend who was also a nun and asked her to send a large photograph of herself. When the friend did that, the young lady cut the face out of the photograph and stuck my face under the nun's habit. [MvR, quoted in Richthofen, ed. Stanley Ulanoff, 1969; p. 118]

On another occasion, Richthofen visited Schulte's Art Gallery in Berlin on a rainy day following what turned out to be an unproductive visit to the aeronautical test center at the Adlershof section of Johannisthal airfield. Because of the weather, he wore his overcoat with the collar turned up. While he was viewing a recent painting of himself in his plane, entitled "Rittmeister Freiherr von Richthofen," a man walked up to examine the picture as well. The Baron shared the brief conversation:

An elderly gentleman came up and stood beside me. I said to him: "I beg your pardon, but I am told I have some likeness to the person in this painting." The gentleman put on his spectacles, looked at the picture, looked at me, and finally said: "I think you can forget that notion." So much for well-known war heroes! [MvR, quoted in Kilduff, 2003; p. 162]

My enemy with his burning machine landed smoothly while I, his conqueror, came down next to him in the barbed wire of our trenches and my machine overturned.
The two Englishmen, who were not a little surprised at my collapse, greeted me like sportsmen.... They had not fired a shot

and they could not understand why I had landed so clumsily. [Richthofen, 1918, p. 104]

It is certainly a good thing if one has a thick head in life. [Following his head injury on July 6, 1917] [Manfred, quoted in Baroness von Richthofen, 1937; p. 137]

To err is human. **Marcus Tullius Cicero**

Because we are human, we are naturally prone to error. This is true whether we transpose numbers in our checkbook or improperly program the advanced weapons system on a modern combat aircraft. Rather than beat ourselves up, it is more productive to simply admit that we are human, build in processes that help prevent errors, remain alert for error-producing situations, correct any mistakes that do occur, and move on down the road. We should also learn to laugh at ourselves. Better yet, we need to learn to laugh *with* ourselves—just as we would laugh *with* others rather than *at* others over some amusing anecdote! We should not allow our natural error proneness short-circuit our productivity or compromise our positive self-esteem.

Self-esteem is a primary aspect of an individual's subjective experience and quality of life.[4] Further, it is highly correlated with variables that influence the "affective tone" of a person's daily experience. Individuals with high self-esteem report more positive effect, more satisfaction with life, lower anxiety, less hopelessness, and fewer symptoms of stress and depression than those with lower self-esteem. For instance, self-esteem is arguably the strongest predictor of satisfaction with life in the United States.

Richthofen possessed in large quantities that typically charming self-awareness and self-assurance, which must be innate, which one can never learn. In his face there was a calm, firm and yet friendly manliness, without any pronounced, determined tenseness, as found in many of our other young heroes. [*Hauptmann* Erich von Salzmann, quoted in Kilduff, 1999; p. 52]

Richthofen was comfortable with who he was and what he needed to accomplish. Because of this, he was able to laugh with others and with himself. He was genuinely amused when he was told that some British airmen believed that "only a girl could sit in the extravagantly painted machine." He also willingly told the stories on himself about his "clumsy" landing next to an aircraft he had just forced to crash-land; about the novice at the abbey who "hid" his picture in a nun's habit; and about being scoffed at when he asked a gentleman at an art gallery in Berlin if he resembled Richthofen.

> Do you accept the fact that you are human and have flaws like the rest of us? Are you confident and comfortable enough to laugh with yourself when you see yourself doing silly or even "brainless" things at times? Compared to unhealthy ways to cope, such as drinking and eating too much, having a sense of humor at such times actually reduces tension, improves one's frame of mind, and boosts self-esteem.

You grow up the day you have your first real laugh—at yourself.
Ethel Barrymore

Chapter 14 Summary

Be Modest in Your Victories. Richthofen measured his service to his country and his success as a pilot by earning the coveted *Pour le Merite* and tracking the aerial victories of himself and his men. His admiration and respect for his mentor Boelcke seemed to kindle his continual quest to live up to that image. In spite of the fact that he would ultimately double Boelcke's victory total, Richthofen always felt that had Boelcke lived, his hero's successes would have surpassed those of everyone else. Unlike several very prominent pilots in the war, the Baron's integrity kept him from padding his victory log, taking credit for the successes of others, or boasting about his accomplishments. It never crossed Richthofen's mind to claim a victory he didn't earn, even when he downed several aircraft that crashed on the other side of the Front and could not be confirmed by German observers. On more than one occasion, he simply didn't claim a legitimate victory. Often he backed off to allow his pilots to attack the enemy while he served as observer and protector. He even attempted to revise policy so that some of his later personal victories could be awarded to his squadron and wing.

Be Humble. Richthofen was somewhat introspective, shy, and reserved. Although he was naturally humble, he derived great pride, satisfaction, and pleasure from serving his country. At the same time, he was never arrogant. Even though he was exceptionally successful as a combat pilot, he always felt that there were others, especially the great Boelcke, who had aviation skills that exceeded his own. Like Boelcke, Richthofen was detailed and methodical, and he understood that as he became more and more experienced to not let arrogance and exuberance replace humility and cautious energy.

In spite of your achievements, do your best to remain humble. Be thankful and take pride in what you have been able to accomplish, but do so without overconfidence, conceit, and arrogance. Be secure in yourself so that you don't feel you have to boast about you talents and blessings. Be willing to admit that many aspects of the person that you have become and the skills that you possess are likely the result of what your parents, mentors, and teachers have passed on to you. Respect others and appreciate their talents, even when they eclipse your own.

Beware of Pride. *Pride*, when seen as a virtue, is a reasonable or justifiable self-respect. It can also manifest itself as a high opinion of one's country, such as national pride. When viewed as a vice, it is often termed vanity, inordinate self-esteem, arrogance, or hubris. In this latter sense, pride is the opposite of humility.

Richthofen was determined to live life fully and couldn't resist the urge to occasionally take an ill-conceived risk such as urging his pilot to make a crash landing or electing to fly through a thunderstorm.

Such actions were probably more the result of exuberance rather than overconfidence and pride.

There is a definite difference between pride in your personal or team accomplishments and arrogant pride based on vanity and a feeling of superiority. Positive pride can motivate and boost creativity. On the other hand, an attitude of superiority and arrogance can alienate and undermine otherwise good leadership.

Manifest virtuous pride in the celebration of the accomplishments of family members, employees, and a personal job well-done. Strive to retain humility and avoid becoming conceited and arrogant.

Laugh *with* Yourself. Because we are human, we are naturally prone to error. Rather than beat ourselves up, it is more productive to simply admit that we are human, build in processes that help prevent errors, remain vigilant for error-producing situations, correct any mistakes that do occur, and move forward. We should also learn to laugh *with* ourselves, just as we would laugh *with* others rather than *at* others! We should not allow our natural error-proneness to compromise our productivity and positive self-esteem.

Self-esteem is a primary aspect of an individual's subjective experience and quality of life. Further, it is highly correlated with variables that influence the "affective tone" of a person's daily experience. Individuals with high self-esteem report more positive effect, more satisfaction with life, lower anxiety, less hopelessness, and fewer symptoms of stress and depression than those with lower self-esteem.

Richthofen was comfortable with who he was and what he needed to accomplish. Because of this, he was able to laugh with others and with himself.

Accept the fact that you are human and have flaws like the rest of us. Be confident and comfortable enough to laugh with yourself when you see yourself doing silly or even "brainless" things at times. Compared to unhealthy ways to cope, such as drinking and eating too much, having a sense of humor at such times actually reduces tension, improves one's frame of mind, and boosts self-esteem.

15 TIE YOUR HANDKERCHIEF TO A STEEPLE
(Value Family and Friends)

One fine day, with my friend Frankenberg, I climbed the famous steeple of Wahlstatt by means of the lightning conductor and tied my handkerchief to the top. I remember exactly how difficult it was to negotiate the gutters. [Richthofen, 1918, p. 23]

"Now you are free.... here everything is permitted." [Baroness von Richthofen, 1937, p. 79]

Psychologists have suggested that no single phenomenon perhaps better reflects the positive potential of human nature than *intrinsic motivation*, which is the inherent individual tendency to seek out innovation and challenge, to extend and exercise capacity, to explore, and to learn.[1] Intrinsically-motivated individuals typically display more interest, excitement, and confidence. Additionally, these characteristics in turn reveal themselves as improved performance, persistence, creativity, vitality, self-esteem, and general well-being. Intrinsic motivation, as it relates to the life span, is more likely to thrive in

271

contexts that provide a sense of security and relatedness. In addition, supportive conditions that facilitate intrinsic motivation include autonomy and competence.

It is commonplace, and typically advantageous, to allow ourselves to be influenced by others, especially family and friends. If we are fortunate, we have had family, friends, managers, or co-workers who have encouraged our greatest aspirations and our most lofty dreams. Richthofen was fortunate to have a mother and a grandmother—and most likely a father as well—who were supportive of his desire to be adventuresome. He was a very healthy and athletically-gifted child and could easily turn standing somersaults and climb the pine trees in the forests of Silesia. One day, deciding to test his skills to the limit, he scaled the famous church steeple at Wahlstatt using the lightning conductor as a rope and tied his handkerchief to the top. He noticed that the handkerchief was still in place ten years later when he visited his brother, Bolko.

Hitch your wagon to a star. **Ralph Waldo Emerson**

Value Family and Friends

I flew towards my brother and we congratulated one another by waving. We were highly satisfied with our performance and flew off. It is a splendid thing when one can fly together with one's brother and do so well. [Richthofen, 1918, p. 180]

So loyal a friend [Lothar] was of inestimable worth for Manfred. [Baroness von Richthofen, 1937, p. 91]

On the ninth of November, 1916, I flew towards the enemy with my little comrade Immelman, who then was eighteen years old. We both were in Boelcke's squadron of chasing aeroplanes. We had previously met one another and had got on very well. Comradeship is a most important thing. [Richthofen, 1918, p. 120]

Richthofen enjoyed a good relationship with his adjutant, *Oberleutnant* Karl Bodenschatz, and with *Hauptmann* Reinhard, who was *JGI's Staffel 6* leader. One of the *Kommandeur's* favorite pilots, however, was *Leutnant* Hans Joachim Wolff.[2] "Little Wolff" had been wounded three times and his aircraft had frequently sustained major damage. Because of his bad luck, Wolff had not been successful in combat in his eight months with the *Geschwader*. But the hapless youngster had once helped his *Kommandeur* out of a jam and Richthofen could sense Wolff's ability. He therefore carefully coached the struggling aviator and patiently waited as Wolff finally developed into one of *Jasta 11's* best fighter pilots.

~

Humans have strong affiliation, belongingness, and validation needs. When individuals share a mutual commitment, they have a greater tendency to deny themselves for the greater good. The need for affiliation and belongingness seems to underscore the human desire to maintain at least a minimum number of interpersonal relationships.[3] Group affiliation—such as that in the workplace—also serves a number of other needs in addition to self-esteem needs, including: psychological, social, comparison, comforting, and practical needs.[4]

Personal relationships on the job are important predictors of job satisfaction. Wide social networks, including support from workers, management, family, and friends relieve strain and serve as buffers against stress.[5] Social support in the workplace appears to moderate physiological stress reactions by reducing the amount of cortisone released, lowering blood pressure, reducing the number of cigarettes smoked, and even promoting complete smoking cessation.

Richthofen enjoyed a close relationship with his family. He was also fortunate to often have his brother Lothar flying at his side. He valued comradeship highly and fostered it openly. He allowed his men to let off steam in any way they liked following a flight. He participated in practical jokes and tolerated a lot, even at his own expense. But he was quick to step in when tempers sometimes flared up between members of his unit.[6] He also recognized individuality and that people sometimes needed to be treated differently. For instance, as stated earlier, he allowed *Leutnant* Hans Joachim Wolff to remain with the *Geschwader* in spite of his initial lack of success in the air.

Do you place appropriate value on family and friends? Do you understand the advantages these strong relationships bring into your life? Being cautious not to become too close to any specific member of your team or organization, do you go out of your way to support those who look to you as their manager or leader?

Chapter 15 Summary

Tie Your Handkerchief to a Steeple. Psychologists have suggested that no single phenomenon perhaps better reflects the positive potential of human nature than *intrinsic motivation*, which is the inherent individual tendency to seek out innovation and challenge, to extend and exercise capacity, to explore, and to learn. Intrinsically-motivated individuals display more interest, excitement, and confidence. Additionally, these characteristics in turn translate themselves into improved performance, persistence, creativity, vitality, self-esteem, and general well-being. Intrinsic motivation, as it relates to the life span, is more likely to thrive in contexts that provide a sense of security and relatedness. In addition, supportive conditions that facilitate intrinsic motivation include autonomy and competence.

Richthofen was fortunate to have parents and a grandmother who were supportive of his desire to be adventuresome. He was a healthy and athletically-gifted child and easily climbed the pine trees in the forests of Silesia. One day, deciding to test his climbing skills to their fullest, he scaled the famous church steeple at Wahlstatt using the lightning conductor as a rope and tied his handkerchief to its peak.

Value Family and Friends. Humans have strong affiliation, belongingness, and validation needs. When individuals share a mutual commitment, they have a greater tendency to deny themselves for the greater good. The need for affiliation and belongingness seems to underscore the human desire to maintain at least a minimum number of interpersonal relationships. Group affiliation—such as that found in the workplace—also serves a number of other needs in addition to self-esteem needs, including: psychological, social, comparison, comforting, and practical needs.

Personal relationships on the job are important predictors of job satisfaction. Wide social networks, including support from workers, management, family, and friends relieve strain and serve as buffers against stress.

Richthofen enjoyed a close relationship with his family. He was also fortunate to often fly side-by-side with his brother. The Baron recognized the value of comradeship and was quick to step in when tempers sometimes flared between members of his unit. He recognized individuality and that people needed to be treated differently in the workplace.

Place appropriate value on family and friends. Understand the advantages these strong relationships bring into your life. Be cautious not to become too close to any specific member of your team or organization, but go out of your way to support those who look to you as their manager, leader, or mentor.

Durwood J. Heinrich, Ph.D.

16 GET A DOG
(Relax)

Dogs are not our whole life, but they make our lives whole.
Roger Caras

The most beautiful being in all creation is the genuine Danish
hound, my little lap-dog, my Moritz. I bought him in Ostend
from a brave Belgian for five marks. His mother was a beautiful
animal and one of his fathers also was pure-bred. I am convinced
of that. I could select one of the litter and I chose the prettiest.
Zeumer took another puppy and called it Max....
Moritz flourished exceedingly. He slept with me in my bed and
received a most excellent education. He never left me while I was
in Ostend and obtained my entire affection. Month by month
Moritz grew, and gradually my tender little lap dog became a
colossal, big beast. Once I took him with me. He was my first
observer. He behaved very sensibly. He seemed much interested
in everything and looked at the world from above. [Richthofen,
1918, pp. 157-8]

In August 1915, Richthofen was transferred to the *Brieftauben-
Abteilung Ostende (BAO)* on the 4th Army Front in Flanders, where he

was teamed for a second time with *Oberleutnant* Zeumer. It was also in Ostende where Richthofen purchased his "little lap-dog" Moritz. As a puppy, the Great Dane initially slept in the same bed as his master, but later became too big. He even flew once with the Baron, calmly assisting with observer duties.

If you have ever owned a pet or grew up with a pet in your family, you most likely understand how an animal can enrich one's life. If you have never owned a pet, perhaps it's time you consider their many pluses. Pets provide social and psychological support.[1] In addition to the obvious benefits such as companionship and affection, pets reduce stress, lower blood pressure, improve one's mood, and "encourage" their owners to get more exercise.[2] Studies of families have shown that pets are especially valued in times of crisis or loss.[3] At such times, pets offer requisite unconditional love, comfort, and security.

Relax

A dog has one aim in life ... to bestow his heart. **J. R. Ackerley**

"Anyone who flies a lot, experiences a lot" was also a maxim of his. "On good days, an average of three take-offs can be made in the morning." Then, of course, he still flew steadily in the afternoons and evenings. The rest of the time he stood with his men on the landing field, pretty much suited-up. [Bodenschatz, 1935, p. 86]

On Sunday, April 21, 1918, *JGI's* airfield at Cappy was fogged in. As always, the pilots of the *Geschwader* were dressed and ready for action, waiting for the weather to clear. Meanwhile, their spirits were still high from the previous evening when they had celebrated their *Kommandeur's* 79th and 80th victories, along with the recent successes of the *Geschwader* itself. Even though the ever-modest Richthofen mentioned little about his 79th and 80th triumphs, he too was in a good mood. Playfully, the *Rittmeister* turned over a cot occupied by the resting and unwary *Leutnant* Richard Wenzl. Moments later, the Baron flipped another pilot onto the damp grass. In retaliation, two officers tied a wheel chock to the tail of Moritz, who, dragging the anchor behind him in circles, sought immediate comfort from his master.[4]

Richthofen recognized that having his dog by his side helped him to relax and cope with the stresses of the war. Moritz helped the Baron to maintain a good mood and get ample exercise when he wasn't flying or tending to squadron or wing business. Moritz also served as a sounding board for the *Kommandeur's* creative ideas. Many officers on both sides of the Front owned pets, especially dogs. For Richthofen, and numerous pilots in the war, pets were a psychological comfort that reminded them of home and afforded unconditional love and companionship in what were horrific conditions. When a comrade was lost in the war, at least the pet was there to provide comfort and support. Companion animals are highly sensitive to the emotions of their masters and instinctively react to changes in moods. Military dogs were also used extensively during the war for guard duty, medical support, and messaging missions.

Are you able to relax? Have you found activities or hobbies that enable you to put aside, at least temporarily, things that cause stress in your life. Better yet, do you make an effort to remove yourself from some of the primary stressors in your life, including negative individuals? Do you exercise regularly, make healthy food choices, and get adequate rest? If you don't yet own a companion pet, have you considered getting one? If you already have a pet, do you make an effort to spend a little more time playing, cuddling, or just "hanging out" with the animal—especially when you are stressed? If you have children, are you aware that studies have shown that pets provide many educational and socialization benefits?[5] For instance, children with pets tend to be more empathetic than those without pets.[6] One parent observed that because of their pets, her children were more responsible, kind, affectionate, and concerned about other living things.[7]

Durwood J. Heinrich, Ph.D.

Count Your Blessings

Reflect upon your blessings, of which every man has plenty, not on your past misfortunes, of which all men have some. **Charles Dickens**

Richthofen's adjutant, Karl Bodenschatz recounted a story about the fact that as the war progressed, there was increasing less likelihood of being able to procure some of the scarce provisions for the *Geschwader*, regardless of the money available for that purpose. He noted that even if he found a vendor who actually had a supply of appealing items, the person would often merely shrug his shoulders or gesture regret with his hands. Finally, one day the adjutant simply reached in his pocket of his tunic and produced a postcard of the Manfred von Richthofen in his finest uniform adorned with his array of medals and signed by the *Rittmeister's* own hand. That little tactic proved to be enormously successful and kept the adjutant from having to return without the proper stores in the future.[8]

~

When we are stressed and overwhelmed with the demands of everyday life, it is important to realize that for each challenge we generally receive many more blessings. Richthofen understood how fortunate he was to become a pilot, to fly in the best fighter aircraft, to win the Blue Max, and then go on to command his own squadron, and ultimately wing, of aircraft:

I joined the Flying Service at the end of May, 1915. My greatest wish was fulfilled. [Richthofen, 1918, p. 60]

I feel very content with my new occupation as a fighter pilot; I believe that no post in the war is as attractive as this one. I am flying a Fokker [E.III *Eindecker* monoplane], which is the airplane with which Boelcke and Immelmann have had their tremendous successes. [MvR letter to his mother, May 3, 1916;

quoted in Richthofen, ed. Stanley Ulanoff, 1969, p. 46]

I had never imagined that it would be so delightful to command a chasing squadron. Even in my dreams I had not imagined that there would ever be a Richthofen's squadron of aeroplanes. [Richthofen, 1918, p. 128]

> Do you engage in destructive self-talk or spend a good deal of your time lamenting over your problems? Or do you recognize that you are blessed many times over? Do you make an effort to keep a pulse on your own attitude? Are you alert for the dangers of "snowballing" and negative thinking? One excellent way to relieve stress is to rediscover nature and animals, much as you did when you were young.

A dog has the soul of a philosopher. Plato

Experience Life Fully

He [MvR] wanted to conquer every day anew. [Baroness von Richthofen, 1937, p. 126]

Richthofen enjoyed life and lived it to the fullest. As previously mentioned, he especially enjoyed family, comradeship, and an occasional practical joke. One day, Supreme Headquarters sent some members of the *Reichstag* (Parliament) to the Richthofen's unit at Lechelle to experience the excitement of the Front. The visitors were lodged in a corrugated iron Nissen building. In the middle of the night, Reinhard, Wolff, and others staged a mock bombing raid by shooting signal flares down through the stove pipe and into the hut. The result was a series of explosions followed by associated crashes and related stench. The occupants rushed out of the hut—suitably terrified, with ghostly faces—and nearly ran over the *Rittmeister* who was enjoying the show from just outside. Fortunately, he was able to slip away into the darkness before they spotted him. Needless to say, the frightened contingent left hurriedly early that morning, even before breakfast.[9]

It was the face [MvR's] of someone who was a decent person down to the last corner of his soul. Within his face lay a resilient energy, an energy without restraint, without nervousness, the wonderful energy of youth.... and the look from his clear, sincere eyes was the look of a man at peace with himself, with the world, and with everything in his past. [Bodenschatz, 1935, p. 11]

On the morning of April 21, 1918, in spite of the fact that Richthofen's units were standing by for immediate launch, the early morning fog at Cappy kept the *Geschwader* pilots grounded. April had been a very successful month for the Wing; and of course, the day before Richthofen himself had added numbers seventy-nine and eighty to his victory list. Therefore, in spite of the weather, the mood was high, and even the *Rittmeister* was more boisterous than usual. Bodenschatz recalled that Richthofen's laughter could be heard frequently across the field as the pilots joked with one another and romped with Moritz. Further, the Baron had another reason to be in a good mood because he and *Leutnant* Wolff were scheduled to go hunting in the Black Forest in just a few days.[10]

∿

On April 30, 1917, the Baron received a wire that he was to meet with the Kaiser on May 2nd. Richthofen had been ordered to take leave after surpassing Boelcke's record of forty victories in mid-April. However, refusing to miss the action during the Battle of Arras, Richthofen protested and was ultimately allowed to remain at the Front until the end of the month. By the time he transferred command of *Jasta 11* to his brother Lothar with an informal handshake on May 1st, he had recorded fifty-two combat victories! Richthofen departed Roucourt with his Technical Officer Konstantin Krefft—in the *Staffel's* all-red two-seat Albatros CIX—for German Army Headquarters at the resort city of Bad Kreuznach. They landed in Cologne where they received a public reception, complete with crowds, flowers, and speeches by town dignitaries. After lunch and a short rest, the crew flew on to Bad Kreuznach, enjoying a low-flying aerial sightseeing tour of the beautiful Rhine River en route:

We flew rather low in order not to lose the sensation that we were traveling along mountains, for after all the most beautiful part of the Rhine are the tree clad hills and castles. Of course we could not make out individual houses. It is a pity that one cannot fly slowly and quickly. If it had been possible I would have flown quite slowly. The beautiful views which we saw vanished only too quickly. Nevertheless, when one flies high in the air one never has the sensation that one is proceeding at a fast pace. [Richthofen, 1918, pp. 189-90]

When the author was in the Air Force and flying jet aircraft, his concerned mother once cautioned him "not to fly too fast!" He responded that should he attempt to fly too slow, the aircraft would simply stall and fall out of the sky due to loss of lift over the wings!

However, like Richthofen's tour over the Rhine, such a concept—flying "slowly and quickly"—certainly has its appeal. In other words, it would be wonderful if one could fly *quickly* to one's destination without losing the obvious advantage of flying *slowly* enough to enjoy the scenery. As the Baron mentioned, flying at higher altitudes *appears* to slow down the "pace" but, of course, affords little in the way of providing an up-close scenic experience.

Richthofen was always enthusiastic and full of life. Early in his career as a pilot, in spite of warnings from more-experienced pilots, he once flew through a severe thunderstorm. Before that, as an observer, he kept badgering his pilot Zeumer to crash the aircraft so that he could experience the resulting sensations:

I had never yet made an attempt to get through thunder clouds but I could not suppress my desire to make the experiment. [Richthofen, 1918, p. 92]

Manfred always begged me to make a crash landing with him…. It wasn't long at all before I put the machine on its head with an awkward landing. Who was not then happier than Manfred! [*Oberleutnant* Georg Zeumer, quoted in Baroness von Richthofen, 1937; p. 135]

Although some might still get a "rush" from deliberately crashing an airplane or deliberately flying through a thunderstorm, there are certainly many other—and safer!—ways to experience life fully. Even Richthofen later acknowledged the folly of his actions and chalked the experiences up as lessons learned. Later, he would advise caution and reprimand his pilots for taking foolish risks.

I shall never again fly through a thunderstorm unless the Fatherland should demand this. [Richthofen, 1918, p. 95]

Psychological studies have shown that happiness is beneficial in reducing stress, improving relationships and social interaction, and enhancing personal well-being. A famous quote by author Ben Sweetland points out that "happiness is a journey, not a destination." Happiness comes from the inside, not from possession of material wealth or even from finally finding that "one special person." Rather, it's an internal choice one must make. Happiness involves understanding yourself, counting your blessings, cultivating your abilities, and applying your strengths in everyday life through interactions with those you love and with those with whom you work.

~

Earlier in Chapter 3, the author mentioned the pilot who lost the battle with cancer in 2002. That individual loved life and almost everyone and everything he encountered. He was never satisfied to sit on the sidelines. He was constantly reading and learning. He volunteered for the difficult tasks that most individuals avoided or were not capable of completing. He was the consummate administrator. He was always ready to join in, to contribute, and to make new friendships. He was perpetually enthusiastic and happy. He always wore a smile and told jokes as only he could, although sometimes to our consternation! But most of all, he loved to fly and was an excellent pilot. There was never a time when he turned down an additional opportunity to fly or failed to volunteer when a pilot was needed for a pop-up non-scheduled flight. But he had more than just a passion for flying. He had an almost childlike exuberance for it. In 1996, he and the author were flying together on a ten-day around the world business trip that included stops at fifteen cities in thirteen countries. Although challenging, extended trips were almost always enjoyable, especially those that were uncommon—such as those that completely circled the globe. The company has a plant in Baguio, a beautiful city in the mountains north of Manila, in the Philippines. It was his leg and he was making his first takeoff from the Baguio Airport that has a single, short runway that somewhat resembles an aircraft carrier deck. When the aircraft rose rapidly above the steep canyon as it launched to the East, he reached over with a smile and presented his hand for a "high-five." He and the author later learned that the passengers saw this gesture through the open cockpit door. The company chairman had looked over at the flight attendant, and asked: "Did they just do a high-five?" She nodded, "I'm afraid so!"

Are you able to fully-experience life? Are you willing to learn, to develop, to explore? Do you have enough confidence and respect for yourself and your abilities that you don't need to constantly search for that elusive construct of "happiness" outside of your existing family, friends, and work associates? Do you take time to smell the flowers and allow yourself to sometimes "fly slowly" enough to appreciate the beauty of the "Rhine River" or the fall colors of the leaves? Are you a positive person with an optimism that spreads to those around you? Are you like your pet when you are around others—always happy to spread warmth and unconditional love?

If there are no dogs in Heaven then, when I die, I want to go where they went. **Will Rogers**

Chapter 16 Summary

Get a Dog. In August 1915, Richthofen was transferred to the *Brieftauben-Abteilung Ostende (BAO)* on the 4th Army Front in Flanders. It was there that Richthofen purchased his "little lap-dog" Moritz. As a puppy, the Great Dane initially slept in the same bed as his master, but later became too big. He even flew once with the Baron and eagerly assisted with his master's observer duties.

If you have ever owned a pet or grew up with a pet in your family, you most likely understand how an animal can enrich your life. Pets provide social and psychological support. In addition to the obvious benefits such as companionship and affection, pets reduce stress, lower blood pressure, improve one's mood, and "persuade" their owners to get more exercise. Studies of families have shown that pets are especially valued in times of crisis or loss. At such times, pets offer welcome unconditional love, comfort, and security.

Relax. Richthofen recognized that having his dog by his side helped him to relax and cope with the stresses of the war. Moritz helped the Baron to maintain a good mood and get ample exercise when he wasn't flying or tending to squadron or wing business. Moritz was also a good listener when the *Kommandeur* vetted his creative ideas. Many officers on both sides of the Front owned pets, especially dogs. For Richthofen, and numerous pilots in the war, pets were a psychological comfort that reminded them of home and afforded unconditional love and companionship in horrific conditions. Companion animals are highly sensitive to the emotions of their masters and instinctively react to changes in moods. When a comrade was lost in the war, the pilot's pet was there to provide comfort and support. Military dogs were also used extensively for guard duty, medical support, and messaging missions throughout the war.

Take the time to relax. Find activities or hobbies that enable you to put aside, at least temporarily, things that cause stress in your life. Make an effort to remove yourself from some of the primary stressors in your daily routine, including negative individuals. Exercise regularly, eat healthy food, and get adequate rest. If you don't yet own a companion pet, consider getting one. If you already have a pet, make an effort to spend a little more time playing, cuddling, or just "hanging out" with the animal, especially when you are stressed. If you have children, be aware that studies have shown that pets provide numerous educational and socialization benefits.

Count Your Blessings. When we are stressed and overwhelmed with the demands of everyday life, it is important to realize that for each problem we generally receive many more blessings. Richthofen understood how fortunate he was to become a pilot, to fly in the best fighter aircraft, to win the Blue Max, and then go on to command his own squadron, and then wing, of aircraft.

Do not allow yourself to engage in destructive self-talk or spend your time lamenting over your problems. Recognize that you are blessed many times over. Make an effort to keep a pulse on your own attitude. Be aware of the negative consequences of "snowballing" and negative thinking. One excellent way to relieve stress is to rediscover nature and animals, much as you did when you were young.

Experience Life Fully. Richthofen was always enthusiastic and full of life. Early in his career as a pilot, in spite of warnings from more-experienced pilots, he once flew through a severe thunderstorm. Before that, as an observer, he kept badgering his pilot Zeumer to crash the aircraft so that he could experience the resulting sensations.

Although some might still get a "rush" from deliberately crashing an airplane or flying through a thunderstorm, there are certainly many other (and safer!) ways to experience life's adventures. Even Richthofen later acknowledged the silliness of his actions and chalked the experiences up to lessons learned. Later, he would caution his pilots and reprimand them if they took foolish risks.

Happiness is a big part of experiencing life fully. Psychological studies have shown that happiness is beneficial in reducing stress, improving relationships and social interaction, and enhancing personal well-being. Remember that "happiness is a journey, not a destination." Happiness comes from the inside, not from the accumulation of possessions or even from finally finding that "one special person." Rather, happiness is an internal choice one must make. Happiness is more about understanding yourself, counting your blessings, cultivating your abilities, and applying your strengths in everyday life through interactions with those you love and with those with whom you work.

Allow yourself to fully-experience life. Be willing to learn, to develop, and to explore. Have enough confidence and respect for yourself and your abilities that you don't need to constantly search for that elusive construct "happiness" outside of your existing family, friends, and work associates. Take time to "smell the roses." Allow yourself the luxury to sometimes "fly slowly" enough to appreciate the beauty of the "Rhine River" and the fall colors of the leaves. Be a positive person with an optimism that spreads to those around you. Become like your pet when you are around others—always willing and happy to spread warmth and unconditional love.

DEBRIEFING
(Conclusions)

Immediately after every *Geschwader* flight a discussion is the most important instructive activity. At this time, everything that happened during the flight from take-off to landing must be discussed. The questioning of individuals can be very useful for clarification. [Richthofen's Air Combat Operations Manual; Kilduff, 1994, p. 234]

Richthofen placed special emphasis on pre- and post-flight briefings so that best-practices could be reinforced and problems, be they individual or mission-related, could be addressed. Every mission was an opportunity to learn and to share lessons learned. Similarly, in modern-day corporate flight operations, the author and his organization recognized the value of spending considerable time in planning, revising those plans as necessary in the dynamic world as the trip progressed, and then debriefing so that any mistakes could be prevented in the future and more effective techniques subsequently incorporated. The author hopes that this final chapter will serve as a useful synopsis and help bring some of the concepts into further focus.

Attack Out of the Sun was essentially divided into three sections. The first five chapters were lessons centered on planning and preparation.

Richthofen and his mentor, Boelcke, were extremely cautious about letting their pilots venture out unprepared for battle. In fact, it was two weeks before Boelcke escorted Richthofen and his other pilots into battle the first time, and more than a week before Richthofen did the same with his men, in spite of the fact that in this latter case they were, supposedly, seasoned pilots. These great managers understood that for their men to be successful, they needed to understand their purpose (Chapter 1), benefit from trusted leadership (Chapter 2) and focused direction (Chapter 3), possess a clear concept of victory (Chapter 4), and become a unified team (Chapter 5).

For someone to expect success, he or she must have a purpose, an exciting vision or dream that makes one want to hit the floor running each morning. Or one might have a series of "Blue Max" objectives that make life challenging, fun, and rewarding. Even a "job" can provide such an avenue of adventure and satisfaction if one systematically develops the requisite skills and is given the tools and the freedom to take it to new heights.

Seldom is it possible to achieve great things without having someone to serve as a pattern for success. Sometimes that mentor is a towering champion who has reached the pinnacle in our chosen profession. Or the mentor might simply be a beloved parent, relative, or friend. In other instances, a combination of inspiring individuals might ebb and flow at vital times in our development. Regardless, most of us need someone we know we can trust, from whom we can learn, and from whom we can expect a helping hand when we inevitably stumble.

In order to achieve our vision, we must set intermediate goals, which should always be specific and attainable. They should include a plan for attainment, a tracking mechanism, and a deadline for achievement. Sometimes after establishing goals, it becomes obvious that we must remove obstacles (things or even negative individuals) that stand in the way of achieving our dreams. At other times, we realize that we must adjust our goals—especially longer range goals—either because our aspirations have changed or a situation has forced us to alter our plans.

It is important that we are able to visualize success. In fact, the more clarity we have in our minds about our goals, the greater the chances for eventual achievement. Sometimes—especially as we increasingly develop skills in our particular professions—we are able to go on "auto pilot" and settle into a kind of "flow," when everything seems to be coming together almost effortlessly. However, it is also important that we don't come to expect or even demand success at the expense of others. The Golden Rule always applies and we should allow for win-win scenarios in dealing with others. In our efforts to achieve success individually or as a team, we should employ our personal and collective strengths and be proactively alert for changing environmental conditions.

Generally, the greater the vision, the greater the need for a team effort to make it a reality. The developing team must not only possess the training background and technical skills but also the wherewithal to function as a unit, utilize synergy, and reinforce each other when faced with problems or opposition. The team also needs a trusted and gifted leader.

The next eight chapters of *Attack Out of the Sun* involved action and included lessons in how to implement your vision and realize success. Richthofen felt that he was a sportsman and never entered any setting with both guns blazing. Rather, he was logical and calculating. He recognized the importance of being responsive and aggressive (Chapter 6), but not without a solid support foundation (Chapter 7). He taught his men to be courageous but to respect the competition (Chapter 8), taking advantage of strengths and utilizing an edge to help ensure victory (Chapter 9). He demonstrated both management efficiency (Chapter 10) and innovative leadership (Chapter 11). He dared to be creative (Chapter 12) and was committed to the needs of his customers (Chapter 13).

Progress towards one's goals is never possible without the willingness to "roll up one's sleeves" and aggressively get to work. However, even aggressiveness should be preceded by adequate preparation—appropriate training, a plan of action, backup strategies, and the patience to wait for the right moment to make an "attack." Further, it is important to consider alternatives when responding to threats or opportunities before taking typically requisite *calculated* risks. The support of a mentor or team can be especially helpful.

Whether one is functioning as an individual or as a member of a team, he or she must do so in "perfect unity," recognizing and minimizing weaknesses while maximizing and capitalizing on harmony and strengths. It is usually more effective to draw on personal talents and core strengths and, when needed, to delegate others to add their special skills. There are normally no short cuts in achieving personal triumphs or business successes. There are more efficient and productive ways of doing things, but no "secrets" or magic formulas, other than old-fashioned hard work. Quality, integrity, and honesty are always the best choices. It is important to employ the right tools and equipment and be well-trained in their usage. Daring and boldness are admirable traits, but not without the willingness to be flexible and admit mistakes when conditions change. Patience and calmness, along with preparation, ensure readiness for opportunities and ability to address adversity.

A chivalrous attitude is one that implies gallantry, courtesy, and honor, not only with family and associates but also with competitors. Competitors should be respected as the opposition and because they may not always be predictable or as vulnerable as we might think. It is essential to know when to leave a "fight," especially if ethics and integrity are involved. It is also important to guard against becoming discouraged as we experience the inevitable setbacks along the way.

Whenever possible, it is wise to secure an advantage to increase the odds of success. Methods of doing this include obtaining extensive training, developing and maintaining core strengths, avoiding distractions, getting adequate rest, and utilizing available resources for increased strategic leverage.

In spite of all the emphasis currently being placed on leadership as the panacea, efficient management remains just as vital to success— and don't forget that one can be both a great manager and a great leader! Whether one is a manager of a project, team, small business, or a large corporation, the position involves duty, responsibility, and commitment. Formal training should be exercised in management, but don't discount rational common sense, especially under unusual conditions or time pressures. Common sense is important in personal life and in business, and it is derived from the sound, practical wisdom that is accumulated, usually over a number of years. Essential responsibilities of a manager are to establish objectives, set priorities, communicate, manage ensuing work, and measure results. Scarce resources must be allocated, opportunities identified and exploited, and problems addressed, all in a timely manner. The best personnel must be recruited, trained, and provided with support and recognition. An environment of trust, safety, and potential for personal growth is critical.

Where efficient management can generate a motivated, high-performance team, effective, charismatic leadership can create the spark that can move mountains. An admired, innovative leader who is trusted and technically-gifted can envision opportunities and lead the charge to huge victories before the competition can even begin to react. The leader accomplishes such feats through determination, confidence, inspiration, encouragement, coaching, and an uncanny ability to adapt and to function in a stellar manner, even in the midst of "battle."

One way to ensure success is to make your product or service stand out. Useful, innovative, quality products that are creative, remarkable, beyond customer expectations—and also beyond the competition's comprehension!—attract attention. The customer not only recognizes quality products coupled with responsiveness and commitment, but also responds with loyalty and provision of unsolicited endorsements.

The final three chapters of *Attack Out of the Sun* presented lessons in methods to evaluate oneself and seek personal renewal and strength. Richthofen understood life's fragility, the need for self-integrity, and the value of laughter (Chapter 14). He greatly treasured family, friends, and fellow soldiers, especially those making the greatest sacrifices in the trenches (Chapter 15). Finally, he recognized the importance of experiencing life fully, along with its many blessings (Chapter 16).

As we journey through life, it is important to remember our roots and the numerous blessings we have received along the way. As we mature into mentors ourselves, it is important that we humbly acknowledge pride in our accomplishments, but without conceit and arrogance. It is always easy to trace the many sources of our success in those who have mentored, taught, and led us unselfishly through the years. It is our responsibility to do the same for others. Further, as humans, we are only a simple recollection away from laughing *with* ourselves about the ridiculous things we have managed to say or do over the years.

We should all be thankful for family and relationships with good friends. Support from family, friends, and important relationships has been found to have positive influences on self-worth and socio-emotional functioning. Similarly, the workplace provides a source of friendships, prestige, social recognition, and an opportunity to exercise creative skills. Each of us possesses an inherent inclination to seek out innovation and change, to explore, and to learn. Those of us who have had parents who were supportive of this natural tendency towards adventure are fortunate. Now, as parents, friends, mentors, and managers, we ourselves can provide supportive conditions that facilitate such *intrinsic motivation* that enhances self-esteem, vitality, performance, creativity, and general well-being for family members and others.

Finally, our day-to-day existence is full of challenges, but also showered with blessings. Pets teach us many things, but primarily how to love unconditionally, relax, how to find joy in the little things, and how to fully-experience life.

ABOUT THE AUTHOR

Dr. Durwood J. Heinrich is a motivational speaker, safety consultant, writer, commercial pilot, and Certified Flight Instructor. He spent most of his 41-year aviation career as the Director of Aviation and Chief Pilot for two major corporations. Prior to joining those companies, Dr. Heinrich served in the U.S. Air Force as a T-38 Master Instructor Pilot and had brief tours as an airline pilot and a jet charter pilot. As an Airline Transport Pilot, Instructor Pilot, and Pilot Examiner, he has accumulated over fourteen thousand accident-free flight hours. Aircraft recently flown as Pilot-in-Command include the Bombardier Global Express, Bombardier Challenger 604, and the Dassault Falcon 2000 aircraft. He also served as the Central Regional Representative for a national business aviation organization that has been assisting businesses in becoming more efficient, productive, and successful since 1947. In this capacity, Dr. Heinrich had responsibility for nine states.

Dr. Heinrich holds a Bachelor's Degree in Aerospace Engineering from Texas A&M University, a Master of Science Degree in Management and Administrative Sciences from the University of Texas, and a Ph.D. in Industrial/Organizational Psychology from Capella University. He is also a graduate of the University of Southern California's Aviation Safety and Accident Investigation School.

Dr. Heinrich has published dozens of papers and conducted numerous presentations, seminars, workshops, and webinars on Manfred von Richthofen and a variety of aviation safety-related topics. Visit his Web site at http://www.redbaronconcepts.com/ to learn more about scheduling a presentation for your organization.

ENDNOTES

Introduction

1. *Jagdstaffel* (*Jasta* or *Staffel*): A pursuit flight squadron of typically nine to twelve aircraft.
2. The author has in his collection a nine millimeter 1917 Artillery Luger pistol, including shoulder stock and holster, a generous gift from Paul H. Smith. The German Army Luger, with its 8-inch barrel, was likely the type of pistol carried by Richthofen as an air observer.
3. The Fokker *Eindecker* was equipped with a machine gun that fired through the propeller arc of the engine using interrupter gear developed by Dutch aircraft manufacturer Anthony Fokker.
4. Manfred von Richthofen, *Der rote Kampfflieger*, trans. Ellis Barker (St Petersburg, FL: Red and Black, 2007), 64.
5. Typically, the student pilot "washout" (failure) rate was 50%.
6. *Orden Pour le Merite*: The Order's badge consisted of a Maltese Cross of deep blue enamel trimmed in gold and worn at the neck, a requirement when in uniform.
7. The Albatros DII—"D" stood for *Doppledecker*, or two wings— was a sleek, maneuverable biplane powered by a reliable 160 hp Mercedes D-III six-cylinder in-line engine, which gave the *"Haifisch"* (Shark) a maximum speed of 109 mph and thereby the ability to engage or break off combat as necessary.
8. The arrival of the formidable "Fees," along with the DH2, and the Nieuport 11 had ushered the end of the "Fokker Scourge," the period of German air superiority fostered by the Fokker *Eindeckers* on the Western Front in late 1915 and early 1916.
9. The *Ehrenbecher* Cup of Honor—inscribed *Dem Siege rim*

Luftkampf, "To the Victor in Aerial Combat"—honored a pilot's first victory, and was commissioned by Kaiser Wilhelm II. The first two were presented to Oswald Boelcke and Max Immelmann on Christmas Eve 1915.

10. German pilots often mislabeled a rear-engine, "lattice-tail" pusher type aircraft, such as the FE2b, a "Vickers" (British Vickers FB5 "Gunbus").

11. H.A. Jones, *The War in the Air*, Vol. II (East Sussex: The Naval & Military Press, 1928), 312ff.

12. Manfred von Richthofen, *Der rote Kampfflieger*, trans. Ellis Barker (St Petersburg, FL: Red and Black, 2007), 105.

13. The Sopwith Scout was nicknamed the Sopwith "Pup" because it was a scaled-down version of the Sopwith Two-Seater, known as the Sopwith Strutter.

14. The official documentation date of Manfred von Richthofen's *Pour le Merite* was January 12, 1917, exactly a year after Oswald Boelcke and Max Immelmann had received their "Blue Max" awards.

15. The Albatros DIII had a lower wing with a single spar and reduced wing chord (wing width) compared with the DII. The designers envisioned that besides improving downward visibility, the DIII would be faster in both forward speed and climb. However—while it did deliver higher climb rates—forward speed did not improve, and high speed dives caused flexing of the lower wing section forward of the spar and ultimate collapse. The DIIIs later had to be grounded for two months for structural modifications.

16. Richthofen chose to paint his Albatros DIII red, possibly because it was the color of his *Uhlan* Regiment. It had also been the color chosen by his mentor, Oswald Boelcke, who had elected to paint the spinners of *Jasta 2's* aircraft red for identification. Regardless, previous attempts made by pilots to use various camouflage schemes proved futile, and Richthofen wanted his aircraft to stand out, not only to his pilots, but also to his opponents. There is evidence that the Baron had painted his Albatros DII red in December 1916 while still at *Jasta 2*, and even as early as October. The author has in his collection a small piece of fabric from the

right wing of Richthofen's Fokker DR.I (425–17), a generous gift from James W. Robertson. Over time, the color has aged to a deep red or maroon.

17. *Staffel* leaders with high scores were given considerable rein to select high-caliber personnel for their units. Headquarters was especially anxious to see Richthofen succeed and had anticipated that he would not disappoint them; and they gave him responsibility for the key *Jasta* location on the Arras Front. In the case of Sergeant Howe, Richthofen decided that he did not possess the requisite qualities and he was posted out on February 17th.

18. Manfred von Richthofen, *Der rote Kampfflieger*, trans. Ellis Barker (St Petersburg, FL: Red and Black, 2007), 109.

19. The narrow, single-spar lower wing of the Albatros DIII suffered the effects of "wing flutter" at high speeds, a phenomenon unknown to engineers at the time.

20. The Halberstadt DII had a top speed of 90 mph. Richthofen's opponents on March 4th, March 24th, and March 25th, respectively, flew much faster aircraft—Sopwith Strutter, +12 mph; Spad VII, +29 mph; Nieuport 17, +20 mph. However, the DII, while having only one machine gun, was a maneuverable aircraft in skilled hands and could safety handle high speed dives.

21. Kurt Wolff, Karl Allmenroder, and Sebastian Festner would become aces under Richthofen's leadership, as would Karl-Emil Schafer and Lothar von Richthofen who joined *Jasta 11* on February 21st and March 10th respectively. All of these men would also receive the *Pour le Merite*—except for Festner who was killed in action (KIA) April 23, 1917.

22. Kunigunde von Richthofen, *Mein Kriegstagebuch*, trans. Suzanne Fischer. (Atglen, PA: Schiffer Military History, 2001), 116.

23. Allmenroder's aircraft was painted red with a white nose and tail; Schafer's, red with black elevators and tail; Wolf's, red with a green spinner and tail; and Lothar von Richthofen's, red with a yellow tail. When they noted the tremendous success of Richthofen's squadron during March and April 1917, other *Staffel* units also soon adopted primary and subsidiary color schemes.

24. The Battle of Arras technically began on April 9th, but the aerial

offensive began five days earlier.

25. *Jasta 11* individual victories in what the British termed "Bloody April" included: Kurt Wolff–22; Manfred von Richthofen–21; Karl-Emil Schafer–16; Lothar von Richthofen–15; Sebastian Festner–10; Karl Allmenroder–4; Konstantin Krefft–1; and Georg Simon–1.

26. On April 29th, Manfred scored four victories and Lothar two victories. The Richthofen brothers alone accounted for thirty-six of the 151 British losses during April.

27. On April 5th, 100 Squadron sent eighteen FE2b night-bombers over La Brayelle to attack *Jasta 11*. However, the unit was alerted that enemy bombers were en route. There were no casualties and only minor damage. They attacked again two nights later.

28. The publisher Verlag Ullstein had suggested to a receptive department of the Adjutant General's Air Service branch responsible for intelligence and press that Richthofen should write his memoirs, to be published in a series of magazine articles and later in a book. Richthofen accepted the project, mainly because he felt it would provide a source of income for his family should he be killed and the war turn out badly.

29. Floyd Gibbons, who wrote Richthofen's first biography in 1927, mentioned that the Baron exchanged daily letters with a young girl with whom he was in love throughout his time at the Front. However, Richthofen feared that he would not survive and therefore would not allow himself to consider marriage until after the war. Details of the relationship and the whereabouts of those letters remain a mystery (Gibbons, *The Red Knight of Germany*, 1927, 66–7).

30. In May 1917, British pilots and ground crews were beginning to gain experience and develop confidence in the newer type fighter aircraft such as the S.E.5, the Bristol Fighter, and the Sopwith Triplane.

31. When Richthofen was given command of *Jagdgeschwader I* (*JGI*), *Oberleutnant* Karl Allmenroder succeeded him as leader of *Jasta 11*. However, Allmenroder was killed in action on June 27th, most likely from British anti-aircraft fire.

32. *JGI's* headquarters was established at Marcke, southwest of

Courtrai. Keeping his *Jastas* as close together as possible, Richthofen had *Jastas 4* and *11* sited at Marcke, *Jasta 6* at Bisseghem, and *Jasta 10* at Heule.

33. The leading FE2d that attacked Richthofen on July 6, 1917, was crewed by Captain Donald Cunnell and observer/gunner Second Lieutenant Albert Woodbridge of 20 Squadron. They did not take credit for the Baron's near disaster. Because of the location of the wound (four inch gash in the left rear of his head), it is also believed that Richthofen may have been struck by a stray bullet from one of his own men while clearing his machine guns for the battle.

34. Dostler, Doring, and Wolff drove to the hospital with Bodenschatz that afternoon. *Oberleutnant* Althaus was required to remain at the airfield in the event that *JGI* was called to respond to another enemy alert.

35. On August 5th, *Hauptmann* Otto Bufe was re-assigned to the 8th Army on the Eastern Front as Officer in Charge of Aviation.

36. Richthofen's nurse, Katie Otersdorf, had been specifically assigned to him. While he was recovering, their frequent walks in the hospital's garden generated rumors that they had developed a romantic relationship.

37. Karl Bodenschatz, *Jagd in Flanderns Himmel*, trans. Jan Hayzlett (London: Grub Street, 1996), 28.

38. On July 17th, *Leutnant der Reserve* Richard Kruger of *Jasta 4* was shot down by a Sopwith Camel and died that evening.

39. Karl Bodenschatz, *Jagd in Flanderns Himmel*, trans. Jan Hayzlett (London: Grub Street, 1996), 29.

40. On July 20th, while visiting his *Geschwader* from the hospital, Richthofen learned that *Leutnant* Hans Adam (*Jasta 6*), *Leutnant* Walter Stock (*Jasta 6*), *Leutnant* Oskar von Boenigk (*Jasta 4*), *Vice Sergeant Major* Kurt Wusthoff (*Jasta 4*), and *Leutnant* Alfred Niederhoff (*Jasta 11*) had all been victorious that morning. Stock and von Boenigk had scored their first successes.

41. As Lieutenant Bird leveled off his Sopwith Pup just before landing, he opened fire on a column of German troops and then deliberately ran his aircraft into a tree so that it couldn't be subsequently used by the Germans.

42. Opposing *Leutnant* Werner Voss in his Fokker Triplane were several of the RFC's top flying aces, including: James McCudden, Richard Mayberry, Keith Muspratt, Reginald Hoidge, Arthur Rhys-Davids, and Verschoyle Cronyn. Their SE5s had a 23 mph speed advantage over the triplane.

43. Lothar von Richthofen was awarded the *Pour le Merite* on May 14, 1917, following his 23rd victory.

44. Karl Bodenschatz, *Jagd in Flanderns Himmel*, trans. Jan Hayzlett (London: Grub Street, 1996), 154.

45. Kunigunde von Richthofen, *Mein Kriegstagebuch*, trans. Suzanne Fischer (Atglen, PA: Schiffer Military History, 2001), 139.

46. An observer, *Leutnant* Arntzen, noticed that the outer tips of Gontermann's triplane upper wing began "flapping," followed by right aileron detachment, wing rib damage, and finally fabric separation.

47. Fokker DRI triplane investigations found condensation in the wings, causing glue joints to weaken, and weak attachment points on the ailerons, exacerbated by heavy loading in steep banks or side-slips.

48. The Pfalz DIII biplane was a sleek and strong aircraft. However, pilots generally criticized its heavy controls, power, speed, and climb rate when compared with the Albatrosses.

49. In late November 1917, *Jasta 11* and the *Geschwader* staff moved to Avesnes-le-Sec, *Jastas 4* and *6* to Lieu-St-Amand, and *Jasta 10* to Iwuy.

50. *Oberleutnant* Erwin Bohme was the pilot who had collided with Richthofen's mentor Oswald Boelcke on October 28, 1916. Bohme scored twenty-four aerial victories and—had he not been killed on November 29th—would have found his *Pour le Merite* waiting at the airfield when he returned.

51. Following Czar Nikolai II's abdication of the throne and subsequent murder, and then the failure of the Kerenski Government's military actions, the war with Russia was over. The peace treaty between the Bolshevik government of Russia and the Central Powers was signed on March 3, 1918.

52. The *Idflieg* (*Inspektion der Fliegeretruppen*—Inspectorate of Flying Troops) was the bureau of the German War Office responsible for

the oversight of German military aviation during WWI.

53. In late 1917, Fokker built the experimental V.11 biplane with a 180 hp Mercedes D.IIIa in-line engine. When he initially flew the V.11, Richthofen found it to be awkward and directionally unstable in a dive. In response, the designer, Reinhold Platz, lengthened the aft fuselage by one structural bay and added a fixed triangular fairing in front of the vertical stabilizer. When he flew the modified V.11, Richthofen declared it to be the best aircraft of the competition. It was so successful that the Armistice ending WWI specifically required that Germany surrender all DVIIs to the Allies. Some 1700 Fokker DVIIs were built in the summer and autumn of 1918.

54. On February, 1918, *JGII*—consisting of *Jastas 12, 13, 15*, and *19*—was formed to support the 7th Army; and *JGIII*—*Jastas 2, 26, 27*, and *36*—established to support the 4th Army.

55. On March 12, 1918, Richthofen flew a predominantly red Fokker DRI Triplane (152/17) for his 64th combat victory. He would pilot triplanes for all subsequent aerial victories (i.e., 65 through 80).

56. Second Lieutenant Henry James Sparks had been victorious over three German aircraft as an observer and had been awarded the Military Cross in September of 1917.

57. Karl Bodenschatz, *Jagd in Flanderns Himmel*, trans. Jan Hayzlett (London: Grub Street, 1996), 63. The envelope contained Richthofen's instructions regarding who should be given command of his *Geschwader* should something happen to him.

58. Ernst Udet, *Ace of the Iron Cross* (New York: Arco, 1981), 49.

59. *Leutnant der Reserve* Ernst Udet later became the highest scoring German ace to survive WWI with 62 victories.

60. The Fokker DRI Triplane (No. 425/17) von Richthofen was flying on April 20, 1918, was all-red, with the exception of a white vertical tail. It was the same aircraft that he was flying when he was killed in action the following day.

61. On April 1, 1918, the Royal Flying Corps (RFC) and the Royal Naval Air Service (RNAS) were merged to form the Royal Air Force (RAF).

62. Most experts believe that Richthofen was killed by ground fire

because the trajectory indicated that the single bullet moved in an upward motion, from the right side, travelled some 600+ yards —indicated by minimal tissue damage from hydrostatic shock— and probably some amount of time following Captain Brown's aerial attack.

63. Richthofen was hit by a single .303 round that caused severe damage to his heart and lungs. It passed directly through the chest from its entry wound at the back of the armpit at the level of the 9th rib—about five inches below the lower level of the outstretched arm—indicating that the bullet was fired from the right side, behind and below the pilot. Sergeant Cedric Popkin's machine gun was in approximately the same plane as the longitudinal axis of the triplane, and the range was consistent with the normal limits for the bullet that was found lodged in the Baron's clothing near the exit wound.

64. At least one observer noted that Richthofen was able to land his aircraft. Another, who was the first to reach the aircraft, indicated that the Baron even spoke briefly before dying. Dr. M. Geoffrey Miller, who in 1998 published a medical study of Richthofen's death, suggested that the Baron would have lost consciousness within twenty to thirty seconds after being struck by the bullet and could not have continued flight (Kilduff, *Red Baron: The Life and Death of an Ace*, 2007, 226). However, because the triplane had to be flown by the pilot at all times, it is unlikely that it landed relatively smoothly without Richthofen's control inputs.

Chapter 1

1. Both Max Immelmann and Oswald Boelcke received their *Pour le Merite* awards on the same day, January 12, 1916.
2. Manfred von Richthofen, *Der rote Kampfflieger*, trans. Ellis Barker (St Petersburg, FL: Red and Black, 2007), 49.
3. Kunigunde von Richthofen, *Mein Kriegstagebuch*, trans. Suzanne Fischer (Atglen, PA: Schiffer Military History, 2001), 83.
4. Manfred von Richthofen, *Der rote Kampfflieger*, trans. Ellis Barker (St Petersburg, FL: Red and Black, 2007), 107.
5. Leon Bennett, *Gunning for the Red Baron* (College Station, TX:

Texas A&M, 2006), 170.

6. Kunigunde von Richthofen, *Mein Kriegstagebuch*, trans. Suzanne Fischer (Atglen, PA: Schiffer Military History, 2001), 91.

7. Kunigunde von Richthofen, *Mein Kriegstagebuch*, trans. Suzanne Fischer (Atglen, PA: Schiffer Military History, 2001), 79.

8. Jerry R. Junkins, President and Chairman of Texas Instruments 1988–96.

9. Kunigunde von Richthofen, *Mein Kriegstagebuch*, trans. Suzanne Fischer (Atglen, PA: Schiffer Military History, 2001), 71.

10. Richard Bickers, *Von Richthofen—The Legend Evaluated* (Annapolis, MD: Naval Institute Press, 1996), 161.

Chapter 2

1. The Fokker *Eindecker* was a single-wing monoplane equipped with a machine gun that fired through the propeller arc of the engine using an ingenious interrupter gear developed by Dutch aircraft manufacturer Anthony Fokker.

2. Barrier patrols consisted of employing lone aircraft scouting along the Front to intercept enemy aircraft.

3. Gary Yukl, *Leadership in Organizations* (Upper Saddle River, NJ: Prentice-Hall, 2002), 388.

4. Paul Muchinsky, *Psychology Applied to Work: An Introduction to Industrial and Organizational Psychology* (Belmont, CA: Wadsworth, 2000), 196.

5. Before he left on his enforced "tour," Boelcke had done his best to outline his recommendations for new air fighter squadrons (*Jastas*) that would apply his combat principles—the famous *Dicta Boelcke*—to regain air dominance in the West. Apparently, his discussions with the *Feldflugchef* (Chief of Field Aviation) paid off and he was allowed to begin selecting pilots for his *Jasta*.

6. *Jasta 2* only had two Fokker DIIIs and a single Albatros DI brought over from *Jasta 1* by *Offizier Stellvertreter* (Acting Officer) Leopold Reimann, although they would receive a refurbished Halberstadt on the 11th.

7. Manfred von Richthofen was given command of *Jasta 11* on January 10, 1917.

Chapter 3

1. The Albatros DIII had a lower wing with a single spar and reduced wing chord (wing width) compared with the DII. The designers envisioned that besides improving downward visibility, the DIII would be faster in both forward speed and climb. However—while it did deliver higher climb rates—forward speed did not improve, and high speed dives caused flexing of the lower wing section forward of the spar, requiring later structural modifications.

2. Richthofen chose to paint his Albatros DIII red, possibly because it was the color of his *Uhlan* Regiment. It had also been the color chosen by his mentor, Oswald Boelcke, who had elected to paint the spinners of *Jasta 2's* aircraft red for identification. Regardless, previous attempts made by pilots to use various camouflage schemes proved futile, and Richthofen wanted his aircraft to stand out, not only to his pilots, but also to his opponents. There is evidence that the Baron may have painted his Albatros DII red in December 1916 while still at *Jasta 2*, and even as early as October.

3. Manfred von Richthofen, *The Red Baron* (S. Yorkshire: Pen & Sword, 2005), 60.

4. Manfred von Richthofen, *The Red Battle Flyer* (New York: Robert M. McBride & Co., 1918), 95.

5. Manfred von Richthofen, *The Red Battle Flyer* (New York: Robert M. McBride & Co., 1918), 181-2.

6. Norman Franks and Greg VanWyngarden, *Fokker Dr I Aces of World War 1* (New York: Osprey, 2001), 9.

7. The Sopwith Scout was nicknamed the Sopwith "Pup" because it was a scaled-down version of the Sopwith Two-Seater, known as the Sopwith Strutter.

8. The official documentation date of Manfred von Richthofen's *Pour le Merite* was January 12, 1917, exactly a year after Oswald Boelcke and Max Immelmann had received their "Blue Max" awards.

9. Typically, the student pilot "washout" (failure) rate was 50%.

10. Paul Muchinsky, *Psychology Applied to Work: An Introduction to Industrial and Organizational Psychology* (Belmont, CA: Wadsworth, 2000), 304.
11. Leon Bennett, *Gunning for the Red Baron* (College Station, TX: Texas A&M, 2006), 72.
12. Karl Bodenschatz, *Jagd in Flanderns Himmel*, trans. Jan Hayzlett (London: Grub Street, 1996), 83.
13. *Jasta 11* individual victories in what the British termed "Bloody April" included: Kurt Wolff–22; Manfred von Richthofen–21; Karl-Emil Schafer–16; Lothar von Richthofen–15; Sebastian Festner–10; Karl Allmenroder–4; Konstantin Krefft–1; and Georg Simon–1.
14. On April 29th, Manfred scored four victories and Lothar two victories. The Richthofen brothers alone accounted for thirty-six of the 151 British losses during April 1917.

Chapter 4

1. Leon Bennett, *Gunning for the Red Baron* (College Station, TX: Texas A&M, 2006), 22.
2. Leon Bennett, *Gunning for the Red Baron* (College Station, TX: Texas A&M, 2006), 5.
3. Maxwell Maltz, *Psycho-Cybernetics* (New York: Pocket Books, 1960), 35.
4. Mihaly Csikszentmihalyi, *Flow* (New York: Harper & Row, 1990). Mihaly Csikszentmihalyi indicated that it is not uncommon for experts in their specific domains to be lost in their work or activities. He described such an experience as *flow*, which involves reaching a kind of optimal experience such that total absorption in an activity results from a match between the task demands and the performance skills of the individual.
5. Kunigunde von Richthofen, *Mein Kriegstagebuch*, trans. Suzanne Fischer (Atglen, PA: Schiffer Military History, 2001), 91.
6. Maxwell Maltz, *Psycho-Cybernetics* (New York: Pocket Books, 1960), 66.
7. Maxwell Maltz, *Psycho-Cybernetics* (New York: Pocket Books, 1960), 72.

8. Steven Ungerleider, *Mental Training for Peak Performance* (Emmaus, PA: Rodale Press, 1996), 94.

9. D.J. Hardy and R. Parasuraman, "Cognition and Flight Performance in Older Pilots," *Journal of Experimental Psychology: Applied* 3, no.4 (1997): 313-48.

10. Robert E. Franken, *Human Motivation* (5th Ed.) (Belmont, CA: Wadsworth Thomson Learning, 2002), 115.

11. John H. Salmela, "Athletes." In *Encyclopedia of Psychology* (Vol. 1). American Psychological Association. (Washington, D.C.: Oxford University Press, 2000), 280.

12. John H. Salmela, "Athletes." In *Encyclopedia of Psychology* (Vol. 1). American Psychological Association. (Washington, D.C.: Oxford University Press, 2000), 281.

13. Opposing *Leutnant* Werner Voss in his Fokker Triplane were several of the RFC's top flying aces, including: James McCudden, Richard Mayberry, Keith Muspratt, Reginald Hoidge, Arthur Rhys-Davids, and Verschoyle Cronyn.

14. Durwood Heinrich, "The Expert Pilot and Situation Awareness" (paper presented at the 47th Annual Corporate Aviation Safety Seminar, Phoenix, AZ, May 24–26, 2002).

Chapter 5

1. Manfred von Richthofen, "Richthofen's Air Combat Operations Manual," in Peter Kilduff, *Richthofen—Beyond the Legend of the Red Baron* (London: John Wiley & Sons, 1993), 233-35.

2. Gary Yukl, *Leadership in Organizations* (Upper Saddle River, NJ: Prentice-Hall, 2002), 327.

Chapter 6

1. Vernon Zunker, *Career Counseling: Applied Concepts of Life Planning* (6th Ed.) (Pacific Grove, CA: Brooks/Cole Publishing Company, 2002), 101-2.

2. John Schermerhorn, James Hunt, and Richard Osborn, *Organizational Behavior* (7th Ed.) (New York: John Wiley & Sons,

2000), 355.

3. Greg VanWyngarden, *Jagdstaffel 2 'Boelcke'* (New York: Osprey, 2007), 12.

Chapter 7

1. H.A. Jones, *The War in the Air*, Vol. II (East Sussex: The Naval & Military Press, 1928), 281.
2. The leading FE2d that attacked Richthofen on July 6, 1917, was crewed by Captain Donald Cunnell and observer/gunner Second Lieutenant Albert Woodbridge of 20 Squadron. They did not take credit for the Baron's near disaster. Because of the location of the wound—four inch gash in the left rear of his head—it is also believed that Richthofen may have been struck by a stray bullet from one of his own men when the wingman cleared his machine guns for the battle.
3. Karl Bodenschatz, *Jagd in Flanderns Himmel*, trans. Jan Hayzlett (London: Grub Street, 1996), 29.
4. H.A. Jones, *The War in the Air*, Vol. III (East Sussex: The Naval & Military Press, 1931), 336–7.
5. H.A. Jones, *The War in the Air*, Vol. IV (East Sussex: The Naval & Military Press, 1934), 396.
6. On April 5th, 100 Squadron sent eighteen FE2b night-bombers over La Brayelle to attack *Jasta 11*. However, the unit was alerted that enemy bombers were en route. There were no casualties and only minor damage. They attacked again two nights later.
7. Alan Stokes and Kirsten Kite, *Flight Stress: Stress, Fatigue, and Performance in Aviation.* (Brookfield, VT: Ashgate Publishing Company, 1997), 217.
8. Alan Stokes and Kirsten Kite, *Flight Stress: Stress, Fatigue, and Performance in Aviation.* (Brookfield, VT: Ashgate Publishing Company, 1997), 178.
9. Dave English, *Great Aviation Quotes*, http://www.skygod.com/quotes/safety.html (accessed December 2, 2003).

Chapter 8

1. Richthofen had eighty confirmed combat victories. All of his opponents were British, except for eight (six Canadians, one Australian, and one United States citizen). Of the pilots, forty-three were killed-in-action (KIA) or missing-in-action (MIA); seven later died of their wounds (DOW), nineteen were made prisoners-of-war (POW), and eleven were slightly injured or unharmed. Of the observers, twenty-eight were KIA or MIA, five DOW, six were POW, and four were slightly injured or unharmed. Therefore, thirty-eight percent of the pilots and twenty-three percent of the observers survived their combat encounters with Richthofen.
2. Richthofen particularly enjoyed a fair fight and posted victories against eight opponents who were also aces (more than five victories) averaging 12.5 victories each. Seven were English and the eighth was Canadian. The Baron was also victorious over eight additional pilots who averaged 2.4 combat victories.
3. Leon Bennett, *Gunning for the Red Baron* (College Station, TX: Texas A&M, 2006), 158.

Chapter 9

1. Mihaly Csikszentmihalyi, *Flow* (New York: Harper & Row, 1990). Mihaly Csikszentmihalyi indicated that it is not uncommon for experts in their specific domains to be lost in their work or activities. He described such an experience as *flow*, which involves reaching a kind of optimal experience such that total absorption in an activity results from a match between the task demands and the performance skills of the individual.

Chapter 10

1. Gary Yukl, *Leadership in Organizations* (Upper Saddle River, NJ: Prentice-Hall, 2002), 5.
2. Arthur Reber and Emily Reber, eds., *The Penguin Dictionary of*

Psychology (3rd Ed.). (London: Penguin, 2001), 135.

3. U. Neisser et al., "Intelligence: Knowns and Unknowns," *American Psychologist* 51(1996): 77–101.

4. R.J. Sternberg, "The Theory of Successful Intelligence," *Review of General Psychology*, 3(1999): 292–316.

5. Manfred von Richthofen, *The Red Baron* (S. Yorkshire: Pen & Sword, 2005), 41.

6. *JGI's* headquarters was established at Marcke, southwest of Courtrai. Keeping his *Jastas* as close together as possible, Richthofen had *Jastas 4* and *11* located at Marcke, *Jasta 6* at Bisseghem, and *Jasta 10* at Heule.

7. Karl Bodenschatz, *Jagd in Flanderns Himmel*, trans. Jan Hayzlett (London: Grub Street, 1996), 15.

8. M.M. Chemers, "Leadership Research and Theory: A Functional Integration," *Group Dynamics: Theory, Research, and Practice* 4(2000): 27–43.

9. W.L. Waag and H.H. Bell, "Situation Assessment and Decision Making in Skilled Fighter Pilots." In C.E. Zsambok & G.A. Klein (Eds.), *Naturalistic Decision Making* (1997): 247–54.

10. C.E. Zsambok, "Naturalistic Decision Making: Where Are We Now?" In C.E. Zsambok & G.A. Klein (Eds.), *Naturalistic Decision Making* (1997): 3–16.

11. David O'Hare and Stanley Rose, *Flightdeck Performance: The Human Factor* (Ames: Iowa State University Press, 1990), 235.

12. Most modern commercial aircraft are now equipped with Full Authority Digital Engine Control (FADEC) systems that automatically control all aspects of aircraft engine performance. In emergencies, crews simply apply full throttle, and the FADEC electronically provides the appropriate power output. In many aircraft, the FADEC system automatically applies full power, and even some additional thrust (Automatic Power Reserve—APR), on the good engine(s) when an engine fails.

13. Flight Safety Foundation, "Principles and Guidelines for Duty and Rest Scheduling in Corporate and Business Aviation," *Flight Safety Digest* 16(1997), 1-11.

14. Flight Safety Foundation Safety Audits, August 21-25, 2000 and December 7-11, 2004

15. G.A. Bonanno, and S. Kaltman, "Toward an Integrative Perspective on Bereavement," *Psychological Bulletin* 125(1999): 760–76.
16. Karl Bodenschatz, *Jagd in Flanderns Himmel*, trans. Jan Hayzlett (London: Grub Street, 1996), 84.

Chapter 11

1. Karl Bodenschatz, *Jagd in Flanderns Himmel*, trans. Jan Hayzlett (London: Grub Street, 1996), 29.
2. Mihaly Csikszentmihalyi, "Creativity." In *Encyclopedia of Psychology* (Vol. 2). American Psychological Association. (Washington, D.C.: Oxford University Press, 2000), 340.
3. Mihaly Csikszentmihalyi, "Creativity." In *Encyclopedia of Psychology* (Vol. 2). American Psychological Association. (Washington, D.C.: Oxford University Press, 2000), 341.
4. Karl Bodenschatz, *Jagd in Flanderns Himmel*, trans. Jan Hayzlett (London: Grub Street, 1996), 85.
5. Karl Bodenschatz, *Jagd in Flanderns Himmel*, trans. Jan Hayzlett (London: Grub Street, 1996), 28-9.
6. Karl Bodenschatz, *Jagd in Flanderns Himmel*, trans. Jan Hayzlett (London: Grub Street, 1996), 53.
7. Karl Bodenschatz, *Jagd in Flanderns Himmel*, trans. Jan Hayzlett (London: Grub Street, 1996), 61.
8. The S-A-F-E (Safety Attitude Focus Encounter) and A-C-T-S (Alternative Concepts Toward Safety) programs consisted respectively of employees "busting" colleagues for displaying an "attitude" of safety and safety-minded individuals submitting ideas to improve safety. If approved by the Safety Council, the person who was "caught" enhancing safety or who submitted a safety-related improvement idea was given a gift certificate to his or her favorite restaurant or store. Further, the individual who "busted" the safety-conscious colleague was also given a gift certificate.
9. John F. Kennedy, Remarks in Heber Springs, Arkansas, at the Dedication of Greers Ferry Dam, October 3, 1963.

Chapter 12

1. The author has in his collection a small piece of fabric from the right wing of Richthofen's Fokker DR.I (425–17). Over time, the color has aged to a deep red or maroon. The fabric patch was a generous gift from James W. Robertson.
2. Lothar von Richthofen. Quoted in Greg VanWyngarden, Richthofen's Circus—Jagdgeschwader Nr 1 (New York: Osprey, 2004), 13.
3. Karl Bodenschatz, *Jagd in Flanderns Himmel*, trans. Jan Hayzlett (London: Grub Street, 1996), 14.

Chapter 13

1. Karl Bodenschatz, *Jagd in Flanderns Himmel*, trans. Jan Hayzlett (London: Grub Street, 1996), 68.
2. Kunigunde von Richthofen, *Mein Kriegstagebuch*, trans. Suzanne Fischer (Atglen, PA: Schiffer Military History, 2001), 155.

Chapter 14

1. Karl Bodenschatz, *Jagd in Flanderns Himmel*, trans. Jan Hayzlett (London: Grub Street, 1996), 61.
2. Karl Bodenschatz, *Jagd in Flanderns Himmel*, trans. Jan Hayzlett (London: Grub Street, 1996), 84.
3. "pride." *Merriam-Webster Online Dictionary*. 2010. Merriam-Webster Online. 29 March 2010 <http://www.merriam-webster.com/dictionary/pride>
4. J. Crocker and C.T. Wolfe, "Contingencies of Self Worth," *Psychological Review* 108 (2001): 593–623.

Chapter 15

1. R.M. Ryan and E.L. Deci, "Self-Determination Theory and the Facilitation of Intrinsic Motivation, Social Development, and Well-Being," *American Psychologist* 55(2000): 68–78.

2. Karl Bodenschatz, *Jagd in Flanderns Himmel*, trans. Jan Hayzlett (London: Grub Street, 1996), 85.
3. R.S. Feldman, *Social Psychology* (3rd Ed.) (Upper Saddle River, NJ: Prentiss Hall, 2001).
4. I.A. Horowitz and K.S. Bordens, *Social Psychology* (Mountain View, CA: Mayfield Publishing Company, 1995).
5. Philip Rice, *Stress and Health* (3rd Ed.) (Pacific Grove, CA: Brooks/Cole, 1999).
6. Karl Bodenschatz, *Jagd in Flanderns Himmel*, trans. Jan Hayzlett (London: Grub Street, 1996), 84-5.

Chapter 16

1. L. Beck and E.A. Madresh, "Romantic Partners and Four-Legged Friends: An Extension of Attachment Theory to Relationships with Pets," *Anthrozoos* 21(2008): 43–56.
2. F. Walsh, "Human-Animal Bonds II: The Role of Pets in Family Systems and Family Therapy," *Family Process* 48(2009): 481–99.
3. A. Cain, "Pets as Family Members." In M. Sussman (Ed.), *Pets and the Family* (1985): 5–10.
4. Karl Bodenschatz, *Jagd in Flanderns Himmel*, trans. Jan Hayzlett (London: Grub Street, 1996), 73.
5. F. Walsh, "Human-Animal Bonds II: The Role of Pets in Family Systems and Family Therapy," *Family Process* 48(2009): 481–99.
6. G.F. Melson, "Child Development and the Human-Companion Animal Bond," *Animal Behavioral Scientist* 47(2003): 31–9.
7. F. Walsh, "Human-Animal Bonds II: The Role of Pets in Family Systems and Family Therapy," *Family Process* 48(2009): 481–99.
8. Karl Bodenschatz, *Jagd in Flanderns Himmel*, trans. Jan Hayzlett (London: Grub Street, 1996), 52.
9. Karl Bodenschatz, *Jagd in Flanderns Himmel*, trans. Jan Hayzlett (London: Grub Street, 1996), 84.
10. Karl Bodenschatz, *Jagd in Flanderns Himmel*, trans. Jan Hayzlett (London: Grub Street, 1996), 73.

GLOSSARY OF GERMAN TERMS AND ABBREVIATIONS

Aufklarung: Reconnaissance
Chef des Generalstabes: Chief of the General Staff
Eisernes Kreuz: "Iron Cross"; medal awarded for valorous service
Feldflugchef: Chief of Field Aviation
Feldgrau: "Field gray"; term used to describe the color of the ordinary
German soldier's tunic
Flieger Abteilung (Fl Abt): Aviation section or unit
Flieger Beobachter Schule: German Air Service School for observer
training
Flieger Ersatz Abteilung (FEA): Aviation replacement section or unit
Fliegertruppe: The Air Service
Flugzeug: Aircraft
Flugzeugwerke: Aircraft Works
Freifrau: German title for a Baroness by marriage
Freiherr (Frhr): German title of Baron
Gefallen: Killed in action
Gefechtsstand: Command post
Generalfeldmarschall: Field Marshal
Geschwader: Fighter wing; unit of four fighter *Staffeln*, as in *JG I*; see
also *Jagdgeschwader*
Grabenkrieg: Trench warfare
Graf: German title of Count
Gruppe: Group
Herr: "Mister"; used before ranks when addressing a person of higher
rank (e.g., *Herr Hauptmann*)

Infanterie: Infantry

Inspekteur der Fliegertruppen (Id Flieg): Inspector of Aviation Troops or Air Service

Jabo (Jagdbomber): Fighter-bomber

Jagdfliegerei: hunting aviation; pursuit flying

Jagdgeschwader (JG): Fighter wing; four *Jagdstaffeln* under a single commander

Jagdgruppe: Grouping of several *Jagdstaffeln* under a single commander

Jagdstaffel (Jasta): A fighter squadron, usually consisting of 9 to 12 aircraft

Jastaschule: German Air Service for the training of fighter pilots

Kanone: German "ace" pilot

Kampfeinsitzer: Single-seat fighter squadrons

Kampfgeschwader (KG): Bomber wing/group; battle group

Kampfgeschwader der Obersten Heeresleitung (Kagohl): Bomber squadrons of the Army High Command

Kampfstaffel (Kasta): A combat flight unit or echelon

Kavallerie: Cavalry

Kette: Flight section

Kommandeur der Flieger (Kofl): The officer in command of the aviation units assigned to a particular army

Kommandierender General der Luftstreitkrafte (Kogenluft): Commanding General of the German Air Service

Kugel: Bullet

Ordonnanzoffizier: Assistant Adjutant

Rumpfdoppeldecker (RDD): A biplane with a solid fuselage

Schlachtstaffel (Schlasta): An attack or ground support unit

Staffel: A flight unit, used here interchangeably with *Jasta* and *Jagdstaffel*

Uhlan: Member of a lancer regiment

GLOSSARY OF GERMAN RANKS WITH THEIR APPROXIMATE EQUIVALENTS

Feldwebel (Fw): Sergeant
Feldwebel Leutnant (Fw Lt): Warrant Officer
Flieger (Fl): Private in the Air Service
Gefreiter (Gefr): Private First Class
General der Flieger: General of Aviation
Generalleutnant (Gen Lt): Lieutenant General
Hauptmann (Hptm): Captain
Leutnant (Lt): Second Lieutenant
Leutnant der Landwehr (Lt d. L.): Lieutenant in the reserves, ages 35 to 45
Leutnant der Reserve (Lt d. R.): Lieutenant of the Reserves
Oberleutnant (Oblt): First Lieutenant
Oberst: Colonel
Oberstleutnant: Lieutenant Colonel
Offizier Stellvertreter (Offz Stellv): Acting Officer
Rittmeister (Rittm): Cavalry Captain
Shirrmeister: Maintenance Technical Sergeant
Unteroffizier (Uffz): Corporal
Vizefeldwebel (Vfw): Vice Sergeant Major

BIBLIOGRAPHY

Baker, David. *Manfred von Richthofen*. London: Outline Press, 1990.

Beck, L. and E.A. Madresh. "Romantic Partners and Four-Legged Friends: An Extension of Attachment Theory to Relationships with Pets." *Anthrozoos* 21(2008): 43–56.

Bennett, Leon. *Gunning for the Red Baron*. College Station, TX: Texas A&M, 2006.

Bickers, Richard. *Von Richthofen—The Legend Evaluated*. Annapolis, MD: Naval Institute Press, 1996.

Bodenschatz, Karl. *Jagd in Flanderns Himmel*. Munich, 1935. Translated by Jan Hayzlett. *Hunting with Richthofen*. London: Grub Street, 1996.

Boelcke, Oswald. *Hauptmann Boelcke's Feldberichte*. Gotha, 1916. Translated by Robert Hirsch. *An Aviator's Field Book*. Nashville: The Battery Press, 1917.

Bonanno, G.A. and S. Kaltman. "Toward an Integrative Perspective on Bereavement." *Psychological Bulletin* 125(1999): 760–76.

Boning, Richard. *The Red Baron*. New York: Barnell Loft, 1975

Burrows, William. *Richthofen: A True History of the Red Baron*. New York: Harcourt, Brace & World, 1969.

Cain, A. "Pets as Family Members." In M. Sussman (Ed.), *Pets and the Family* (1985): 5–10. New York: Haworth Press.

Chemers, M.M. "Leadership Research and Theory: A Functional Integration." *Group Dynamics: Theory, Research, and Practice* 4(2000): 27–43.

Connors, John. *Albatros Fighters in Action*. Carrollton, TX: Squadron/ Signal Publications, 1981.

Corum, James. *Wolfram von Richthofen*. Lawrence, KS: University

Press of Kansas, 2008.

Coursen, H.R. *After the War*. Chico, CA: Heidelberg Graphics, 1981

Covey, Steven. *The Seven Habits of Highly Effective People*. New York: Simon & Schuster, 1989.

Crocker, J. and C.T. Wolfe. "Contingencies of Self-Worth." *Psychological Review* 108(2001): 593–623.

Csikszentmihalyi, Mihaly. *Flow: The Psychology of Optimal Experience*. New York: Harper & Row, 1990.

Csikszentmihalyi, Mihaly. "Creativity." In *Encyclopedia of Psychology* (Vol. 2, 337-42). American Psychological Association. Washington, D.C.: Oxford University Press, 2000.

English, Dave. *The Air Up There*. New York: McGraw-Hill, 2003.

Feldman, R.S. *Social Psychology* (3rd Ed.). Upper Saddle River, NJ: Prentiss Hall, 2001.

Flight Safety Foundation. "Principles and Guidelines for Duty and Rest Scheduling in Corporate and Business Aviation." *Flight Safety Digest* 16(1997), 1-11.

Franken, Robert E. *Human Motivation* (5th Ed.). Belmont, CA: Wadsworth Thomson Learning: 2002.

Franks, Norman, Hal Giblin, and Nigel McCrery. *Under the Guns of the Red Baron*. London: Grub Street, 1995.

Franks, Norman. *Albatros Aces of World War 1*. New York: Osprey, 2000.

Franks, Norman and Alan Bennett. *The Red Baron's Last Flight*. London: Grub Street, 2006.

Franks, Norman and Greg VanWyngarden. *Fokker DR I Aces of World War I*. New York: Osprey, 2001.

Franks, Norman and Hal Giblin. *Under the Guns of the German Aces*. London: Grub Street, 1997.

Gibbons, Floyd. *The Red Knight of Germany*. New York: Bantam Books, 1927.

Guttman, Jon. *Sopwith Camel vs Fokker DrI*. New York: Osprey, 2008.

Hardy, D.J. and R. Parasuraman. "Cognition and Flight Performance in Older Pilots." *Journal of Experimental Psychology: Applied* 3, no.4 (1997): 313-48.

Heinrich, D. "Safer Approaches and Landings: A Multivariate

Analysis of Critical Factors." Ph.D. dissertation, Capella University, 2004.

Heinrich, Durwood. "Teams and Team Leadership in Aviation." Paper presented at the 49th Annual Corporate Aviation Safety Seminar, Tucson, AZ, April 27–29, 2004.

Heinrich, Durwood. "The Expert Pilot and Situation Awareness." Paper presented at the 47th Annual Corporate Aviation Safety Seminar, Phoenix, AZ, May 24–26, 2002.

Horowitz, I.A. and K.S. Bordens. *Social Psychology*. Mountain View, CA: Mayfield Publishing Company, 1995.

Jones, H.A. *The War in the Air*, Vol II. East Sussex: The Naval & Military Press, 1928.

Jones, H.A. *The War in the Air*, Vol III. East Sussex: The Naval & Military Press, 1931.

Jones, H.A. *The War in the Air*, Vol IV. East Sussex: The Naval & Military Press, 1934.

Kilduff, Peter. *Richthofen—Beyond the Legend of the Red Baron*. London: John Wiley & Sons, 1993.

Kilduff, Peter. *The Red Baron Combat Wing—Jagdgeschwader Richthofen in Battle*. London: Arms and Armour, 1997.

Kilduff, Peter. *The Illustrated Red Baron—The Life and Times of Manfred von Richthofen*. London: Arms and Armour, 1999.

Kilduff, Peter. *Talking with the Red Baron*. London: Brassey's, 2003.

Kilduff, Peter. *Red Baron—Beyond the Legend*. London: Cassell, 1994.

Kilduff, Peter. *Red Baron—The Life and Death of an Ace*. Cincinnati, OH: David & Charles, 2007.

Leaman, Paul. *Fokker Dr.I Triplane*. Surrey: Air War Classics Publications, 2003.

Lindbergh, Charles. *The Spirit of St. Louis*. New York, NY: Avon Books, 1953.

Maltz, Maxwell. *Psycho-Cybernetics*. New York: Pocket Books, 1960.

McGuire, Frank. *The Many Deaths of the Red Baron: The Richthofen Controversy 1918–2000*. Calgary: Bunker to Bunker Publishing, 2001.

McManus, Peter. *Richthofen Jagdstaffel Ahead*. London: Grub Street, 2008.

Melson, G.F. "Child Development and the Human-Companion

Animal Bond." *Animal Behavioral Scientist* 47(2003): 31–9.

Muchinsky, Paul. *Psychology Applied to Work: An Introduction to Industrial and Organizational Psychology* (6th Ed). Belmont, CA: Wadsworth, 2000.

Neisser, U., G. Boodoo, T.J. Bouchard, A.W. Boykin, N. Brody, S.J. Ceci, D.F. Halpern, J.C. Loehlin, R. Perloff, R.J. Sternberg, and S. Urbinda. "Intelligence: Knowns and Unknowns." *American Psychologist* 51(1996): 77–101.

Nowarra, H.J. and Kimbrough Brown. *von Richthofen and the Flying Circus*. Edited by Bruce Robertson. Fallbrook, CA: Aero Publishers, 1958.

Nowarra, Heinz. *Fokker Dr.I in Action*. Carrollton, TX: Squadron/Signal Publications, 1989.

O'Connor, Mike and Norman Franks. *In the Footsteps of the Red Baron*. Barnsley, South Yorkshire: Pen & Sword Military, 2004.

O'Hare, David and Stanley Rose. *Flightdeck Performance: The Human Factor*. Ames: Iowa State University Press, 1990.

Reber, Arthur and Emily Reber, Eds. *The Penguin Dictionary of Psychology* (3rd Ed.). London, England: Penguin, 2001.

Rice, Earle. *Manfred von Richthofen*. Philadelphia, PA: Chelsea House, 2003.

Rice, Phillip. *Stress and Health* (3rd Ed.). Pacific Grove, CA: Brooks/Cole, 1999.

Richthofen, Kunigunde, Freifrau von. *Mein Kriegstagebuch*. Berlin: Verlag Ullstein, 1937.

Richthofen, Kunigunde, von. *Mein Kriegstagebuch*. Berlin, 1937. Translated by Suzanne Fischer. *Mother of Eagles*. Atglen, PA: Schiffer Military History, 2001.

Richthofen, Manfred von. *Der rote Kampfflieger*. Middlesex: Echo Library, 2008.

Richthofen, Manfred von. *Der rote Kampfflieger*. Berlin, 1918. Translated by Ellis Barker. *The Red Fighter Pilot*, St. Petersburg: Red and Black, 2007.

Richthofen, Manfred von. *Der Rotte Kampfflieger*. Berlin: Verlag Ullstein, 1917. *The Red Air Fighter*. London: Greenhill Books, 1999.

Richthofen, Manfred von. *The Red Baron*. Translated by Peter Kilduff.

Edited by Stanley M. Ulanoff. Fallbrook, CA: Aero Publishers, 1969.

Richthofen, Manfred von. *The Red Baron*. South Yorkshire: Pen & Sword, 2005.

Richthofen, Manfred von. *The Red Battle Flyer*. New York: Robert M. McBride & Co., 1918. Translated by J. Ellis Barker. *The Red Baron*. Edited by Hans-Peter Oswald. Breinigsville, PA: Books on Demand, 2010.

Richthofen, Manfred, Freiherr von. *The Red Battle Flyer*. New York: Robert M. McBride & Co., 1918. Translated by J. Ellis Barker. Breinigsville, PA: BiblioLife, 2010.

Richthofen, Manfred, Freiherr von. *The Red Battle Flyer*. New York: Robert M. McBride & Co., 1918. Translated by T. Ellis Barker. Breinigsville, PA: Nabu, 2010.

Ryan, R.M. and E.L. Deci. "Self-Determination Theory and the Facilitation of Intrinsic Motivation, Social Development, and Well-Being." *American Psychologist* 55(2000): 68–78.

Salmela, John H. "Athletes." In *Encyclopedia of Psychology* (Vol. 1, 277-82). American Psychological Association. Washington, D.C.: Oxford University Press, 2000.

Schermerhorn, J.R., J.G Hunt, and R.N. Osborn. *Organizational Behavior* (7th Ed.). New York: John Wiley & Sons, 2000.

Sykes, Claud. *Richthofen, The Red Knight of the Air*. Bristol, UK: Cerberus, 2004.

Sternberg, R.J. "The Theory of Successful Intelligence." *Review of General Psychology* 3(1999), 292–316.

Stokes, Alan and Kirsten Kite. *Flight Stress: Stress, Fatigue, and Performance in Aviation*. Brookfield, VT: Ashgate Publishing Company, 1997.

Treadwell, Terry and Alan Wood. *Images of Aviation–Richthofen's Flying Circus*. Gloucestershire: Tempus, 1999.

Udet, Ernst. *Mein Fliegerleben*. Berlin, 1935. Edited by Stanley Ulanoff. *Ace of the Iron Cross*. New York: Arco, 1981.

Udgerleider, Steven. *Mental Training for Peak Performance*. Emmaus, PA: Rodale Press, 1996.

VanWyngarden, Greg. *'Richthofen's Circus'—Jagdgeschwader Nr 1*. New York: Osprey, 2004.

VanWyngarden, Greg. *Albatros Aces of World War 1 Part 2*, New York: Osprey, 2007.

VanWyngarden, Greg. *Jagdstaffel 2 'Boelcke.'* New York: Osprey, 2007.

Waag, W.L. and H.H. Bell. "Situation Assessment and Decision Making in Skilled Fighter Pilots." In C.E. Zsambok & G.A. Klein (Eds.). *Naturalistic Decision Making*, 247–254. Mahwah, NJ: Lawrence Erlbaum Associates, 1997.

Walsh, F. "Human-Animal Bonds II: The Role of Pets in Family Systems and Family Therapy." *Family Process* 48(2009), 481–99.

Wilberg, Jim. *Rittmeister—A Biography of Manfred von Richthofen.* Fairfield, IA: First World, 2007.

Wolfe, Tom. *The Right Stuff.* New York, NY: Bantam Books, 1979.

Wright, Nicolas. *The Red Baron.* New York: McGraw-Hill, 1976.

Yukl, Gary. *Leadership in Organizations* (5th Ed.). Upper Saddle River, NJ: Prentice-Hall, 2002.

Zbiegniewski, Andre. *Richthofen's Eleven—Jasta 11*. Lublin: Kagero, 2005.

Zsambok, C.E. "Naturalistic Decision Making: Where Are We Now?" In C.E. Zsambok & G.A. Klein (Eds.). *Naturalistic Decision Making*, 3–16. Mahwah, NJ: Lawrence Erlbaum Associates, 1997.

Zunker, Vernon G. *Career Counseling: Applied Concepts of Life Planning* (6th Ed.). Pacific Grove, CA: Brooks/Cole Publishing Company, 2002.